On Campus

東京大学教養学部英語部会 編
Department of English, The University of Tokyo, Komaba

東京大学出版会
University of Tokyo Press

On Campus
Department of English, The University of Tokyo, Komaba
University of Tokyo Press, 2006
ISBN 4-13-082118-0

[TRADITION] Summit of Mauna Kea, Hawai'i

[POETRY] A "waka" in Waitangi, Aotearoa

[VIEW] "Austria," 1997, by Martin Bruch

[VIEW] "Liechtenstein," 1999, by Martin Bruch

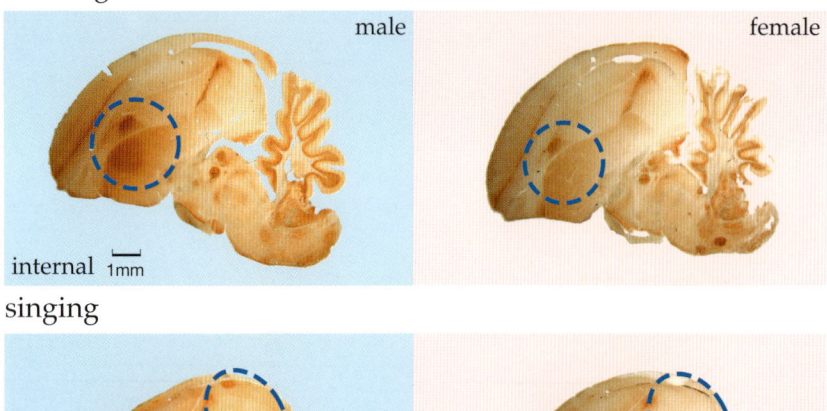

[SONG] a. The brains of male and female finches

[SONG] b. Japanese finches and koshijirokinpara

On Campus

まえがき

このテクストの成り立ちと狙い

　本書は，平成18（2006）年度以降，東京大学教養学部（以下「駒場」と表記）の1年生全員に対して使用される英語Ⅰのリーディング教材です。英語Ⅰとは，授業1回で，このリーディング教材の1章と，それと密接に関連するマルチメディア教材とを組み合わせて学習していく英語授業で，駒場では1993年から行われているものです。これまでに，その教科書として *The Universe of English, The Expanding Universe of English*，そのおのおのの続編が刊行されてきました。

　制作担当者を新たにして編集された本書は，基本的には前著の伝統を踏襲しています。たとえば文科生と理科生がともに興味をもって学べるよう，文系理系両方にまたがる多様なテーマの文章を，それぞれ週1コマで読み切れる長さで配列しています。また，「英語を読む」というよりは「英語で読む」という読者の意識をひきだせるよう，現在の大学生が知的におもしろいと感じられるような内容のものを選びました。

　そのような教科書のイメージをもって教科書制作をはじめたわたしたち制作班4名は，しかし週に1度くらいの割合で開かれた「制作会議」をとおして，独自のアイデアも楽しむようになりました。それは，学問分野の多様性を体現している駒場の多くの先生方にわれわれの教科書制作にさまざまなかたちで関わっていただくことで，よりおもしろい教科書をつくることができるのはないかというものでした。そうすることで，各分野でもっともおもしろいトピックを，一線の研究者からダイレクトに供給してもらえることになるし，また，先生方に書いていた

だくオリジナル・テクストは，どの学問分野でも英語でのコミュニケーションが必要であることを表現することになるのではないか。わたしたちはそう考えました。

　そのアイデアにそって，駒場の教員紹介一覧を頼りにさまざまな先生方に連絡をとらせていただき，実際に研究室をお訪ねしました。そして参考となるお話をお伺いしたり，おもしろそうなテクストや（駒場内外の）協力者を紹介していただいたり，本文となる文章を提供していただいたり，イントロやコラムの執筆をお願いしたり，注を付けていただいたり……，とほんとうにいろいろなかたちで協力していただくことになりました。それは，わたしたちにとってはほんとうに貴重な，思い出すだに楽しい時間でした。ご協力いただいた先生方にはこの場を借りて，心よりのお礼を申し述べさせていただきます。ありがとうございました。

　というわけで本書は，さまざまな分野の研究者の力が1冊に結集されたものとなっています。そのようなものとして本書は全体として，もちろん体系的ではありませんが，さまざまな研究分野の総合的イントロダクションになるよう意図されています。それぞれの学問分野に若い人たちを誘うものとなるよう意図されています。

　本書が以上の意味で，現代の大学における教養のあり方のひとつを体現しているものとなっていることをわたしたちは望んでいます。そしてそういう意味をこめて本書を *On Campus* と名づけました（1年生冬学期用の続編も同様の意味をこめて *Campus Wide* と名づけてあります）。たしかに平凡なタイトルですが，大学のキャンパスのなかに学問の多様な宇宙があることを実感していただければという思いをこめました。

細かなお断り

1. スペリングや引用形式に関して英・米いずれのスタイルを選ぶかは，文章内で統一されているかぎりは，原著者のスタイルに従っています。
2. 注の作成にあたっては，いくつかの辞書，事典を参照しましたが，頻繁に利用した以下のものについては煩瑣となることを避けてその都度の出典の明記はしていません。以下にまとめて記して感謝申しあげます。*The Oxford English Dictionary* (2nd. ed.), 『平凡社 CD-ROM版世界大百科事典』，『研究社 リーダーズ＋プラス』，『小学館 ランダムハウス英和大辞典』。その他，Web上の『ウィキペディア（Wikipedia）』も折りにふれて参照しました。
3. 注は前著 *Universe* より多めにつけ，英語がそれほど得意でない人でも躓かずに，あるいは内容に集中して読めるよう工夫しました。辞書がなくても流れが

追える程度の注が用意されていますので，それをひととおり読んでからテクストを読みはじめるというのも一法かもしれません。コンテクストを意識しながら流れに乗って読むという経験が重要です。

4. 注をつける場合，イディオムというほどではないけれどもよく用いられる単語の組み合わせには注意を促すことにしています。それが結局は英文の理解にも役立つし，と同時に「発信型」の英語力の養成にも役立つのではないかと考えたからです。また，覚えておくと使えそうな類似例を，e.g. (for example) や cf. (compare) というかたちで載せてあります。

5. 注については本書をつうじて記述に重複があり，適宜クロスレファレンスを指示してもいます。その趣旨は，かならずしも第 1 章から順番に本書を読まなくてもいいということです。

6. この「まえがき」の直後にある「Word Network List」は，本書に複数回あらわれるテーマやコンセプトやキーワードを相互にたどるための見取り図です。読む順序の参考にしていただければ幸いです。

謝　辞

まずは有形無形のさまざまなご協力をいただいた英語部会の同僚諸氏に感謝申しあげます。

各章のイントロダクションの執筆者および注作成の協力者（章の順で，敬称略）は，以下のとおりです。

1. 斎藤兆史（英学）
2. 石井直方（運動生理学）
3. 矢口祐人（アメリカ研究）
4. 斎藤毅（数論幾何）
5. 藤垣裕子（科学技術社会論）
6. 村田純一（哲学）
7. 石橋純（文化人類学）
8. 丹治愛（英文学・英文化研究）
9. 臼井隆一郎（ドイツ文学・思想）
10. 中尾まさみ（英語圏現代詩）
11. 野矢茂樹（哲学）
12. ホーンズ・シーラ（空間論・テクスト分析）
13. 坪井栄治郎（言語学）
14. 永田敬（分子物理化学）
    朽津耕三（物理化学／東京大学名誉教授・長岡技術科学大学名誉教授）

このうち，斎藤，坪井，中尾，ホーンズ，矢口，丹治以外は，英語部会外からご協力をいただいた方であり，心から御礼を申しあげます。また，第 14 章に関して，本文についても注についても惜しみない協力を提供してくださったニュー

トリノ物理学の権威，梶田隆章教授（東京大学宇宙線研究所・附属宇宙ニュートリノ観測情報融合センター）にも，この場を借りて特別の感謝を申し述べたいと思います．

さらに，編集の過程でさまざまなかたちで協力してくれた以下の方たちにも感謝申しあげます．

古賀裕章，佐藤元状，設楽靖子，古川敏明，森仁志（以上，東京大学大学院博士課程），砂田恵理加（一橋大学大学院博士課程），有井秀子（東京大学事務嘱託）

注作成の補助で信じがたいほど多大な時間を割いてくれた設楽氏には，感謝よりもむしろお詫びすべきなのかもしれません．さらにさらに，本作りに関していつも的確なアドバイスをしてくださったうえに，遅れに遅れた編集作業を少しでも早めるために，制作会議にいろいろな差し入れまでしてくれた東京大学出版会編集部の後藤健介氏にも心からの感謝を申し述べなければなりません．

本作りの常識として，それぞれの責任を明確にするために，わたしたちの役割分担も記しておくべきかもしれません．しかしわたしたち4名の制作班は，ほんとうに長いあいだ一緒の時間を過ごすうちに，あらゆる仕事も責任も感情も結局は共有するようになったと感じています．したがって本書という結果にたいしては，「浮かぶも一緒，沈むも一緒」という責任のとり方をしたいと思います．そのようなかたちの仕事になったということについては，また，学ぶことの多い有意義な仕事だったということについても，ただただ感謝と感慨あるのみ．（AT）

西村義樹 / ホーンズ・シーラ / 矢口祐人 / 丹治　愛

WORD NETWORK LIST

This word network list has two main purposes. First, it is designed to enable readers to explore the way in which the meanings of apparently simple terms vary in subtle ways according to context. By tracking a single word as it appears and reappears throughout this book, readers will be able to see how context-dependent its meaning is, and how it makes sense differently in different contexts. The term 'space,' for example, which appears in eight different chapters, shifts its meaning almost every time, asking us constantly to rethink what it means. Reading along, we move from the blank space to be found in the margins of a printed page to 4-dimensional mathematical space, from the native Hawaiian concept of the Great-Expanse-of-Space to a geographer's view of space as the product of interrelations, and from underground space to social space, virtual space, public space, and outer space. In each case, 'space' means something slightly different, and as readers we have to constantly resituate ourselves and rethink our understanding of what 'space' means.

The second reason that we have included this word network list is that we wanted to make easily visible the way in which certain themes surface and resurface throughout the text. We hope that the word network list will in this way show how texts which at first sight seem to be firmly situated within distinct academic disciplines or traditions, located at a distance from each other, are in fact 'networked,' engaged in implicit conversation, and approaching shared concerns from different perspectives. In this sense, we hope that the word network list will function as a metaphor for the creative potential of interdisciplinary collaboration, for us one of the most exciting aspects of life on campus.

（抄訳）この「ワードネットワーク・リスト」には主にふたつの趣旨があります。まず，ひとつの英単語や語句が，いかに多層的な意味を持ちうるかを理解するための手がかりを示すものです。たとえば「space」という言葉は，単純に「空間」と和訳されがちですが，その意味は文脈によって実に多様です。またこのリストは，ある種のテーマが本書で頻出していることを示す指針にもなっています。一見すると，それぞれのレッスンは異なる学問分野の話であると思われるかもしれません。しかしこのリストから，学問全体に通底する学際的なテーマがあることがわかるでしょう。いろいろな分野に興味を抱き，積極的に知の枠組みを広げていくためのヒントとしてください。

astronomy（天文学）	tradition, physics
calculation（計算，予測）	mathematics, objectivity
culture/cultural（文化，文化の）	you, tradition, objectivity, voice, gender, coffee, poetry, space
emotion(s)（感情，情緒，気持ち）	you, tradition, subjectivity, voice, gender, poetry
environment(al)（環境［の］，周囲［の］）	tradition, objectivity, gender, coffee
geography/geographical（地理，土地，地理の，土地に関する）	coffee, poetry, space
global(ization/isation)（グローバル，グローバリゼーション）	objectivity, voice, coffee, space
illness/disease（病，疾患）	fat, gender, view
indigenous（先住の，土着の，その土地に固有な，元来からある）	tradition, coffee, poetry
knowledge（知識，情報，学識，学問）	you, tradition, mathematics, objectivity, subjectivity, poetry, physics
language（言語，言葉，語学）	you, tradition, mathematics, voice, coffee, poetry, song
nature/natural（自然，環境，性質，自然の，当然の）	you, fat, tradition, gender, coffee, physics
network(s)（ネットワーク，つながり，関係）	voice, gender, coffee, physics

normative（基準の，標準の，規範となる）	gender, view
originality/creativity（オリジナリティ，独創性，創造力）	you, tradition, physics
poetry（詩）	tradition, poetry
point of view(s)/view(s)（視点，見解）	fat, tradition, subjectivity, gender, poetry, view,
perspective（視点，視座，考え方，見解，思考）	space, song
relations/relationships/interrelations/interact(ions)（関係，関連，つながり，相互作用）	you, fat, voice, tradition, mathematics, subjectivity, voice, gender, coffee, view, poetry, space, song, physics
research（研究，探求，調査）	fat, mathematics, objectivity, voice, gender, song, physics
science/scientific（科学，科学的な，科学に関する）	fat, tradition, objectivity, gender, song, physics
song（歌）	tradition, voice, song
sound（音）	subjectivity, view, song
space/spaces（空間，距離，スペース，間隔，期間）	tradition, mathematics, voice, coffee, poetry, view, space, physics
tradition(s)（伝統，伝説，しきたり，慣習）	you, tradition, voice, poetry
universe（宇宙，世界）	tradition, mathematics, physics
value(s)（価値，価値観，打ち，大切さ，有益であること）	fat, tradition, mathematics, objectivity, coffee, poetry

* 上記の日本語は厳密な「和訳」ではありません。それぞれの英単語・語句の意味を適切に捉えるためには，各レッスンを参照し，前後の文脈の中で考えてみてください。

TABLE OF CONTENTS

1 • YOU 2
Introduction by Saito Yoshifumi
"Only You," by Norma Field

2 • FAT 12
Introduction by Naokata Ishii
"Walking Off Your Fat," by Naokata Ishii

3 • TRADITION 22
Introduction by Yujin Yaguchi
"Why is Mauna Kea so Sacred to the Native Hawaiian People?," by The Royal Order of Kamehameha I & Mauna Kea Anaina Hou,
"There's room for everybody," by Michael West

4 • MATHEMATICS 34
Introduction by Takeshi Saito
"Fermat's Enigma," by Simon Singh

5 • OBJECTIVITY 46
Introduction by Yuko Fujigaki
"Objectivity and the Assessment Process," by Yuko Fujigaki

6 — SUBJECTIVITY · 56
Introduction by Junichi Murata
"Dying a Death," by Allan Kellehear

7 — VOICE · 68
Introduction by Jun Ishibashi
"In Search of a Voice," by Casey Man Kong Lum

8 — GENDER · 82
Introduction by Ai Tanji
"Biobehavioral Responses to Stress in Females," by Shelley E. Taylor, et al.

9 — COFFEE · 96
Introduction by Ryuichiro Usui
"Coffee and Globalization," by Ryuichiro Usui

10 — POETRY · 108
Introduction by Masami Nakao
"Whetu Moana, Ocean of Stars," by Albert Wendt, Reina Whaitiri and Robert Sullivan

11 — VIEW · 126
Introduction by Shigeki Noya
"The Fall Guy," by Samantha Ellis

12 — SPACE · 136
Introduction by Sheila Hones
"For Space," by Doreen Massey

13 — SONG · 148
Introduction by Eijiro Tsuboi
"Finchsong," by Kazuo Okanoya

14 — PHYSICS · 162
Introduction by Takashi Nagata and Kozo Kuchitsu
"The Thrill of Experiments," by Masatoshi Koshiba

出典一覧

Grateful acknowledgment is made for permission to reprint excerpts and figures from the following publications:

TEXTS

1. YOU: Norma Field, "The Aims of Education Address," in *The University of Chicago Record*, Vol. 33, No. 1 (October 29, 1998). Reprinted by permission of The University of Chicago Record, cited from their Website (http://www.uchicago.edu/docs/education/record/10-29-98).
2. FAT: 石井直方「ウォーキングの生理学」，株式会社健康体力研究所のウェブサイト（http://www.kentai.co.jp/column/physiology/p026.html）より抜粋，英訳。
3. TRADITION: The Royal Order of Kamehameha I and Mauna Kea Anaina Hou, "Mauna Kea — The Temple: Protecting the Sacred Resource," cited from www.kahea.org/maunakea/pdf/the-mk-temple-2001.pdf22/ Michael West, "There's room for everybody on Mauna Kea," appeared in *The Honolulu Advertiser* (February 17, 2003), cited from http://www.the.honoluluadvertiser.com/article/2003/Feb/17/op/op04a.html. Reprinted by permission of The Honolulu Advertiser.
4. MATHEMATICS: Excerpt from Simon Singh, 1997, *Fermat's Enigma* (Anchor Books [Random House] edition), pp. 171–185. Permission requested from Walker's & Co.
5. OBJECTIVITY: 藤垣裕子『専門知と公共性：科学技術社会論の構築へ向けて』（東京大学出版会，2003 年）より抜粋，英訳して再構成．／コラム（藤前干潟）：特定非営利活動法人藤前干潟を守る会のウェブサイト（http://www.fujimae.org/fujimae_eng.htm）から抜粋。
6. SUBJECTIVITY: Allan Kellehear, 1997, *Eternity and Me*, Michelle Anderson Publishing. Reprinted by permission of Michelle Anderson Publishing (http://www.michelleandersonpublishing.com).
7. VOICE: Casey Man Kong Lum, 1996, *In Search of a Voice* (Laurence Erlbaum Associates), pp. 1–3, 76, 79–82, 97. Reprinted by permission of the author and Laurence Erlbaum Associates.
8. GENDER: Shelley E. Taylor, Laura Cousino Klein, Brian P. Lewis, Tara L. Gruenewald, Regan A. R. Gurung, and John A. Updegraff, 2000, "Biobehavioral Responses to Stress in Females," *Psychological Review*, 107(3), 411–429. American Psychological Association.
9. COFFEE: 臼井隆一郎「コーヒー：ドイツ—メキシコ間に漂う苦いアロマ」『アエラムック 77 文化学がわかる』2002 年，朝日新聞社，64–68 頁より再構成して英訳。
10. POETRY: "Honda Waka," by Robert Sullivan, in *Star Waka*, 1999, Auckland University Press / "Introduction," by Albert Wendt, Reina Whaitiri, and Robert Sullivan, "Homecoming," by Jean Tekura Mason, "Over Ponsonby," by Albert Wendt, in Wendt et al. (eds.), 2003, *Whetu Moana*, *Ocean of Stars*, Auckland

University Press. Reprinted by permission of Auckland University Press.
11. VIEW: "The Fall Guy," copyright © 2002 by Samantha Ellis. First appeared in *The Gurdian*, April 29, 2002. Reprinted by permission of the author.
12. SPACE: Doreen B. Massey, 2005, *For Space*, Sage Publications. Reprinted by permission of Sage Publications Ltd. Copyright © Doreen B. Massey, 2005.
13. SONG: 岡ノ谷一夫「動物のおしゃべり解読学」(5、6)『日経サイエンス』2002年4月号(94–96頁)、5月号(68–70頁)より抜粋、英訳して再構成。
14. PHYSICS: Masatoshi Koshiba, "Commencement Address by Emeritus Professor Koshiba at the University of Tokyo in March 2002," 東京大学大学院理学系研究科ウェブサイト(http://www.s.u-tokyo.ac.jp/koshiba/shukuji_e.html)、小柴昌俊『ニュートリノ天体物理学入門』(講談社[ブルーバックス]、2002年、34–35頁)、小柴昌俊(高橋真理子によるインタビュー)『イリューム ILLUME』32号(2004年12月)、東京電力株式会社、以上3つのコメントから再構成して英訳。

FRONTISPIECE

"Summit of Mauna Kea," photo by Yujin Yaguchi (2005).
"Maori war canoe, waka, in Wairoa Bay," PhotoNewZealand.com / Andy Reisinger.
"Austria, 1997" and "Liechtenstein, 1999," photos by Martin Bruch.
"The brains of male and female finches,"『日経サイエンス』2002年4月号、95頁、"Japanese finches and koshijirokinpara,"『日経サイエンス』2002年4月号、94頁(撮影・高橋美樹)。

PLATES

1. YOU: "Norma Field," photo by Sheila Hones.
2. FAT: "Walking and Running," from Dickinson, M. H. et al., *Science*, vol. 288, 2000.
4. Mathematics: "Circle Limit IV (1960)." All M. C. Escher works © Escher Holding B. V., Baarn, the Netherlands. / Huis Ten Bosch, Japan.
5. OBJECTIVITY: "Fujimae tidal flats," photo by Ai Tanji (2005).
7. VOICE: "China Town," photo by Yujin Yaguchi (2004).
8. GENDER: "Darwin," in *Hornet*, 1871 / "Mill," in *Punch*, 1867.
9. COFFEE: "City of Dubrovnik in 2002," photo by Toshio Ohori.
11. VIEW: "Hall in Tirol, 1999," by Martin Bruch.
12. SPACE: "Tenochtitlán: Aztec depiction," The Bodlean Library / "Tenochtitlán: Spanish depiction," The Newberry Library. Reprinted from *For Space*, Sage Publications.
13. SONG:「アラームコール」『日経サイエンス』2002年5月号、69頁「ジュウシマツとコシジロキンパラの歌の比較」『日経サイエンス』2002年4月号、96頁。
14. PHYSICS:「カミオカンデ」田賀井篤平編『小柴昌俊先生ノーベル賞受賞記念 ニュートリノ』(東京大学総合研究博物館、2003年、58頁)。

1
YOU

Introduction
Saito Yoshifumi

In his introduction to *The Games of Robert J. Fischer* Harry Golombek, the English chess player and author, describes the collection of games recorded in the book as a demonstration of 'the unique quality of Bobby Fischer as a player'. Bobby Fischer is a legendary American chess player who became world champion in 1972 but then mysteriously withdrew from serious play soon after, rejecting all the conditions for another championship game and consequently relinquishing his title by default.

But what kind of 'unique quality' of a chess player can a collection of printed games demonstrate? Does this collection of Fischer's games convey to us how uniquely this grandmaster behaved — or misbehaved even — during the World Championship at Reykjavik? Is it a record of something uniquely different from conventional chess in terms of rules or strategy? Not at all. What the book contains is nothing other than a collection of the most beautifully played chess games; Fischer's 'unique quality' shows itself in the superhuman way he accurately combines a very limited number of appropriate moves, chosen from an astronomical number of possible ones, into a series of devastating attacks and stout defenses. In other words, his uniqueness manifests itself within the rigidly fixed code of chess. Golombek hastens to justify his use of the word 'unique' by stating:

> I am not saying that his play has been entirely uninfluenced by those that have gone before him. No player starts off from, as it were, a vacuum and every one of us, from the veriest tyro to the superlative grandmaster, is part of a continuous and unbroken chain in the development of chess throughout the ages.[1]

Saito Yoshifumi: 本テキストの英文では基本的に日本語の氏名は欧米と同様に，「名」「姓」の順で記している。しかし近年の英文では，言及される人物の文化を尊重する意識を込めて，敢えて氏名の順を変えない表記の方法も見られる。日本の氏名が「姓」「名」の順で記されることは学術書などでは珍しくない。ここでは，著者の希望と近年のこのような傾向をふまえ，「姓」「名」の順で日本の氏名を表記している。

[3] **as a demonstration:** demonstration とすぐ後に出て来る demonstrate に，日本語でも使われる「デモ（行進をする）」以外に「実証（する）」という重要な意味があることに注意（9 章 [114]）(cf. She *illustrated* her point by giving some interesting examples.)。

[3] **the unique quality:** unique は本来「他に類がない」「特有の」という意味である（したがってこの意味では very で強調されることも比較級になることもありえない）ことも覚えておきたい (e.g. The giant panda is *unique* to China.)。ただし，日本語の「ユニークな」と同じような意味で用いることもある (e.g. He's very *unique*.)。

[4] **Bobby Fischer:** Robert James Fischer (1943–)。14 歳から全米チェス選手権で 8 連覇を達成した伝説のチェス・プレイヤー。1972 年，アイスランドのレイキャビクでの世界選手権で世界チャンピオンとなる。1975 年，防衛戦の運営をめぐり世界チェス連盟と対立し，不戦敗で失冠。

[8] **relinquishing his title by default:** relinquish [rɪlíŋkwɪʃ] は「（権利などを）放棄する」で，「やむなく」という意味合いを伴うことが多い。default は「義務・約束などの不履行」。winning [losing] a match by default は「不戦勝／不戦敗」。

[14] **in terms of . . . :**「…の観点から」「…に基づいて」といった意味で頻繁に用いられる非常に重要な表現（12 章 [153]）(e.g. The essence of metaphor is understanding and experiencing one kind of thing *in terms of* another. / cf. Let's think about the problem *in* strict mathematical *terms*.)。

[15] **nothing other than . . . :**「…以外の何ものでもない」「…に他ならない」。あるものが何（通例驚くべきもの）であるかを強調して述べる時の決まり文句のひとつ (cf. Can you guess who I bumped into on campus yesterday? It was *none other than* Professor Field!)。

[16] **in the superhuman way . . . :**「…する方法」と言う場合，このように way の直後に…の内容を表す文がそのまま来ることも多い。

[19] **devastating attacks and stout defenses:**「相手に壊滅的な打撃を与える攻撃と相手の攻撃にびくともしない防御」(cf. a *devastating* critique of his theory)。

[20] **manifests itself:**「具体的な形を取って現れる」(cf. Many scholars believe that the capacity for language is *a manifestation of* the unique way the human mind works.)。

[20] **within the rigidly fixed code of chess:**「厳格に決められたチェスの規則体系の範囲内で」。rigid の反意語は flexible。code は本来「法典」(e.g. *code* of ethics/conduct「倫理規約／行動規範」) だが，「暗号（体系）」(e.g. Punch in your *code* number.)，「遺伝暗号」(e.g. genetic *code*) などの意味でもよく用いられる。

[25] **from the veriest tyro to the superlative grandmaster:**「全くの初心者から最上級のグランドマスターまで」。

[26] **a continuous and unbroken chain:** continuous (cf. continuum) も unbroken も，連綿と切れ目なく続くことを表す。continuous の反意語は discrete。

Perhaps we can generalize a moral from this specific remark made about this particular maverick chess genius, one which should always be kept in mind in this age of individualism: you cannot come up with something truly 'unique' and 'original' without learning the basic rules of the activity you are to be involved in and becoming deeply immersed in its long-established traditions and conventions.

Another important point to make in this context is that uniqueness or originality is not a goal you should aspire to attain, but a quality which you unconsciously acquire as a result of, and in proportion to, the efforts you make to improve yourself in that activity. It is very much like a mischievous angel who quickly flies away the instant you ask for his help but comes down unnoticed to assist you when you are exerting yourself to accomplish something he approves of.

Pablo Picasso's early artistic career demonstrates how uniqueness and originality emerge as a result of long and arduous efforts made primarily within a pre-established framework of tradition and convention. We are so familiar with his cubist-style paintings that we tend to think that he was born with a God-given talent for looking at the world in that 'unique' way, but that is not the case. Picasso started out as a conventional representational painter in his early teens and, after going through a massive self-imposed course of training in rudimentary sketching, gradually moulded his own painting style. One of his closest friends testifies to the staggering fact that the piles of his discarded sketch sheets provided sufficient fuel for a stove all winter long. You may be able to become one of Picasso's obscure epigones simply by imitating his artistic style, but you can never become a Picasso if you skip the process he went through.

Individualism is one of the basic tenets of democracy, and the belief that individuals take priority over the aggregate they make up together — family, community, society, nation — has found its way into various codes of conduct at different levels of human relationships. People try to stand out as individuals and be 'uniquely' different from others. American TV programmes encourage you to 'be yourself'. But a casual attempt to be different from other people quite often ends up being just an eccentricity. We should always be mindful that we can only meaningfully behave 'like ourselves' within the whole system of human society, and therefore that we need to make strenuous efforts to learn that system in the first place.

The text for this session is taken from an address made to the

[29] **this particular maverick chess genius:** Bobby Fischer のこと。maverick は「独立独行の（人）」「一匹狼（の）」。

[31] **come up with . . . :**「…を見つけ出す，考え出す」の意味で非常に広く一般的に用いられる表現 (e.g. We'll have to *come up with* some new ideas to get this project off the ground.)。

[33] **becoming deeply immersed in . . . :** become immersed in . . . は「…に浸る，没頭する，熱中する」。

[36] **is not a goal you should aspire to attain:**「達成を目指すべき目標ではない」(cf. He *aspires to* a political career.)。

[39] **It is very much like . . . :** a mischievous [místʃivəs] angel は「いたずら好きの天使」(cf. mischief)。the instant . . . は「…した瞬間に」。the instant が接続詞的に使われていることに注意 (cf. She said she'd give me a call *the moment* she got to the station.)。exert oneself は「最大限の努力をする」。

[44] **arduous:**「（仕事や旅などが）多大な労力を要する」。

[48] **but that is not the case:** 前言の内容を否定する時の決まり文句のひとつで，この場合の the case は「事実」「実情」といった意味 (2 章 [103]) (e.g. If that's *the case*, why don't we call the whole thing off?)。

[49] **in his early teens:** 日本語では時として「ローティーン / ハイティーン」と言うが，それらに当たる英語の表現は (in) one's early [late] teens であることに注意。

[52] **One of his closest friends testifies to . . . :** close friend は日本語の「親友」に相当するよく使われる表現。testify to . . . は「…が事実であると証言する」(e.g. The author's new novel amply *testifies to* her creative talent.)。staggering は「驚くべき」(cf. I was *staggered* by his remarks at last week's meeting.)。

[54] **become one of Picasso's obscure epigones . . . :** obscure は「無名の」，epigone [épɪgòun] は「（思想家や芸術家の）亜流」。「本家」に劣るという意味合いを伴う。become a Picasso は「第二のピカソ [それほど優れた画家] になる」。不定冠詞がついているのは「ピカソのような人」という意味であるため。(cf. He owns *a Picasso*. / *A Mr. Tanaka* called while you were out.)。skip は「（すべきことや普段はすることを）飛ばす，抜く」(e.g. I'm afraid I'll have to *skip* lunch today.)。

[58] **the basic tenets of democracy:**「民主主義の基本原理」。

[58] **the belief . . . :** take priority over . . . は「…に優先する」(cf. be given priority over . . .)。aggregate [ǽgrɪgət] は「集合体」。find one's way は，人を主語にして「目的地にたどり着く」(e.g. Are you sure you'll be able to *find your way* back?) という意味でよく用いられる他に，ものを主語にしてこのように「（いつの間にか）ある場所に入り込んでいる」と言う場合に使うこともある。

[62] **stand out:**「目立つ」「目を引く」の意味でよく用いられる重要な表現 (cf. an *outstanding* performance)。

[64] **But a casual attempt to . . . :** この場合の casual は「軽々しい」という感じ。end up . . . は「（計画したわけではないのに）結局は…ということになる」といった意味でよく用いられる重要な表現で，このように後に . . . ing 形を伴う他に前置詞 + 名詞句が来ることもある (e.g. If he goes on like this, he might *end up* in prison.)。eccentricity < eccentric:「（行動などが）常軌を逸した」(eccentric は「変人」「奇人」という意味の名詞にもなる)。

[65] **be mindful that . . . :**「…ということを心に留めておく」。

[68] **make strenuous efforts:**「大いに努力する」「奮闘する」。

incoming Class of 2002 by Professor Norma Field at the University of Chicago. Read this, and think about what *you* should do now in order to develop your true self.

Only You

Norma Field

I don't know how many of you have read *Robinson Crusoe*, but you probably know that it is an early eighteenth-century novel about a man marooned on a desert island who manages to singlehandedly reproduce the basics of civilization. Well, not quite singlehandedly because he has the assistance of "his" man Friday after rescuing him from the cannibals. Crusoe was a model figure for many eighteenth-century thinkers, who saw in him the ideal individual creating culture by mastering nature. Karl Marx was scathing about the way in which these thinkers mistook Crusoe the isolated individual as something sprung fullblown out of nowhere, or rather, out of nature. They ignored the historical processes necessary to *producing* something as complicated as the individual. (I am sure each of you thinks of yourself as an individual and as complicated, and rightly so.) "The human being," he wrote, " . . . is not merely a gregarious [social] animal, but an animal which can individuate itself only in society." To think about human activity

Norma Field

- [70] **Class of 2002:** 2002 年卒業（予定）の学生たち。つまり 1998 年の入学生。
- [70] **Norma Field:** シカゴ大学教授。専門は日本文学・日本近代文化。著書に *In the Realm of a Dying Emperor*（1991）（『天皇の逝く国で』みすず書房）などがある。

- [73] *Robinson Crusoe*: イギリスのジャーナリスト・小説家であるダニエル・デフォー（Daniel Defoe, 1660–1731）の代表作（1719 年刊）で，イギリス近代小説の原点とも評される。主人公 Robinson Crusoe は，漂着した無人島で，28 年間にわたって，最初はひとりで，のちには Friday という従僕と二人で自給自足の生活を送る。
- [75] **a man marooned on a desert island:**「無人島に置き去りにされた男」。maroon はこのように過去分詞形で用いることが多い（cf. Because of the typhoon, many flights were cancelled or delayed, leaving hundreds of tourists *stranded* at the airport.）。a desert [dézərt] island「（絶海の孤島としての）無人島」も決まった言い方（cf. an uninhabited island）。
- [76] **singlehandedly reproduce the basics of civilization:** singlehandedly は「（他人の助けを借りずに）独力で」。日本語の「女手ひとつで（子供を育て上げる）」などと同じ発想の表現（e.g. She raised two boys *singlehandedly*.）。the basics of . . . は「…の一番基本になること[もの]」という意味の決まり文句（e.g. I wish I could say I always enjoy teaching *the basics of* English grammar. / cf. This book is an excellent introduction to *the fundamentals of* physics.）。
- [76] **Well, not quite singlehandedly:** well はこのように直前の自分の発言を少し修正する際に用いることがある。not quite . . . はいわゆる部分否定（3 章 [2]）で「完全に…というわけではない」といった意味（e.g. I'm still *not quite* myself.「まだ本調子というわけではありません」）。
- [77] **"his" man Friday:** Friday は Robinson Crusoe の忠実なしもべの名前で，そこから man Friday と言えば「忠実な男のしもべ」という一般名詞としても使われるようになった（cf. *one's* [*a girl*] *Friday*）。his が引用符に入っているのは，Friday が実際に Robinson Crusoe の所有物であるわけではないことを強調するため。
- [78] **cannibals:**「人食い人種」（cf. cannibalism）。
- [79] **saw in him . . . :** see . . . in someone は「人に…（魅力，長所など）を見出す」「人が…であると思う」という意味の表現（e.g. I just can't figure out *what* you *see in* him.「あんなやつのどこがいいのかさっぱりわからないね」）。
- [80] **Karl Marx was scathing about . . . :** be scathing about . . . は「…を痛烈に非難する」（e.g. a *scathing* review of his new book）。マルクスがロビンソン・クルーソーに言及しているのは，『経済学批判』の準備として 1857–61 年に執筆した草稿の一部においてである。この草稿は，20 世紀になってから『経済学批判要綱』として整理されるが，クルーソーへの言及はその「序」の冒頭部分に見られる。
- [82] **something sprung fullblown out of nowhere:** spring は「突然現れる」「急に飛び出す」。fullblown は「完全に発達した」「本格的な」（cf. full-fledged / fully fledged）。out of nowhere は「どこからともなく（現れる）」（9 章 [44]）（cf. (appear) out of thin air）。
- [86] **and rightly so:** 前言の内容について「それで正しいのですよ」「それは当然のことなのです」と言う場合の決まり文句（cf. for [with] good reason）。
- [88] **individuate itself only in society:** individuate は「同種の他の個体と明確に異なるものにする」。したがって individuate oneself は「個を確立する」といった感じ。「社会」を意味する society が無冠詞であることにも注意（e.g. *Japanese society* is not nearly as homogeneous as some popular books make it out to be.）。

outside society, he continued, "is as much of an absurdity as is the development of language without individuals living *together* and talking to each other."[2] Notice that he is not denying that individuals exist. They do, of course, but as made up of what he refers to as social relations.

Marx mostly elaborates social relations in terms of economic processes relying on and producing differences in power. All too often, scholars (and bankers and policy experts) forget to think about how economic processes translate into the details of human life that are far removed from dollars and cents. So let's get at it from the other end, and think about social relations in terms of who you are. In saying that you are the product, most literally, of your parents, we also have to think about everything that brought them together; we have to think about other family members, the places where you grew up, the kinds of schools you went to, the movies you saw, the language of your parents and the language of your friends (even if they're both English, they could be quite different), the clothes you wore. It's not just things, including places, that count. It's the relations — resources of income, knowledge, skills, friends and neighbors — that made those things part of your life. For instance, were your clothes chosen for you? If you were able to buy them, was it with money you earned or money given to you? Did you have access to a car? Or did you become expert in getting around on public transportation?

What are your capabilities, you who are unique beings embodying a diversity of backgrounds? Having so emphasized the ways in which we have been socially produced — the breaking down part — I want to focus for a moment on the rebuilding part, or rather, the concrete persons you are now. I'm going to do this by quoting from a letter by a children's book editor to a very young author, or author to be, someone still in high school, in fact:

> And never forget that what you told me is something ONLY YOU know about; no one else knows just what you know about anything. And that is why it will be so important for you to put down your thoughts and emotions in picture book form.[3]

The editor's name is Ursula Nordstrom, and she was director of Harper's Department of Books for Boys and Girls from 1940 to 1973. She was an innovator, someone who sought to make "good books for bad children," and she was responsible for books that many of you may remember, such as *Goodnight Moon, Charlotte's Web,* or *Where the Wild Things Are.* This quotation is from a letter to

[89] **is as much of an absurdity as is . . .**:「…と変わらないほどばかげている」。is just as absurd as is . . . とほぼ同じ意味。このように比較表現の as や than の後では倒置がしばしば起こる。

[92] **as made up of what he refers to as social relations:**「(マルクスが)社会的関係と呼ぶものから構成された存在として」。refer to A as B で「A を B と呼ぶ」。

[94] **elaborates:** < elaborate: add more information to or develop further.

[95] **All too . . .**: 程度のはなはだしさを表すのによく用いられ，このようにネガティブな気持ちが込められていることが多い (e.g. In an emergency like this, it's *all too* easy to jump to a faulty conclusion.)。

[96] **how economic processes translate into . . .**: A translates into B は「A (抽象概念など)が形を変えて B (現実など)になる」(e.g. His words hardly ever *translate into* action.)。

[97] **are far removed from . . .**: are removed from . . . は「…からかけ離れた」。dollars and cents は「経済」や「お金」に関することを表すのによく用いられる組み合わせで，ここではすぐ前の economic processes の言い換え。この表現のもじりから生まれた dollars and sense という表現もある。

[98] **get at . . .**:「…を突き止める」(e.g. We are determined to *get at* the truth.)。

[100] **literally:**「文字通りに」。反意語は figuratively「比喩的に」。

[101] **everything that brought them together:**「父と母がそもそも出会った理由のすべて」。bring . . . together はここでは「…を出会わせる」。「(より)親しくさせる」「仲直りさせる」の意味を表すこともある (e.g. The crisis *brought* us closer *together*.)。

[106] **It's not just . . . that count:**「重要なのは…だけではありません」。この場合の count は「重要である」という意味の自動詞 (e.g. It's the thought that *counts*.「大切なのは気持ちです」)。

[110] **have access to . . .**:「…を使う[…を見る，…に入る]ことができる(立場にある)」(cf. Very few people are *allowed access to* the lab.)。

[111] **on public transportation:** public transportation は「(電車，バスなどの)公共交通機関」を表す集合不可算名詞。*on* the train, *on* the bus などの場合と同じく *on* public transportation となっていることにも注意。

[113] **embodying:** embody は「(抽象概念などを)体現する」(cf. He is *the embodiment of* kindness.)。

[118] **author to be:**「後に作家になる人」。. . . -to-be (普通はハイフンを入れる)は「将来…になる人」「未来の…」(e.g. a bride-*to-be* / cf. a *would-be* author「作家志望の人[自称作家]」)。

[122] **put down . . .**: 普通「…を書き留める」(e.g. Let's *put* some ideas *down* on paper.) だが，この場合には絵本なので文字や数字だけではなく，絵で表現することも含まれている。

[125] **Harper's:** 1817 年創業の J. & J. Harper 社に連なるニューヨークの老舗出版社。特に人文系，児童書の出版で有名。

[127] **she was responsible for . . .**: A is responsible for B (「A は B に対して責任がある」) は通常「B (ネガティブな物事)が生じたのは A のせいである」という意味 (e.g. It didn't take Holmes long to determine who *was responsible for* the murders.)。しかし，このように「B (よい物事)が生じたのは A のおかげである」という意味を表すこともある (e.g. She's *responsible for* most of the ideas that have made this project a big success.)。

[128] ***Goodnight Moon, Charlotte's Web,* or *Where the Wild Things Are***: いずれも 1950 年代から 60 年代にかけて Harper 社から出版された児童書。

African-American author and illustrator John Steptoe.

When I first read this letter, with "only you" all in capital letters, I thought instantly that this was not only a wonderful thing for an editor to say to a fledgling author, but for teachers to tell their students. And it is something that can be said truthfully to every student, for the reasons I have been trying to lay out. But notice that Nordstrom follows up the claim that "no one else knows just what you know about anything" with the injunction to "put down your thoughts and emotions." I think she was emphasizing the importance of letting the world see the unique knowledge of a talented young man, but I also believe Steptoe himself needed to put down his "thoughts and emotions" in picture book form in order to really know what he knew. And this is what you will be asked to do, over and over, though probably not in picture book form, and with the emphasis on thoughts, not emotions. (Keep in mind, though, that emotional investment plays a considerable role in shaping knowledge.) You might even think of your education as a continuing encounter with what you know through your developing capability to externalize it. This, in turn, will give you greater clarity about the new knowledge demanding to be let in.

I am using the language of inside and outside metaphorically, of course. What we know from our experiences is precisely what we learn through interaction with the world, including the world of books and CDs and videos. "Only you know" what you know not because that knowledge was miraculously generated inside you out of nothing, but because each of you is a unique historical accumulation of interaction with the world. There is no end to that process, but the more we can be conscious of it, the more actively we can give to and take from the world.

---

¹ Harry Golombek, "Fischer the Artist," Robert G. Wade and Kevin J. O'Connell, eds., *The Games of Robert J. Fischer* (London: B.T. Batsford Ltd., 1972, pp. 13–20).
² "Introduction of 1857," *Grundrisse: Foundations of the Critique of Political Economy* (Harmondsworth: Penguin Books, 1993), pp. 83–84. Emphasis in the original.
³ Leonard S. Marcus, ed., *Dear Genius: The Letters of Ursula Nordstrom* (New York: HarperCollins, 1998), pp. 240–41.

[130] **John Steptoe:** 本文にあるとおり，アフリカ系アメリカ人の絵本作家・絵本画家（1950–89）。16歳から書きはじめた *Stevie* が 1969 年に Harper 社から出版され，一躍脚光を浴びた。代表作は，*Mufaro's Beautiful Daughters*（1988）。

[133] **a fledgling author:** 前出の author to be の言い換え。fledgling は（「羽が生えかけの」から）「…になりたての」「駆け出しの」という意味（cf. full-fledged / fully fledged / full-blown）。

[134] **something that can be said truthfully to every student:**「どんな生徒に対して言ってもあてはまること」。

[135] **lay out:** express or present clearly.

[136] **Nordstrom follows up the claim ...:** follow up A with B は「A をした後（その効果をより確かなものにするなどのために）B をする」（e.g. When you make an appointment with him, I suggest that you *follow up* your phone call *with* an e-mail message. / cf. a *follow-up* experiment）。the claim that ... は「…という主張」（cf. He claimed that he had done nothing wrong.）。injunction: a piece of advice.

[144] **Keep in mind, though, that ...:**「でも，…ということは忘れないで下さい」。though が「でも」「しかし」の意味で用いられる際にはこのように文の途中（または最後）に来ることに注意。

[145] **emotional investment:** involving your feelings.

[146] **You might even think of ...:** think of A as B は「A を B であると考える」（e.g. I *think of* him *as* my mentor.）。

[147] **your developing capability to externalize it:** it は what you know を指す。externalize「外在化する」とは，例えば自分の考えを書き留める（put down your thoughts）こと。developing はそのような能力が今も発達し続けていることを表現している。

[148] **This, in turn, will:** in turn は「すぐ前で述べたことの結果として今度は…という事態が生じる」という場合によく用いられる表現。

[149] **to be let in:** let ... in または let in ... は「…を中に入れてやる」（cf. *Let* me *out*.）。外にある知識が中に入れてくれと要求しているという比喩。この場合の let in はすぐ前の externalize（= let out）と対になっている。

[150] **metaphorically:**「内側」「外側」というのが metaphor（隠喩，喩え）であり，すぐ後で述べるように，正確な表現ではない（内と外が容器のように截然と分かれているわけではない）ことに注意を促している。

[156] **There is no end to that process:**「そのプロセスには終わりはありません」（cf. *There is a limit to* the amount of work you can do in a week.）。前出の a *continuing* encounter ... や your *developing* capability ... などと響き合う表現。

2. FAT

Introduction
Naokata Ishii

Take a look around you while you are on the train to school. You will no doubt find the word *daietto* somewhere along the way. According to the editors of weekly and monthly magazines, "anything that has an article related to diet will always sell well." Our society is full of so-called "diet" foods and exercise equipment that promise consumers effective ways of losing weight. Why are people so interested in "losing weight"?

First of all, before we even start to deal with this question, we have to remember that being "fat" has nothing to do with the innate value of a person. In fact, a person who is on the heavy side is quite often thought of as being rather relaxed and kind, whereas a thin person may be regarded as a bit nervous. Social preference for particular body shapes changes over time. It is quite possible that in the future there may come a time when a heavier body type is preferred.

On the other hand, as long as humans are biological creatures, "staying healthy" will be something that remains an absolute value. For an average male between the ages of 20 and 30, 40% of body weight consists of muscle and 20% consists of fat. Not all of this fat is unnecessary baggage. One gram of fat has 9 kcal of energy. This figure is twice that of the energy level of glucose. In other words, fat is the best source of energy for the human body. Medically speaking, when body fat is less than 10%, various functions of the body go into decline. In contrast, when body fat exceeds 25% — a condition characterized as "obesity" — the chances of diabetes and heart diseases increase.

Regardless of social preferences for particular body shapes, it is important to keep the percentage of the body fat between 10 and

[4] **will always sell well:**「(…は)常によく売れる」。sell の主語が売られるものになっているのは,(売る人の能力や努力ではなく)そのものに備わった特性ゆえに売れるという行為が実現することを強調するため (cf. His latest book on philosophy *reads* like a thriller.)。

[6] **promise consumers effective ways of losing weight:** promise は「人にものを(与えると)約束する」という場合にこのように二重目的語構文でよく用いられる (e.g. My parents *promised* me a new car if I passed the entrance exam.)。lose weight は「やせる」という時の決まった表現のひとつ (cf. gain [put on] weight)で, weight の前に their などの所有代名詞がつかないことに注意(someone's weight はその全体重を意味する)。

[10] **on the heavy side:**「太目の」(cf. He's a bit *on the* short *side* for a basketball player.)。

[19] **Not all of this fat is unnecessary baggage:**「この脂肪がすべて不必要な手荷物というわけではない」。baggage は「旅行の際に持ち歩く荷物」だが, ここではもちろん比喩的に使われている。複数のものを(目的, 機能などの観点から)まとめて指す baggage, luggage, furniture, stationery などが不可算名詞(以下では集合不可算名詞と呼ぶ)であることにも注意(3 章 [131], 10 章 [196])。

[25] **obesity** [oʊbíːsəti]:「肥満」(cf. overweight)。形容詞は obese [oʊbíːs]。

[25] **the chances of diabetes and heart diseases increase:**「糖尿病や心臓病にかかる可能性が高くなる」。chance はこのように「可能性」「見込み」という意味を表すことも多い (e.g. There *is a chance that* …「…という可能性がある」/ She *has a very good chance of* full recovery.)。*(The) chances are* …「多分…」, "Fat chance!"「まさか」「ありえないよ」などの決まった言い方も chance のこの用法の応用例。diabetes [daɪəbíːtiːz] は「糖尿病」(cf. diabetic「糖尿病患者」)。

20% for men and 15 and 25% for women simply in order to stay healthy. It is quite popular today to try to reduce body fat by diet or by limiting the amount of food intake, but this method results in the loss of muscle as well as fat. This, in turn, leads to the decline of the basal metabolism — the consumption of energy necessary to maintain life — and this actually makes the body more prone to gaining weight. This session introduces some recent findings about the relationship between body fat and health, and discusses an effective way of reducing body fat through the everyday activity of walking.

Walking Off Your Fat

Naokata Ishii

I am a body builder, but because I've been rather busy lately I have not been getting much exercise. I can feel a little bit of fat around my belly. In technical terms, this "spare tyre" I've been acquiring is made up of subcutaneous fat, or body fat, and in the field of sport science there has been a rapid development of research on this topic lately. Body fat is clearly not a good thing. It's bad not only for athletes but for all of us, because too much fat affects our body shape and threatens our health. Clinical studies clearly show that obesity can lead to such serious illnesses as heart failure, brain damage, and diabetes. However, the actual mechanism of how obesity triggers these illnesses is not yet clear. Although scholars have come up with many complicated and sophisticated theories about the connection, they still find it rather difficult to answer the simple question, "why is it bad to be on the heavy side?" However, recent studies showing that fat tissue is actually a kind of endocrine organ are now helping us to understand the relationship between health and fat.

Fat tissue is mainly made up of fat cells. Some time ago, it was discovered that these fat cells secrete a hormone called "leptin." This was quite a discovery because it showed that fat tissue is actually an endocrine organ. The leptin is secreted when fat cells accumulate neutral fat. This leptin affects the central nervous system

[32] **This, in turn, leads to the decline of the basal metabolism:** in turn は「(すぐ前で述べたことの結果として)今度は(…という事態が生じる)」という場合によく用いられる表現(1章[148])。basal metabolism は「基礎代謝」。

Walking Off Your Fat:「歩いて脂肪を落とす[減らす]」。日本語では動詞を2つ使わなければ表現できないことが英語では動詞1つで言い表わされることに注意 (cf. *work off* a few calories, *shout* oneself *hoarse*, *laugh* an actor *off* the stage)。

[41] **this "spare tyre":** お腹のまわりの贅肉はしばしばこのように「スペアタイア」に喩えられる (cf. a potbellied man)。

[42] **made up of subcutaneous fat:**「皮下脂肪でできている」(cf. a *subcutaneous* injection「皮下注射」)。

[46] **Clinical studies clearly show that . . . :**「臨床研究で…ということが明らかになっている」。

[49] **how obesity triggers these illnesses:**「肥満がどのようにしてこれらの病気の誘因になるのか」。trigger は「(銃の)引き金」から派生した「誘因」の意味をもつが,さらにこのように「…の引き金[誘因]になる」という因果関係を表す動詞としてもよく使われる(9章[158])。

[50] **scholars have come up with many complicated and sophisticated theories:** come up with ... は非常に広い守備範囲をもつ重要表現(1章[31], 5章[93])であるが,ここでは「考え出す」「思いつく」「考案する」に相当する。sophisticated は「(理論,仕組みなどが)高度で複雑な」。

[53] **fat tissue:**「脂肪組織」。

[54] **endocrine organ:**「内分泌器官」。

[56] **fat cells:**「脂肪細胞」。

[57] **secrete** [sɪkríːt] **a hormone:**「ホルモンを分泌する」。

[60] **neutral fat:**「中性脂肪」。

and decreases the appetite while at the same time activating the sympathetic nervous system and encouraging the fat to dissolve, thereby thinning the cell that had begun to fatten. You can see why leptin came to be considered the ultimate weapon in the struggle to lose weight. More recent research, however, has shown that there are large secretions of leptin in routine obesity, so it's obvious that leptin secretions don't necessarily lead to weight loss. Another hormone called "adiponectin" has also been discovered recently. This hormone appears to speed up the metabolism of fatty acids by affecting the liver and skeletal muscles. These two hormones, leptin and adiponectin, can thus be thought of as "good hormones" that improve your fat metabolism.

Other research has shown, however, that fat cells also secrete a hormone that has a negative effect on your body. This "bad" hormone, named "resistin," hinders the work of insulin on fat cells, the liver, and skeletal muscles. Under normal circumstances, insulin is secreted from your pancreas once your blood glucose level increases. In the right amounts, its effect is beneficial in that it reduces your blood glucose levels. But if there is too much resistin, this insulin becomes less effective, and your blood glucose level may not go down after all. This condition is called "insulin resistance" — which is why this troublesome hormone is called "resistin." "Insulin resistance" is basically an early symptom of diabetes. In other words, it can be said that fat cells secrete a substance that triggers diabetes.

In addition to resistin, fat cells secrete several hormonal substances called "cytokines." It seems likely that one of these cytokines leads to the depositing of a fatty substance in your blood vessels, thereby triggering the hardening and narrowing of your arteries, which is obviously not a good thing. In short, it seems that fat cells secrete substances that cause myocardial infarction and brain infarction. So we have reached at least some understanding of the precise reasons why fat cells are not good for our bodies. Having got this far, what are we going to do to get rid of those unhealthy spare tyres we tend to develop? What are some of the practical steps we can take to resist encroaching fat? Steps, actually, may be the key word. Let's think about walking.

Walking has become quite a popular form of exercise in recent years. It's categorized as a type of aerobics, just like jogging. However, unlike jogging it has the advantage of not putting too much stress on your joints and circulatory system. Serious athletes might dismiss walking as too easy an exercise to have any effect on the

- [62] **sympathetic nervous system:**「交感神経系」。
- [62] **encouraging the fat to dissolve:**「脂肪の分解を促す」。
- [63] **thereby thinning the cell:** thereby「それによって」はこのように分詞構文の分詞節の先頭に用いて主節と分詞節の内容の因果関係を表すことが多い（e.g. We have managed to simplify the design of our products, *thereby* making them user-friendly.）。
- [66] **large secretions of leptin:**「レプチンの大量分泌」。
- [69] **fatty acids:**「脂肪酸」。
- [70] **skeletal muscles:**「骨格筋」。
- [77] **pancreas:**「膵臓」。
- [83] **an early symptom of diabetes:**「糖尿病の初期症状」。
- [88] **the depositing of a fatty substance in your blood vessels:**「脂肪物質が血管に蓄積すること」。
- [89] **the hardening and narrowing of your arteries:**「動脈が固く狭くなること」。hardening of the arteries は「動脈硬化」。
- [91] **myocardial infarction:**「心筋梗塞」。
- [95] **What are some of the practical steps . . . ?:**「忍び寄る脂肪に抵抗するために実行できる手段としてはどんなものがあるであろうか」。What are some of the . . .（複数名詞）? は具体的に例を挙げることを求める際によく用いられるパターン（e.g. I understand you're a movie buff. *What are some of the* films that made you cry?）。take steps (to . . .) は「（…という目的を達成するために)対策[措置]を講じる」「（…するように）対処する」（e.g. We'd better *take immediate steps* to keep our reputation from declining any further.）。この場合の steps は「特定の目的を達成するまでに踏むべき諸段階」といった意味であり，歩く時の一歩，二歩，…という場合の step(s) の基本的用法の比喩的な転用。すぐ後の "Steps, actually, may be the key word." ではこの原義との関連が活用されている。
- [100] **it has the advantage of . . . :** have the advantage of . . . は「…という利点がある」という場合の決まった言い方。このように advantage には「利点」「長所」という意味があることはよく覚えておきたい（e.g. Both candidates have their *advantages and disadvantages*.）。また発音は [ədvǽntɪdʒ] で日本語のアドバンテージとは相当異なることにも注意が必要。
- [101] **joints and circulatory system:**「関節と循環器系」。
- [102] **dismiss walking as . . . :** dismiss は「重要でないと考えてまともに取り合わない」「一笑に付す」の意味で，このように as . . .（「…として」）を伴うことがよくある（e.g. He *dismissed* my suggestion *as* impractical.）。

body, but actually that is not the case. Taking a long walk is a highly effective way of burning body fat. What's more, because walking is something you have to do every day, if you consciously utilize it as a form of exercise you will be able to get a very good cumulative result.

Walking and running are entirely different forms of exercise. Running is commonly defined as a movement in which there is a clear moment when both feet are off the ground. Here are two simple models of running and walking [fig. 1]. In walking, your center of gravity is at its highest when it is right above one of your legs. In other words, in walking we move forward efficiently when the right and left legs move alternately like a "reverse pendulum." This move is often characterized as "a rolling egg movement." On the other hand, when you are running, your center of gravity is at its lowest point when it is located directly above a leg — actually, the leg that is touching the ground. This leg serves as a kind of spring that propels you forward by directing your center of gravity to move diagonally ahead. This action enables you to get a strong propelling force but it also actually breaks your speed because you have to wait until your center of gravity is right above your leg again before you can start pushing yourself forward again.

In 1973, T. J. Dawson and C. R. Taylor published a very interesting article in the famous science journal *Nature* analyzing the energy cost of locomotion in kangaroos. Kangaroos propel themselves along using their arms, legs, and tail until their speed reaches 6 km/h. Until this point, the amount of energy consumed increases in proportion with the increase in speed. Once the kangaroos reach the speed of 6 km/h, however, they start hopping. At this point, interestingly, the amount of energy consumed remains the same despite the increase in speed. This is because their long Achilles' tendons serve as effective springs. Although human beings do not have long Achilles' tendons like kangaroos, a similar phenomenon can be observed. According to R. Margaria (1938), up until a speed of 7.5 km/h, walking requires less energy than running on a flat surface. But the reverse is true when the speed is higher. What this means is that when one reaches a speed of 7.5 km/h, it requires less energy to run than to walk. This is why human beings quite naturally begin to run when reaching this speed. If they decided to keep on walking, it would require more and more energy as their speed increased.

The reason why it requires less energy to walk when moving at less than 7.5 km/h is probably because human beings have acquired an efficient way of walking with two legs — the reverse pendulum

- [103] **that is not the case:** すぐ前で述べられた意見について「そうではない」「それは間違っている」と言う時の決まり文句のひとつ（1章 [48]）。この場合の the case は「事実」「実情」という意味（e.g. If *that's the case*, we may have to consider taking legal action.「それが事実なら，法的措置を講じることを考えなければならなくなるかもしれない」）。
- [104] **What's more:**「その上」「それに」。前言に付け加える時の決まり文句のひとつ（cf. in addition/besides）。
- [114] **the right and left legs move alternately:**「右足と左足が交互に動く」。
- [118] **serves as . . . :**「…の役割を果たす」「…として働く」という場合の決まった言い方（e.g. If you want to stay here overnight, this sofa will *serve as* a bed.）。
- [119] **propels:**「推進させる」。
- [120] **move diagonally ahead:**「斜め前方に移動する」。
- [121] **breaks your speed:** この場合の break は「（力や勢いを）弱める，減じる」の意味（e.g. They managed to *break* his fall with a mattress.「落下の衝撃を和らげる」）。
- [125] **the energy cost of locomotion in kangaroos:**「カンガルーの運動のエネルギーコスト」。「エネルギーコスト」はこの場合，一定距離，例えば 1 km を移動するのにどれだけエネルギーを必要とするかを示す。自動車でいえば「燃費」に相当する。
- [128] **in proportion with . . . :**「…に比例して」。
- [132] **their long Achilles'** [əkiliːz] **tendons:**「カンガルーの長いアキレス腱」。日本語で「弱点」という意味で比喩的に用いられる場合の「アキレス腱」に相当する英語は one's Achilles' heel（e.g. Bill's lack of confidence is his *Achilles' heel*.）。

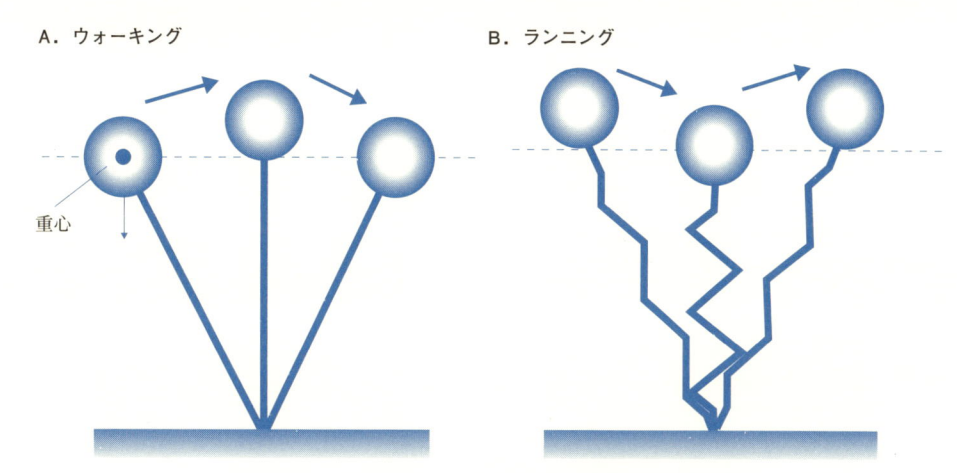

fig. 1 ヒトの歩行（A）と走行（B）の単純な力学モデル
Dickinson, M. H. et al., *Science*, vol. 288, 2000 より改変。

method illustrated in the diagram. It is generally understood that the walking speed which requires the least energy per kilometer would be 3 km/h to 5 km/h. This is because the movement of our legs has a natural frequency of oscillation and when you walk according to that natural movement your speed would be somewhere between 3 km/h and 5 km/h.

You have probably heard that the standard speed for walking is 4 km/h, and this is clearly the most desirable speed from the perspective of energy conservation. When utilizing walking as exercise, however, it is necessary to walk at a speed that requires more than the minimum expenditure of energy. When you walk at the speed of 7.5 km/h, it requires as much energy as jogging at the same speed. Moreover, you can prevent the long-term muscle fatigue associated with jogging that is caused by the stretching movement involved in running. So if you walk at 7.5 km/h for 30 minutes, you will consume 300 kcal of energy. If the speed was only a little slower, at 5.5 km/h, you would have to walk for 70 minutes to consume the same amount of energy. Furthermore, what's significant is that half of this energy expended through walking will be taken from your body fat. So you can see that by exercising this way, it is possible to lose almost 1 kg of body fat within a matter of a single month!

[148] **a natural frequency of oscillation:**「固有振動数」。重力以外の外力を加えず，振り子のように自然振動させたときの振動数。

[165] **within a matter of a single month:**「ほんの1ヶ月で」。a matter of seconds [hours/days/inches] 等は時間や距離の短さを強調する場合の決まった表現型（e.g. Things returned to normal *within a matter of weeks*.）。

3.
TRADITION

Introduction
Yujin Yaguchi

Many people associate Hawai'i with warm sunshine and beautiful beaches. While that image is not entirely inaccurate, the landscape of Hawai'i is actually far more varied than most people imagine. Particularly striking are the high mountains and deep valleys created by volcanic activity thousands of years ago. When the famous American novelist Mark Twain visited the island of Kauai in 1866, he was so astounded by the grandeur of Waimea Canyon, which is more than 3,600 feet deep, that he decided to call it the "Grand Canyon of the Pacific." Other islands boast similar scenery. Mt. Haleakala in Maui is over 12,000 feet high. The island of Hawai'i has Mauna Loa, standing at 13,367 feet. And adjoining this peak is the tallest mountain in the Hawaiian island chain, Mauna Kea, soaring up to 13,796 feet.

Mauna Kea means "white mountain" in the Hawaiian language, and the mountain was named that way because in the winter the summit is often capped by snow. Over the past several decades, astronomers have taken advantage of the fact that this high mountain peak offers one of the best environments in the world for observing the sky. The elevation, clear and dry air, stable weather, and distance from city lights allow scientists to carefully and accurately measure infrared and sub-millimeter radiation from celestial sources, and this has enabled them to make some important discoveries. As a result, the summit of Mauna Kea is now the largest astronomical facility in the world. The W. M. Keck Observatory, for example, has the world's largest optical and infrared telescopes. Each telescope is eight stories tall! Japan's National Astronomical Observatory has a large and extremely sophisticated telescope called Subaru. Other

- [1] **Many people associate Hawai'i with . . . :** associate A with B は「A を B と結びつけて考える」「A と言うと B を連想する」。
- [1] **Hawai'i:** ハワイ州は，ハワイ諸島からなるアメリカ合衆国第 50 番目の州(州となったのは 1959 年)。この章の舞台となる Mauna Kea のあるハワイ島は，ハワイ諸島最大の島。アメリカ連邦政府は，従来より Hawaii という表記を州の正式名称としてきた。しかし地元ハワイにおいては，現在，ハワイ語に沿った Hawai'i という表記のほうが普及しており，州政府，ほとんどの公的機関，および主要なメディアもこの表記を用いている。発音は「ハワイイ」に近い(ただし，形容詞として用いる際は Hawaiian という英語表記になる)。
- [2] **that image is not entirely inaccurate:**「そのイメージは全く不正確というわけではない」。not entirely . . . はいわゆる「部分否定」(1 章 [76])で「全く…というわけではない」という意味を表す (e.g. I guess you are right. But I'm still *not entirely* convinced.)。しばしば批判的な発言の口調を和らげるために用いる。
- [4] **Particularly striking are . . . :** . . . を主語とする倒置の構文。主語が新たに導入される話題である場合にはこのように倒置構文がしばしば用いられる(5 章 [64], 13 章 [208]) (e.g. *Beside the shed was* the motorcycle. / *Among the topics to be covered in today's lecture is* the vital importance of cross-cultural communication skills.)。
- [7] **grandeur** [grǽndʒər]:「壮大さ」。
- [9] **Other islands boast similar scenery:**「他の島々も同じような景色を誇っている」。日本語の「誇る」と同様，boast は「場所や組織（A）に優れた特長（B）がある」という場合に A boasts B という形で用いることができる (e.g. This university *boasts* a number of outstanding scholars specializing in a wide range of disciplines.)。scenery が集合不可算名詞であることに注意 (e.g. Her house is surrounded by magnificent *scenery*./cf. Such a scene will make her cry.)。
- [11] **And adjoining this peak is . . . :**「そしてこの頂に隣接しているのが…である」。再び倒置の構文。adjoin は be next to と同義。この場合，(意味は相当変わってしまうが)もし主語を文頭にもって来て普通の語順にもどすと，"The tallest mountain . . . *adjoins* this peak." となることにも注意 (cf. A tacit assumption underlies his argument./Underlying his argument is a tacit assumption.)。
- [16] **capped by snow:**「頂上が雪に覆われた」(cf. a *snow-capped* mountain)。
- [25] **optical and infrared telescopes:**「光学望遠鏡と赤外線望遠鏡」。
- [27] **a large and extremely sophisticated telescope:** sophisticated はこのように「（機械や方法などが）高度に発達した」「高性能の」という意味を表すことがよくある (e.g. a highly *sophisticated* security system)。口絵参照。

countries, such as France, Britain, and Germany, also have their own telescopes with which to conduct investigations into the celestial system from this ideal spot in the Pacific.

This "astronomy industry" is commonly thought to bring material benefits to the Hawaiian economy, by creating jobs and boosting tourism. Besides, many residents find it exciting to think that their island is a place where great discoveries are being made. At the same time, however, in recent years a growing number of people have become ambivalent about, or, at times, downright opposed to the presence of astronomers at Mauna Kea. This is because Mauna Kea is considered a sacred mountain by Native Hawaiian people.

Today's Native Hawaiians are the descendants of the indigenous people who were living on the islands when Captain James Cook and other Europeans and Americans arrived in the late eighteenth century. Over the centuries, their nation, the Hawaiian Kingdom, has been destroyed and many of their cultural traditions have changed. But many Hawaiian people have retained their sense of identity as Native Hawaiians. Through the contemporary political movement for minority rights to be recognized by the local and federal governments, more and more Native Hawaiians (and people who support them) are realizing the importance of salvaging and maintaining traditional Hawaiian values, beliefs, and language. To these people, the state of the Mauna Kea summit today seems like an insult, because the telescopes are standing on a site that was, and still is, a sacred temple for Native Hawaiians.

The astronomers disagree. They argue that Mauna Kea is indispensable to the advancement of human knowledge. They want to keep using the summit and introducing ever more advanced telescopes, so that they can continue to make new discoveries for the sake of all humankind, of course including Native Hawaiians.

The following two articles explain the different positions of the two sides. It is important to remember that this disagreement is not a clash between the primitive and the advanced. Native Hawaiians are modern and modernized people, just as much as the astronomers. They are trying to exercise the rights they are entitled to as a minority people in today's modern society. And astronomers are not necessarily believers in science for science's sake. They understand, at least to a certain degree, the importance in the contemporary world of recognizing Native Hawaiian values as well as protecting the environment. That is precisely what makes assessing the different claims of the two positions rather difficult. But this kind of

[31] **"astronomy industry":** 引用符に入っているのは，結果として「産業」と同様の経済効果をもたらしているので比喩的に「産業」と呼んでいる，という含み。

[32] **by creating jobs and boosting tourism:** create jobs はよく用いられる決まった組み合わせで，日本語の「雇用を創出する」という表現に対応する (cf. jobs *creation*「雇用創出」)。boost: improve, increase, make more successful (e.g. The manager's pep talk helped *boost* the team's morale. / cf. That song was a great morale *boost*.)

[35] **a growing number of . . . :**「…が増えている」という場合によく用いられる表現 (e.g. *A growing number of* teenagers find it hard to get by without their cell phones even for a single day.)。

[36] **become ambivalent about . . . :** come to have mixed feelings or conflicting ideas about . . .

[36] **at times, downright opposed to . . . :**「時として完全に…に反対する気持ちになることがある」。downright はネガティブな表現の意味をさらに強める場合によく用いられる副詞 (e.g. I found his remarks *downright* rude.)。

[39] **the descendants of the indigenous people:**「ハワイにもともと住んでいた人々の子孫」。

[40] **Captain James Cook:** イギリスの探検航海者（1728–79）。3回の太平洋航海を行い，第3回航海の途上，1778年にハワイ諸島を訪れたが，翌年再訪した際，島民との対立で殺害された。

[42] **the Hawaiian Kingdom:** ハワイ王国。カメハメハ一世がハワイ諸島を統一した1810年から，リリウオカラニ女王が白人住人を中心とする勢力によるクーデターによって退位させられた1893年まで，ハワイ諸島にあった王国。その後1898年，ハワイはアメリカに併合された。

[49] **traditional Hawaiian values:**「価値観」という意味の values は常に複数形で用いられることに注意(10章[193]) (e.g. moral *values*)。

[56] **for the sake of all humankind:**「人類すべてのために」。「人類」という意味の mankind に代わってこのように humankind を使うことが多くなっている。「男性」をも意味しうる言葉で人類全体を表現することは「政治的に正しくない」（politically incorrect）という立場から。

[60] **a clash:**「集団（例えば警官隊とデモ隊）間の物理的衝突」「（意見などの）衝突，対立」という意味でよく用いる (cf. Police *clashed* with demonstrators. / It is not uncommon for my interests to *clash* with his.)。「(車の)衝突」「(飛行機の)墜落」などを表す crash（および同じ形の動詞）と混同しないように注意が必要 (e.g. a plane *crash* / His car *crashed* into a tree.)。

[62] **exercise the rights they are entitled to:** 動詞 exercise は（「運動する」「練習する」以外にも）このように「（権利，権力などを）行使する」という意味でよく用いられる。be entitled to . . . は「…（権利や資格）を与えられている」という意味で，to 以下には名詞句のほか不定詞句が来ることもある (e.g. Members of this association *are entitled to* (receive) the biannual journal.)。

[64] **believers in science for science's sake:** cf. *believe in* science for science's sake.

[65] **the importance in the contemporary world of . . . :**「現代世界における…の重要性」。importance と結びついている of . . . 以下が長いため the contemporary world の後に置かれていることに注意。

clash is likely to increase in the future in other parts of the world, including Japan, as the valued traditions of particular groups of people become threatened by scientific progress.

Why is Mauna Kea so Sacred to the Native Hawaiian People?

The Royal Order of Kamehameha I & Mauna Kea Anaina Hou

The summit of Mauna Kea represents many things to the indigenous people of Hawai'i. The upper regions of Mauna Kea reside in Wao Akua, the realm of the Akua — Creator. It is also considered the Temple of the Supreme Being and is acknowledged as such in many oral and written histories throughout Polynesia, which pre-date modern science by millennia. It is the home of Na Akua (the Divine Deities), Na 'Aumakua (the Divine Ancestors), and the meeting place of Papa (Earth Mother) and Wakea (Sky Father) who are considered the progenitors of the Hawaiian People. Mauna Kea, it is said, is where the Sky and Earth separated to form the Great-Expanse-of-Space and the Heavenly Realms. Mauna Kea in every respect represents the zenith of the Native Hawaiian people's ancestral ties to Creation itself.

The Mauna Kea issue has been a long and emotionally charged controversy. This is so because, throughout the deliberations, some very basic fundamental rights have been ignored and abridged, the right to freedom of religion, the right to have a spiritual relationship with the land of our birth.

From the Native Hawaiian perspective, the issue surrounding Mauna Kea is neither political nor economic. The issue is of a religious and spiritual nature. It is so because the upper regions of Mauna Kea reside in Wao Akua, the realm of the Akua — Creator. Mauna Kea is a Temple or House of Worship. The Temple of Mauna Kea differs from other temples because it was not created by man. Akua built it for man, to bring the heavens to man. Therefore, the

[70] **the valued traditions of particular groups of people:** 形容詞 valued「貴重な」「大切な」は元来「大事にする」「重んじる」という意味の動詞 value (e.g. I've always *valued* her judgment.) の過去分詞形。particular が「特別の」ではなく「特定の」であることにも注意。

Mauna Kea Anaina Hou: ハワイ語。「マウナケアを守る新しい団体」という意味。

[74] **Wao Akua:** ハワイ語。A distant mountain region, believed to be inhabited only by spirits (akua).

[75] **is acknowledged as such:** such は直前の the Temple of the Supreme Being を指す (cf. The group is a dire threat to national security and should be treated *as such*.)。

[76] **many oral and written histories:** history「歴史(史料)」というと最初から書かれたもの (written history) を想像しがちだが，oral history とは口述記録として残されている歴史(およびそれに基づく著作)のこと。

[80] **the progenitors:**「(直系の)先祖」。

[81] **Mauna Kea, it is said, is where . . . :** it is said はこのように挿入的に用いられることもよくある (cf. She is, *I believe*, one of our most talented colleagues.)。

[83] **the zenith of . . . :**「…の頂点」。

[83] **the Native Hawaiian people's ancestral ties to Creation itself:** tie は「つながり」「結びつき」「きずな」という意味の場合このように複数形になるのが普通。「(神による)天地の創造」という場合の Creation はこのように通例大文字で書き始める。

[85] **a long and emotionally charged controversy:** charged には(「充電された」「帯電した」から派生した)「(状況などが)感情や気分に満ちている」(e.g. The atmosphere was *charged* with excitement.)という意味があるが，(be) emotionally charged や (be) *charged* with emotion は「関係者の感情が高ぶっていて一触即発の」という感じ。controversy には [kάntrəvə̀ːrsi] と [kəntrɔ́vəsi] の2つの発音があるので，聞いた時にはいずれでもわかるようにしておきたい。

[86] **deliberations:**「話し合い」「議論」という意味の場合にはこのように複数形になることが多い。

[87] **ignored and abridged:** abridge の基本的な意味は「(本や映画などを)簡約化する」(e.g. an *abridged* version of the film) だが，ここでは「(権利などを)制限する」。

[87] **the right to freedom of religion:** the right to 以下にはこのように名詞句と不定詞句のいずれも来ることができる (cf. 本章 [62] be entitled to . . . の注)。

[91] **The issue is of a religious and spiritual nature:** be of a . . . nature は「…という性格[性質]のもの[人]である」という意味の決まった表現 (cf. The issue is religious and spiritual *in nature*.)。

[96] **the heavens:** 文語的な用法で「空」「天」を意味する。

[96] **the laws of man do not dictate its sanctity:**「人」「人類」の意味で用いられる場合の man はこのように単数形で無冠詞 (e.g. *Man* is mortal.)。dictate は(「指示する」から)「(法則，状況などが)…を決定する，左右する」といった意味 (e.g. Company policy *dictates* that we should respond immediately to consumer complaints.)。sanctity は「神聖さ」。

laws of man do not dictate its sanctity, the laws of Heaven do.

Although Mauna Kea is not a typical house of worship by dominant cultural standards, it is, in our cultural understanding and cosmology, a temple of the highest order. The reverence of a place is determined by the essence of the place and on Mauna Kea, when we walk upon the sacred 'āina, we do not walk in the province of our will but rather in the province of Heaven's will. For it is here that the very life breath can be seized in a moment never to return. It is only here that the life-giving waters originate. Only here do the heavens open so that man can be received, blessed, freed and transformed in the ways of Heaven. As kahu (religious guardians) of this place, our kuleana (responsibility) to this temple is ancient. It is our duty to proclaim its sanctity and work to protect it, so that its greatness and purpose can be shared with all of mankind. We must be allowed to continue our work there.

Unfortunately, the history of Hawai'i Nei has shown all too clearly that our land was seized, our culture bastardized, and our essence consumed and transformed beyond recognition. At this time in our existence, we acknowledge that, though physical things may be taken from us, our duty to Heaven cannot be abridged.

As each culture has its gifts to give mankind, so too has the native Hawaiian culture. We have asked Akua to allow us to continue on our path so we can contribute the wisdom of our ancestors to the collective knowledge of mankind. We also ask those listening to accept the responsibility to maintain reverence and respect for the laws of Wao Akua and its place in the context of Creation, for it is said that all who enter the temple of Heaven are bound by the laws of Heaven. And so it is. Aloha nō.

There's room for everybody

Michael West

If Queen Lili'uokalani had lived today, she might have been an astronomer. This thought occurred to me as I spent a few enjoyable hours sailing under the starry skies with a group of Big

[100] **a temple of the highest order:** この場合の order は「等級」「階級」「階層」(e.g. a movie director of the first *order*)。

[102] **'āina:** ハワイ語で「大地」を意味する。

[105] **Only here do the heavens open ...:** 否定の意味を含む表現が強調のために文頭に置かれるとこのように倒置の構造が生じる (e.g. *Under no circumstances must the safe* be left unlocked.)。

[107] **religious guardians:**「宗教上の守護者」。

[112] **Hawai'i Nei:** nei とはハワイ語で名詞の後に続き，愛情を含んだ指示代名詞となる。したがって「この愛するハワイ」(this beloved Hawai'i) の意。ハワイではしばしば Hawai'i Nei という表現を耳にする。

[113] **our land was seized, our culture bastardized, and our essence consumed and transformed:** culture と bastardized，essence と consumed の間に was が省略されている。このように動詞を共有する同じ構造の文が並列される場合には2番目以降の文ではその動詞が省略されることが多い (9章 [96])。bastardize: make something worse by changing its good parts.

[114] **beyond recognition:**「以前に知っていた…だということがわからなくなるほど(変わってしまった)」という意味の決まった言い回し (cf. He had changed so much that I could hardly *recognize* him.)。

[118] **continue on our path:**「これまでどおりの道を進み続ける」(cf. She steadfastly *continued on her course*.)。path はもちろん比喩的な意味で使われている。

[119] **the collective knowledge of mankind:**「人類が共有する知識」。collective: shared.

[124] **Aloha nō:** ハワイ語の英訳辞書を見ると，aloha は "love, affection, compassion, mercy, sympathy, pity, kindness, sentiment, grace, charity; greetings, salutation regards; sweetheart, lover, loved one ...." などと多様な意味があることがわかる。この場合は，greetings に近い。nō は強調を表す。

[125] **Queen Lili'uokalani:** リリウオカラニ (1838–1917)。ハワイ王国最後の国王(在位 1891–93)。ハワイアンの名曲「アロハ・オエ」の作曲者としても名高い。

[126] **This thought occurred to me:**「こういう考えが頭に浮かんだ」。

[127] **under the starry skies:**「星空の下」。sky は "I saw an airplane flying high up in *the sky*." のように the sky という形で用いるのが最も一般的だが，空模様や空の大きさを語る時には複数形になることもある (e.g. ... and *the skies* are not cloudy all day. アメリカ民謡「峠の我が家 (*Home on the Range*)」の歌詞)。

Island astronomers and Native Hawaiians aboard the Hawaiian voyaging canoe Makali'i.

Lili'uokalani, Hawai'i's last reigning monarch until her overthrow in 1893, was a woman of great intelligence and creativity. She had a passion for poetry. She composed over a hundred songs, including the famous "Aloha Oe." She spoke several languages. She dined with presidents, queens and kings. She fought tirelessly for the rights of the Hawaiian people after the illegal takeover of their kingdom.

But above all, Lili'uokalani had an unquenchable thirst for knowledge. As she wrote in her 1898 autobiography, *Hawai'i's Story by Hawai'i's Queen*, "the acquisition of knowledge has been a passion with me during my whole life, one which has not lost its charm to the present day."

I imagine that, if she were alive today, Lili'uokalani would feel saddened that two of her greatest passions — her love for the Hawaiian people and her desire for knowledge — should have so much difficulty coexisting on the summit of Mauna Kea. The many amazing discoveries about the universe that are made by the telescopes on the "White Mountain" would surely have fascinated her.

And who knows, perhaps as a young girl Lili'uokalani might even have been inspired to pursue a career in astronomy.

As the Makali'i glided across the water, I thought about how we're all explorers of one sort or another. It's part of our human nature. The same curiosity to find out what lies beyond the horizon that inspired the ancient Polynesians to set sail for new lands is what inspires astronomers today to search the heavens to learn about distant worlds across the cosmic ocean.

So why is there so much controversy surrounding Mauna Kea today?

Much of the blame belongs to astronomers. For many years, the astronomy community was, through ignorance or arrogance, insensitive to the sanctity of Mauna Kea to some Hawaiians. In their eagerness to build bigger and better telescopes, astronomers forgot that science is just one way of looking at the world, and that we must be respectful of world views that differ from our own. Mauna Kea was a sacred site to the Hawaiian people long before there were ever telescopes there, and so astronomers have a moral obligation to help preserve the dignity of this holy place.

But sensitivity to other cultures is a two-way street. Science, too, is a culture, an ancient one whose roots go back to the dawn of

[129] **Makali'i:** ハワイ語で「小さい」の意。

[130] **Hawai'i's last reigning monarch:** 「ハワイを最後に統治した君主」。

[130] **overthrow** [òuvərθróu]:「(指導者や政府の)転覆,打倒」。意味的に対応する動詞も同じ綴りだが,アクセントの位置が変わって [óuvərθròu] となることに注意。

[131] **She had a passion for poetry:** 「…に夢中である」「…が大好き」という場合の passion を用いた決まった言い方 (e.g. She *has a passion for* teaching.)。poetry (cf. poem(s)) が集合不可算名詞 (1 章 [111], 2 章 [19], 10 章 [196]) であることにも注意 (cf. cutlery, imagery, scenery, stationery)。

[135] **the illegal takeover:** takeover は「(企業などの)買収,乗っ取り」という意味でよく用いられる名詞 (e.g. a hostile *takeover*「敵対的な乗っ取り」/ cf. His company *was taken over* by a multinational corporation.)。illegal というのは 1893 年の白人クーデターをハワイ在住アメリカ領事が連邦政府に無断で支持したことを指す。1993 年の王朝転覆百周年に際して,当時のクリントン大統領はネイティヴハワイアンに対して謝罪の意を表明した。

[137] **had an unquenchable thirst for knowledge:** 「抑えがたい知識欲の持ち主だった」。have a thirst for ... は本来「のどの渇き」を表す thirst を用いた「…を強く求める」という意味の定型表現。「のどの渇きを癒す」という意味の動詞 quench から派生した unquenchable は知識欲 (a thirst for knowledge) の強さを表すのに相応しい形容詞 (14 章 [60])。

[142] **Lili'uokalani would feel saddened that ...:** sadden: make someone feel sad. 驚きや意外などの感情を表す形容詞や過去分詞に伴う(感情の原因となる事態を表す) that 節の中で用いられる should には「…とは(驚きだ,意外だ,遺憾だ)」という意味合いを付け加える働きがある (e.g. It's funny that you *should say* that.)。

[148] **who knows ...:** 基本的には「だれも知らない」という意味を表す修辞疑問文だが,そこから派生してこのように「ひょっとすると…(who knows 以下で述べられること)がないともかぎらないですよ」と言いたい場合に使うこともある。

[148] **might even have been inspired to ...:** inspire A to B は「A (人) を B したいという気にさせる」「A (人) に B できるという自信をもたせる」。

[149] **pursue a career in ...:** 「…(職種)を(生涯の)仕事にする」という意味の決まった言い方。

[153] **set sail for new lands:** 「新しい世界を求めて船出する」。set sail は「船出する」という意味の決まり文句。

[155] **the cosmic ocean:** ここでは宇宙を海に喩えている。cosmic < cosmos.

[162] **we must be respectful of world views:** 「(自分たちのものとは異なる)世界観を尊重しなければならない」。be respectful of ... は動詞 respect とほぼ同義 (cf. His behavior is *indicative* of his disrespect for the law. / His behavior *indicates* his disrespect for the law.)。world views は「世界観」。

[166] **help preserve:** help はこのように直後に不定詞句 (to はあってもなくてもよい) を伴って「…するのを助ける」「…するのに役立つ」という意味を表すことがよくある (e.g. Coffee *helps* (to) *keep* me alert. / cf. This book might *help you* (to) *find* out what cultural geography is all about.)。

[167] **a two-way street:** 文字通りには「両方向に車が走れる道路」だが,「2 人の当事者双方が対等に努力することを要請するもの」といった比喩的な意味を表すのが普通 (cf. Teaching a class shouldn't be like driving down *a one-way street*. / unilateral/bilateral)。

[168] **whose roots go back to the dawn of human civilization:** 「起源が人類の文明の黎明にまで遡る」。

human civilization. Today the science of astronomy transcends race, religion and language. Calls from some Native Hawaiian and environmental groups for the dismantling of telescopes on Mauna Kea or banning future development there are also culturally insensitive because they ignore the kinship astronomers feel with the mountain as they explore the cosmos in what is ultimately a spiritual quest for them, too.

Sure, there will always be some astronomers who view the Hawaiian reverence for Mauna Kea as merely a quaint relic of an ancient belief system that is out of place in the modern world and who believe that astronomers should be allowed to build whatever telescopes they wish on Mauna Kea.

Likewise, there will always be some Native Hawaiians who view the presence of astronomers on Mauna Kea as a very visible example of the continuing occupation of their nation by foreign invaders, and who will settle for nothing less than the removal of all the telescopes and a return of the mountain to its original state.

But between those two extreme views lies the common ground occupied by most of us. There's enough aloha spirit in these Islands to ensure that our keiki, whether of Hawaiian or non-Hawaiian blood, will always feel welcomed on Mauna Kea to worship as they wish, to practice their cultural heritage, and to study the stars. We can't live in the past, consumed by anger or guilt over earlier injustices.

As Queen Lili'uokalani said herself, "The world cannot stand still. We must either advance or recede."

As the Makali'i docked in Hilo Bay and we returned to shore, Hawaiians and non-Hawaiians, astronomers and non-astronomers, I thought to myself that if Lili'uokalani were alive today, she'd surely say that there's room for everybody on the summit of Mauna Kea.

- [169] **the science of astronomy transcends:** transcend は「（通常の限界などを）超越する」。
- [171] **for the dismantling of telescopes:** for ... は calls と結びついていることに注意。calls for ... は「…を求める声」(cf. Some members *called for* his resignation.)。dismantle は「撤去する」。
- [173] **they ignore the kinship ... :** kinship は（「親族関係」から派生した）「親近感」という意味で，with の目的語 the mountain がそれを感じる相手 (cf. I somehow felt a *kinship* with him the moment I saw him.)。
- [176] **Sure, there will always be ... :** sure「なるほど」「確かに」の意で，直後の文の内容を（この場合は Likewise で始まる次の文の内容も）肯定しつつ，後出の But 以下でそれと対立する（より重要な）内容を提示するというパターンが利用されていることに注意（6 章 [14]，9 章 [80]）。
- [177] **a quaint relic of an ancient belief system:** quaint は「古風であるために変わっていて趣がある」といった意味 (e.g. a *quaint* old tavern) を表すことが多いが，ここでのように価値判断が逆転して「時代遅れで奇妙な」という意味になる場合もある。belief system「信念の体系」はよくある組み合わせで，複数の信念（例えば「天地はこのようにして創造された」「人類はこのようにして誕生した」）が関連し合って体系化したもの（一貫した世界観など）を表す。
- [181] **Likewise:** ここでは「同じように」という意味の文副詞。similarly にも同様の用法がある。
- [184] **who will settle for nothing less than ... :**「…しないかぎりは満足しない」。settle for ... は「（満足できるものではないが仕方がないので）…で我慢する」(e.g. Since there was nothing better to eat, I had to *settle for* a bowl of instant ramen.)。
- [186] **But between those two extreme views lies the common ground:** 再び倒置の構文。common ground は「異なる立場に共通の基盤」(e.g. It is hardly surprising that apparently incompatible theories should have some *common ground*.)。
- [188] **keiki:** ハワイ語で「子供」を意味する。
- [191] **consumed by ... :** は「…（強い感情）に心を奪われる」という意味の定型表現 (cf. The old temple was quickly *consumed* by fire.)。
- [193] **stand still:**「静止している」という意味の決まった組み合わせで，このように比喩的に用いることも多い (cf. Negotiations are *at a standstill*.)。
- [195] **Hilo Bay:** ハワイ島の東部の湾。その湾に面しているヒロ市はハワイ島最大の町。
- [198] **there's room for everybody on ... :**「…にはみんなの居場所がある」。「特定の人 [もの / 活動] のための空間 [余地]」という意味の room はこのように不可算名詞であることに注意 (e.g. I'm afraid there won't be enough *room* in the refrigerator for all the food we've bought.)。

4
MATHEMATICS

Introduction
Takeshi Saito

The history of Fermat's Last Theorem began when Pierre de Fermat, a 17th-century French mathematician, wrote the following tantalizing sentences in Latin in the margin of a mathematics book he was reading: "It is impossible for a cube to be the sum of two cubes, a fourth power to be the sum of two fourth powers, or in general for any number that is a power greater than the second to be the sum of two like powers. I have discovered a truly marvelous demonstration of this proposition that this margin is too narrow to contain."

Fermat is asserting that the equation $x^n + y^n = z^n$ has no nontrivial, i.e. $xyz \neq 0$, integral solution if $n \geq 3$. But he doesn't have enough space in the margin, he says, to write down the marvelous proof he has found. This assertion was to challenge any number of great mathematicians in the centuries that followed. It is known as Fermat's Last Theorem because it was the last one to be proved among the several mathematical statements Fermat made without providing proof.

More than three hundred years after Fermat made his unproven assertion, two young Japanese mathematicians, Yutaka Taniyama and Goro Shimura of the University of Tokyo, found a crucial clue to its solution, a clue that was tied to Fermat's Last Theorem by a connection that was quite unknown at the time. The clue was the totally unexpected and surprising link between two of the main subjects of mathematics: elliptic curves and modular forms. While the study of elliptic curves has a long history dating back to ancient Greece, with Fermat himself playing a prominent role in its revival, the study of modular forms is a relatively new field, dating back only to the 19th century. As these origins suggest, the two were considered to have been very different subjects, and establishing

- [1] **Fermat's Last Theorem:**「フェルマーの最終定理」。Pierre de Fermat はフランスの数学者 (1601–66)。後期ヘレニズムの数学者ディオファントスの『数論』の余白に、「n が 3 以上の自然数のときには、不定方程式 $x^n + y^n = z^n$ は $xyz \neq 0$ であるような整数解をもたない」という定理を書き記し、これについての「驚くべき証明を発見したが、その証明を記すにはこの余白は狭すぎる」という言葉を残した。この謎めいた言葉に触発されて、この定理は多くの優れた数学者の興味を引いてきたが、長い間、解決されることがなかった。しかしついに 1994 年、Andrew Wiles によって完全に証明されることになった。
- [4] **It is impossible for a cube to be . . . :**「3 乗の数は 3 乗の数 2 つの和にはならず、4 乗の数は 4 乗の数 2 つの和にはならない。そして一般的に 2 乗より大きな任意の累乗の数は同じ指数の累乗の数 2 つの和にはならない」。
- [9] **nontrivial:**「自明でない」。ここでは、x, y, z のどれかが 0 であるような解を自明な解と考え、x, y, z のどれも 0 でない解が自明でない解。
- [18] **Yutaka Taniyama:** 谷山豊。数学者 (1927–58)。
- [19] **Goro Shimura:** 志村五郎。数学者 (1930–)。大阪大学教授、プリンストン大学教授を歴任。
- [23] **elliptic curves:**「楕円曲線」。たとえば $y^2 = x^3 - x$ のような 3 次方程式 (cubic equation) で定義される、xy 平面内の曲線。楕円曲線は、楕円とは違う。名前の由来は、楕円の長さを表す積分との関係から。
- [26] **modular forms:**「モジュラー形式」「保型形式」。複素数平面 (complex plane) の上半分で定義された関数 (analytic function) の中で、特別に重要な種類のもの。本文中にもあるように、それをわかりやすく説明するのは難しいが、例としては $q = e^{2\pi \sqrt{-1} z}$、とおいて、無限積 $q \prod_{n=1}^{\infty} (1 - q^n)^{24}$ で定義される関数などがある。

the link between them was considered a great mathematical achievement.

In 1993 Andrew Wiles announced a proof of a large part of the link discovered by Taniyama and Shimura, and thereby concluded at last the solution of Fermat's Last Theorem. His announcement was the result of seven years of isolated endeavor. But his announcement was not quite yet the happy end to the story of Fermat's Last Theorem. Shortly after the announcement, a serious gap was found in the proof. Wiles had to endure one more year of struggle in the full glare of intense worldwide interest before Fermat's Last Theorem was finally and conclusively solved in 1994.

This session introduces you to the story of how Taniyama and Shimura met on the campus of the University of Tokyo and how they worked closely together to produce a theory that would eventually lead to one of the most important discoveries in the history of mathematics.

Fermat's Enigma

Simon Singh

In January of 1954 a talented young mathematician at the University of Tokyo paid a routine visit to his departmental library. Goro Shimura was in search of a copy of *Mathematische Annalen*, Vol. 24. In particular he was after a paper by Deuring on his algebraic theory of complex multiplication, which he needed in order to help him with a particularly awkward and esoteric calculation.

To his surprise and dismay, the volume was already out. The borrower was Yutaka Taniyama, a vague acquaintance of Shimura who lived on the other side of the campus. Shimura wrote to Taniyama explaining that he urgently needed the journal to complete the nasty calculation, and politely asked when it would be returned. A few days later, a postcard landed on Shimura's desk. Taniyama had replied, saying that he too was working on the exact same calculation and was stuck at the same point in the logic. He suggested that they share their ideas and perhaps collaborate on the problem. This chance encounter over a library book ignited a part-

[31] **Andrew Wiles:** イギリス生まれの数学者（1953– ）。プリンストン大学教授。

[46] **paid a routine visit to . . . :**「いつものように…を訪れた」。pay a visit to . . . は「…を訪れる」という意味の決まった言い方（cf. I *paid him a visit* for the first time in five years.）。

[47] **a copy of . . . :**「…のコピー」ではなく，「…の1冊」であることに注意（cf. I bought *two copies* of the novel, one for myself and the other for a friend./Her latest novel has sold 300,000 *copies*.）。

[48] **he was after a paper by . . . :**「…の書いた論文を探していた」。be after . . . はすぐ前の be in search of . . . と同様，「…を探している」という意味（e.g. The police *are after* him./cf. She's finally decided to *go after* the job.）。「論文」の意味の paper はこのように可算名詞（e.g. read *a paper* at a conference「学会で論文を発表する」）。

[48] **Deuring:** マックス・ドイリング（Max Deuring, 1907–84）。ドイツの数学者。ゲッティンゲン大学教授。

[49] **complex multiplication:**「虚数乗法」。方程式 $y^2 = x^3 - x$ で定義される楕円曲線の点 (x, y) を $(-x, \sqrt{-1}y)$ にうつす変換のような，楕円曲線の点を同じ楕円曲線の点にうつす変換のうち特別なもの。数論への応用が大きい。

[50] **a particularly awkward and esoteric calculation:**「特に厄介で難解な計算」。

[51] **To his surprise and dismay, the volume was already out:**「その巻はすでに貸し出されていたので，驚くと同時に困ったなと思った」。to one's surprise も to one's dismay も決まった言い方（cf. to one's delight/disappointment）。

[52] **a vague acquaintance:**「そう言えばそういう人もいたなあ，という程度の知り合い」。

[55] **the nasty calculation:**「厄介な計算」。nasty は awkward and esoteric の言い換え。

[57] **he too was working on the exact same calculation:**「彼も全く同じ計算に取り組んでいて」。この場合の work on . . . は「…（仕事，研究，制作など）に従事する，取り組む」という意味。the exact same は「全く同じ」で，exactly the same とも言う。

[58] **was stuck:**「行き詰まっていた」（9章 [180], 12章 [37]）。

[58] **He suggested that they share their ideas and perhaps collaborate on the problem:** suggest はこのように原形動詞を述語とする that 節をともなって「…してはどうかと提案する」という意味を表すのによく用いられる（e.g. I *suggested* that she *buy* another computer./cf. I said to her, "Why don't you buy another computer?"）。should + 原形動詞を述語にすることもある（e.g. I *suggested* that she *should buy* another computer.）。that 節の内容は提案の時点では実現されていないことに注意（cf. John *demanded* that he [*should*] *be* promoted.）。share their ideas は「考えを出し合う」といった感じ（cf. It's good to have someone you can *share* your feelings with.）。

[60] **This chance encounter over a library book:**「1冊の図書館の本をめぐるこの偶然の出会い」。この場合の chance は「偶然の」という意味の形容詞（11章 [53]）。

[60] **a partnership which would change the course of mathematical history:**「数学史の流れを変えることになる共同研究」。change the course of . . . は「…（歴史など）の流れを変える」と言う場合の決まり文句。過去のある時点に基準をおいて，そこからそれより後に（発話時点から見ればやはり過去の）ある事態が生じる［起こる］ことになる，という「過去から見た未来」を表す would の用法にも注意。

fig. 1:   M. C. Escher's rendition of hyperbolic space, *Circle Limit IV*.

nership which would change the course of mathematical history.

When they met in 1954, Taniyama and Shimura were just beginning their mathematical careers. The tradition was for young researchers to be taken under the wing of a professor who would guide the fledgling brain, but Taniyama and Shimura rejected this form of apprenticeship. During the war real research ground to a halt, and even by the 1950s the mathematics faculty had still not recovered. According to Shimura, the professors were "tired, jaded and disillusioned." In comparison the post-war students were passionate and eager to learn, and they soon realized that the only way forward would be for them to teach themselves. The students organized regular seminars, taking it in turn to inform each other of the latest techniques and breakthroughs. Despite his otherwise lackadaisical attitude, when it came to the seminars Taniyama provided a ferocious driving force. He would encourage the more senior students to explore uncharted territory, and for the younger students he acted as a father figure.

Taniyama was the epitome of the absentminded genius, and this was reflected in his appearance. He was incapable of tying a decent knot, and so he decided that rather than tie his shoelaces a dozen times a day he would not tie them at all. While Shimura was fastidious, Taniyama was sloppy to the point of laziness. Surprisingly this was a trait that Shimura admired: "He was gifted with the special capability of making many mistakes, mostly in the right direction. I

[64] **be taken under the wing of . . .**:「…の指導を受ける」。「ひな鳥が親鳥の羽の下で保護される」というイメージから。数学者としてこれから独り立ちしようとする若手研究者をひな鳥に喩える。すぐ後に用いられている fledgling brain も、いかにも「これから巣立ちしようとする頭脳」という感じ (fledgling は「羽が生えたての [鳥]」)。

[66] **apprenticeship**:「見習いの期間」。apprentice は「徒弟」「見習い」。

[66] **real research ground to a halt**:「実質的な研究は停止してしまった」。grind to a halt は「ぎーっと音を立てて止まる」(cf. come *to a halt*/bring . . . *to a halt*/screech *to a halt*/skid *to a halt*)。

[67] **the mathematics faculty**:「数学の教授陣」。この場合の faculty は「大学の特定学部に所属する教員全員」という意味の集合名詞 (a *faculty* meeting は「教授会」)。すぐ後に出てくる the professors は the mathematics faculty と同じ人たちを指す。

[68] **"tired, jaded and disillusioned"**:引用符は志村自身のことばであることを示す。jaded は tired とほぼ同じ意味だが、「疲弊してやる気をなくしている」という感じ。disillusioned は「幻滅している」。

[70] **the only way forward**:「前進する唯一の方法」(cf. That's *a big step forward*.)。

[72] **taking it in turn to inform each other of . . .**:「順番に…を教え合った」。take it in turns to do . . . は「順番に…する」。take turns to do [in doing . . .] とも言う (e.g. It's pretty common nowadays for a married couple to *take turns in doing* the housework.)。

[73] **Despite his otherwise lackadaisical attitude, when it came to . . .**:「普段は投げやりな (lackadaisical) 谷山であったが、…となると話は別で」。otherwise「その他の点では」とは when it came to 以下のことを除いては、という意味。when it comes to . . . は「…ということになると」という言い回し (6 章 [183]) (e.g. *When it comes to* eating, he's a world champion.)。

[75] **a ferocious driving force**:「猛烈な推進力」。このように、driving force は事業などを推進する要になる人を指して使われることも多い (13 章 [24], 14 章 [37]) (e.g. She's been *the driving force behind* the whole project.)。

[76] **explore uncharted territory**:「未知の領域を探究する」。uncharted は「海図に載っていない」だが、このように uncharted territory という比喩表現の中で用いることが多い (cf. *uncharted waters*)。

[77] **he acted as a father figure**:「彼は父親的な役割を果たした」。father figure は「(理想的な父親のように) 適切な指導や助言によって後進から尊敬される人物」という意味でよく用いられる表現 (cf. a mother figure)。

[78] **the epitome of the absentminded genius**:自分の専門や目下の関心事に没頭しているために他のことには気が回らず、うっかりして (absentmindedly) あきれるような失敗をしたりする人という、ある種の天才 (genius) についてわれわれが抱くイメージにぴったり合っている人。the epitome [ipítəmi] of . . . は「…の典型」「…の権化」「…を絵に描いたような人」。

[81] **fastidious**:「潔癖な」「几帳面な」。

[82] **sloppy to the point of laziness**:「怠惰と言ってもよいほどだらしない」。sloppy は fastidious の反対の意味の形容詞。to the point of . . . はこのように程度や段階を表す時によく用いられる (cf. He got *to the point* where he just couldn't go on.)。

[83] **a trait that Shimura admired**:「志村が素晴らしいと思った特性」。trait は人の性格特性などを表すことが多い (e.g. personality *traits*)。

[83] **He was gifted with . . .**:be gifted with . . . は「…(才能など) に恵まれている」(e.g. She *is gifted with* a brilliant brain./cf. *gifted* children「天才児」/He has a *gift for* languages.)。

envied him for this and tried in vain to imitate him, but found it quite difficult to make good mistakes."

Because the students were isolated from the West, the seminars would occasionally cover subjects that were generally considered passé in Europe and America. One particularly unfashionable topic that fascinated both Taniyama and Shimura was the study of modular forms. Modular forms are some of the most bizarre and wonderful objects in mathematics. They are one of the most esoteric entities in mathematics, and yet the twentieth-century number theorist Martin Eichler rated them as one of the five fundamental operations: addition, subtraction, multiplication, division, and modular forms. The interesting property of modular forms is that they exhibit infinite symmetry. The modular forms studied by Taniyama and Shimura can be shifted, switched, swapped, reflected, and rotated in an infinite number of ways and still they remain unchanged, making them the most symmetrical of mathematical objects.

Unfortunately, drawing, or even imagining, a modular form is impossible because modular forms live in a four-dimensional space called hyperbolic space. The hyperbolic universe is tricky to comprehend for humans, who are constrained to living in a conventional three-dimensional world, but four-dimensional space is a mathematically valid concept, and it is this extra dimension that gives the modular forms such an immensely high level of symmetry. The artist M. C. Escher was fascinated by mathematical ideas and attempted to convey the concept of hyperbolic space in some of his etchings and paintings. Figure 1 shows Escher's *Circle Limit IV*, which embeds the hyperbolic world into the two-dimensional page.

Modular forms stand very much on their own within mathematics. In particular, they would seem to be completely unrelated to elliptic equations. The modular form is an enormously complicated beast, studied largely because of its symmetry and discovered only in the nineteenth century. The elliptic equation dates back to the ancient Greeks and has nothing to do with symmetry. Modular forms and elliptic equations live in completely different regions of the mathematical cosmos, and nobody would ever have believed that there was the remotest link between the two subjects. However, Taniyama and Shimura were to shock the mathematical community by suggesting that elliptic equations and modular forms were effectively one and the same thing. According to these two maverick mathematicians, they could unify the modular and elliptic worlds.

In September 1955 an international symposium was held in Tokyo. It was a unique opportunity for the many young Japanese

- [89] **passé** [pæséɪ]:「流行遅れの」(cf. Life-time employment is quickly becoming *a thing of the past*./That singer is just *a has-been*.)。
- [91] **bizarre:** extremely strange.
- [93] **Martin Eichler:** マルティン・アイヒラーはドイツの数学者 (1912–92)。
- [96] **infinite** [ínfɪnət] **symmetry:**「無限の対称性」。cf. finite [fáɪnaɪt]「有限の」。
- [100] **making them . . . :** which makes them . . . と言っても同じ意味。このように分詞節はしばしば主節の内容の結果ないし帰結を表現する(8章[215]) (e.g. More than two thirds of Japan is forested, *making* it one of the world's most heavily forested nations.)。
- [103] **hyperbolic space:**「双曲空間」。ふつうの幾何学で考える平面とは異なり、直線の外に点をとると、その点を通りしかももとの直線に平行な直線が、2つ以上引けるような平面を、双曲平面という。複素数平面の上半分は双曲平面と考えることができて、そうすると、モジュラー形式は双曲平面上の関数とも考えられる。Simon Singhのこの部分の記述には、双曲平面と4次元の双曲空間の混同に起因すると思われる混乱が見られる。
- [103] **tricky:** difficult to deal with.
- [104] **who are constrained to living in . . . :**「…で暮らすことを余儀なくされている」。constrain:「制約(constraint)を課す」(cf. I limit[restrict] myself to one bottle of beer a day)。conventional:「陳腐な」「ありきたりの」「平凡な」。
- [108] **M. C. Escher:** マウリッツ・コルネリス・エッシャー (Maurits Cornelis Escher, 1898–1972) はオランダの版画家。存在不可能な立体的な構造物を二次元の空間の中に描き出すなど、数学的な趣向の強い作品を数多く残した。
- [111] **which embeds the hyperbolic world into the two-dimensional page:**「hyperbolic な世界を二次元のページにはめ込む (embed)」。
- [112] **stand very much on their own:** stand on one's own は「自立している」(cf. It's hard to believe that he wrote this essay *on his own*.)。
- [114] **elliptic equations:**「楕円方程式」。ここでは elliptic curve を定義する方程式のこと。elliptic curve と同じ意味で使われている。
- [114] **an enormously complicated beast:**「とてつもなく複雑なもの」。この場合の beast は「(特定の性質をもった)もの」といった意味の口語的な用法 (e.g. This area of Shinjuku is a completely different *beast* at night.)。
- [116] **dates back to . . . :**「…に遡る」という起源の意味を表す (cf. This building *goes back* over a century.)。
- [119] **the mathematical cosmos:**「数学の宇宙[世界]」。cosmos [kázməs] の代わりに universe と言ってもほぼ同じ意味。
- [119] **nobody would ever have believed that there was the remotest link between the two subjects:**「この2つのテーマ[modular form と elliptic equation]の間にわずかでもつながりがあろうなどとは誰も信じたりしなかったであろう」。ever も the remotest も nobody で始まる否定の環境ゆえに生じている (cf. I don't have *the slightest* idea what you're talking about.)。
- [122] **effectively one and the same thing:**「実質的には同一のものである」。この場合の effectively は (「効果的に」ではなく)「実質上」(cf. *In effect*, their views are identical.)。one and the same は「同一の」という意味の決まった言い方。

researchers to show off to the rest of the world what they had learned. They handed around a collection of thirty-six problems related to their work, accompanied by a humble introduction — *Some unsolved problems in mathematics: no mature preparation has been made, so there may be some trivial or already solved ones among these. The participants are requested to give comments on any of these problems.*

Four of the questions were from Taniyama, and these hinted at a curious relationship between modular forms and elliptic equations. These innocent questions would ultimately lead to a revolution in number theory. All of the questions handed out by Taniyama at the symposium were related to his hypothesis that each modular form is really an elliptic equation in disguise. The idea that every elliptic equation was related to a modular form was so extraordinary that those who glanced at Taniyama's questions treated them as nothing more than a curious observation. Taniyama's only ally was Shimura, who believed in the power and depth of his friend's idea. Following the symposium, he worked with Taniyama in an attempt to develop the hypothesis to a level where the rest of the world could no longer ignore their work. Shimura wanted to find more evidence to back up the relationship between the modular and the elliptic worlds. The collaboration was temporarily halted when in 1957 Shimura was invited to attend the Institute for Advanced Study in Princeton. Following his two years as a visiting professor in America he intended to resume working with Taniyama, but this was never to happen. On November 17, 1958, Yutaka Taniyama committed suicide.

During his short career Taniyama contributed many radical ideas to mathematics. The questions he handed out at the symposium contained his greatest insight, but it was so ahead of its time that he would never live to see its enormous influence on number theory. Barry Mazur, a professor at Harvard University, witnessed the rise of the Taniyama-Shimura conjecture. "It was a wonderful conjecture but to begin with it was ignored because it was so ahead of its time. When it was first proposed it was not taken up because it was so astounding. On the one hand you have the elliptic world, and on the other you have the modular world. Both those branches of mathematics had been studied intensively but separately. Then along comes the Taniyama-Shimura conjecture, which is the grand surmise that there's a bridge between these two completely different worlds. Mathematicians love to build bridges."

The value of mathematical bridges is enormous. They enable com-

[127] **show off to the rest of the world what they had learned:**「世界の他の国々の研究者に自分たちが学んだことを誇示する（show off）」。the rest of the world はこのように「世界の他の国（の人々）」という意味でよく用いられる表現（cf. Are you going to live in Japan *for the rest of your life*?）。

[130] *no mature preparation has been made*:「じっくり準備したわけではありません」。この場合の mature は「慎重な」「熟慮した」。

[131] *trivial*: 普通は of little importance or value（cf. trivia, triviality）という意味だが，ここでは「自明な」。

[138] **an elliptic equation in disguise:**「姿を変えた楕円方程式」。in disguise は「変装した」（cf. Holmes *disguised himself* as an old lady./e.g. This is *a blessing in disguise*）。

[141] **Taniyama's only ally:**「谷山の唯一の理解者」。ally [ǽlaɪ] は本来「同盟国」だが，このように比喩的に「支持者」「（苦しい時に）援助してくれる人」の意味で用いることも多い。

[142] **who believed in the power and depth of his friend's idea:**「谷山の考えには力と深さがあると信じていた」。believe in ... は，単に「...を信じる」ではなく，「...が存在すると信じる」「...には価値があると信じる」という意味を表す表現（e.g. Very few friends of mine *believe in* God. / He seems to *believe in* calling a spade a spade.）。

[143] **in an attempt to develop the hypothesis to a level where ... :**「その仮説を...のレベルにまで発展させようとして」。in an attempt to ... は「...しようとして」という意味の決まった言い回し。

[147] **was temporarily halted:** temporarily は「一時的に」（cf. a *temporary* measure「暫定的措置」）。halt は「停止させる」の意味で動詞として用いられている。

[150] **but this was never to happen:**「しかし，この共同研究は決して再開されることはなかった」。いわゆる「運命」を表す be to ... の用法の例。

[155] **but it was so ahead of its time that he would never live to see its enormous influence on number theory:**「しかし谷山の洞察はあまりにも時代に先んじていたために，それが数論に計り知れない影響を与えるのを彼自身が生前に見届けることはなかった」。ahead of one's time は「同時代の人々よりも（考えなどが）進んでいるために理解されない」という意味の決まった言い方。

[157] **Barry Mazur:** アメリカの数学者（1937–　）。ハーヴァード大学教授。

[158] **the Taniyama-Shimura conjecture:**「谷山-志村予想」。conjecture はすぐ後に出てくる[164] surmise と同じく「推量」「予測」という意味。数学では，statement not yet proved but undoubtedly correct という意味で使われる。

munities of mathematicians who have been living on separate islands to exchange ideas and explore each other's creations. Mathematics consists of islands of knowledge in a sea of ignorance. For example, there is the island occupied by geometers who study shape and form, and then there is the island of probability where mathematicians discuss risk and chance. There are dozens of such islands, each one with its own unique language, incomprehensible to the inhabitants of other islands. The great potential of the Taniyama-Shimura conjecture was that it would connect two islands and allow them to speak to each other for the first time. The Taniyama-Shimura conjecture enabled mathematicians to tackle elliptic problems that had remained unsolved for centuries by approaching them through the modular world.

- [171] **geometers** [dʒiámətərz]:「幾何学者」。
- [176] **allow them to speak to each other for the first time:** allow A to B はこのように「A が B することを可能にする」という，すぐ後の enable A to B と同じ意味で用いることが多いパターン（5 章 [105]）。
- [178] **tackle elliptic problems that had remained unsolved for centuries:**「それまで何世紀もの間未解決のままであった楕円問題に取り組む」。remain + un-過去分詞は「…されないまま」という意味を表す頻出表現型。

5. OBJECTIVITY

Introduction
Yuko Fujigaki

Things seem to take on a life of their own when they are turned into numbers. Think about *hensachi* for example, or TV ratings — even educational and research evaluations. Once things are transformed into numbers, they start to seem objective and globally applicable, things that have no context and can be applied everywhere.

The text for this session argues for the importance of going back to the moment when a particular number gets defined and thinking carefully about the process that produced it. It's a good idea to stop and consider what has been ignored and what has been considered important in the definition of that number. Or, to put it another way, how have "noise" and "signal" been differentiated? Depending on this kind of judgment, the methods of approximation will differ and hypotheses for calculation will vary, and this, in turn, will lead to different numbers. It is a serious mistake to skip over the process of approximation and the construction of hypotheses and treat calculated numbers as objective results that are universally applicable.

"Globalization" is a catchphrase everywhere in today's world. Talk of universals such as "the global standard" promotes the idea that there actually are such things as global standards and variables that are applicable to every context and every culture. However, is it really true that there is a standard variable that is universally applicable? In fact, important variables are always deliberately selected, and depend on the subject and the purpose of the particular research project in question. Important variables are for this reason likely to vary in accordance with cultural and historical context. It seems worryingly possible that globalization will lead to the enforced export of culturally specific variables: the variables of a powerful culture could easily become imposed on other cultures, where

- [1] **take on . . . :**「…(意味や性質など)を持つようになる，帯びる」。
- [2] *hensachi*: 英語に訳すと adjusted standard deviation score となる。ただし，英語圏では一般的に用いられないのでここでは *hensachi* とある。
- [2] **TV ratings:**「視聴率」(cf. The Prime Minister's *approval rating* has been on the decline lately.)。
- [5] **things that have no context and can be applied everywhere:** いずれも直前の globally applicable の言い換え。次の段落に出てくる universally applicable も同じ意味。
- [6] **The text for this session argues for . . . :** argue for [in favor of] . . . は「…(が正しい[妥当である]こと)を主張する」「…に賛成の議論をする」(cf. argue against . . .)。
- [10] **Or, to put it another way:**「あるいは別の言い方をすると」と言う場合の決まり文句 (cf. Let me *put* it this way.)。
- [11] **"noise" and "signal":**「雑音(ノイズ)」と「信号」。測定器の品質を示すうえで「信号対雑音比(SN比)」が用いられる。ここでは情報理論に転用されているので，引用符で囲まれている。伝達されるべき情報(信号)と，無視すべき不要な成分(雑音)というような意味。後出の [48] S/N ratio 参照。
- [12] **approximation:**「近似化」(e.g. Isaac Newton's method of *approximation* for the extracting of roots./cf. approximate; approximately)。
- [14] **skip over . . . :**「…(普段はすることや本来すべきこと)を省く，飛ばす」(cf. I was so busy I had to *skip* lunch.)。
- [19] **variables:**「変数」。
- [28] **could easily become imposed on . . . :**「たやすく…に押しつけられてしまいかねない」。

they may well be entirely inappropriate. This is one of the major issues at the heart of science and technology studies today.

Objectivity and the Assessment Process

Yuko Fujigaki

The theoretical frameworks of modern laboratory-based sciences such as physics and chemistry are based on hypothetical or idealized systems. As a physicist friend of mine once said, physics is a science of approximation. In other words, it is always striving to distinguish between the essential and the negligible. Only those factors which it takes to be essential are expressed in its various formulae: everything that can be safely ignored is tossed out. Its problems, therefore, are always solved through approximation.

In high-school physics, for example, friction and air resistance are ignored in order to derive an elegant equation of motion. But what we have to remember is that the friction and air resistance which are ignored in high-school approximations, as well as in laboratories and in idealized systems, actually constitute a large part of the real essence of on-the-job practical or applied science. Understanding "signal" (S) as that which must be considered, and "noise" (N) as that which can be ignored, we have to keep sight of the fact that the S/N ratio may be very different in laboratory (or theoretical) science and in field (or actual) science.

The importance of this kind of difference, or even disagreement, over the definition of signal and noise, or the significant and the insignificant, can be very clearly seen in the dispute over the filling-in of a tidal flat that happened in the Nagoya area in the 1990s. Between 1994 and 1998, the city of Nagoya and the Nagoya Port Authority conducted an assessment of a project designed to fill in some tidal flats in the Fujimae area. Public hearings were held in order to debate the official assessment of the potential environmen-

[30] **science and technology studies:**「科学技術社会論」を指す。科学／技術と社会との接点の問題を研究対象とする。詳細については藤垣裕子編『科学技術社会論の技法』（東京大学出版会，2005）を参照。

[32] **hypothetical or idealized systems:** hypothetical は hypothesis「仮説」と関連する「仮説の」「仮説的な」という意味の形容詞で，actual の反意語。idealized「理想化［理念化］された」とは，すぐ後で述べられるように，この文脈では「実際には（actually）存在する要因のいくつかを negligible と考えて捨象し，essential と想定した要因のみを対象とする」といった意味であるから hypothetical と実質的に同義。

[36] **Only those factors which it takes to be essential:** it は physics を指す。take A to be B は「A を B と解釈する」。

[37] **formulae** [fɔ́ːrmjəliː]**:** formula [fɔ́ːrmjələ]「公式」の複数形。

[37] **everything that can be safely ignored is tossed out:**「無視しても差し支えない要因はすべて捨てられる」。この場合の safely は It is *safe* to say ...「…と言っても差し支えない」などと言う場合の safe と比較するとよい。toss out は throw out とほぼ同じ意味で「(不要なものを)捨てる」。

[41] **derive an elegant equation of motion:** derive は「引き出す」「導く」。equation は「方程式」。

[45] **on-the-job practical or applied science:** on-the-job は「職務中になされる」(e.g. *on-the-job* training「社内研修」)。practical と applied はほぼ同じ意味で，いずれも theoretical「理論的」の反意語 (cf. in theory「理論上は」/in practice「実際上は」)。

[47] **keep sight of the fact:** keep sight of ... は lose sight of ... の反意表現で「…を見失わないようにする」。

[48] **S/N ratio:** signal-to-noise ratio の略。「信号対雑音比」「SN 比」。電気信号においては，意図した信号以外に，不要な成分(雑音)が混入するが，もともと SN 比とは，この不要成分の混入の度合いを示す通信工学上の尺度である。

[53] **a tidal flat:**「干潟」。

[55] **a project designed to fill in ... :**「…を埋めることを目的とするプロジェクト」。(be) designed to ... は「…することを目的としている」「…するためのものである」(8 章 [129]) (cf. by design「計画的に」)。

[56] **tidal flats in the Fujimae area:** 伊勢湾，名古屋港内に残る約 89 ha の藤前干潟は，シギ (snipe)，チドリ (plover) 類などが飛来する渡り鳥の中継地点として国際的に知られる。名古屋市はこの地にゴミ埋め立て処理場をつくる計画を発表したが，環境保護団体や住民による干潟保全運動が盛り上がりを見せるなか，1999 年，計画を断念。2002 年 11 月，藤前干潟は，「特に水鳥の生息地として国際的に重要な湿地」としてラムサール条約 (The Ramsar Convention on Wetlands) に登録された。ラムサール条約登録で，国と地元自治体は，湿地保全計画の策定や生態系の維持に努めることが義務付けられた。

[57] **debate the official assessment:** debate はこのように「…について(結論や解決策を出すために)正式に議論する」という意味の他動詞として用いられることが多い (e.g. How and where language originated remains a hotly *debated* issue)。

tal impact of the project. Local residents were strongly opposed to the project and flatly disagreed with the environmental assessment of the official report. In the end, the mayor of Nagoya was forced to give up the project in 1999.

The crucial question was how to calculate the "use rate," which was the data intended to show how much birds like snipe and plover used the area targeted by the proposed project. At the heart of the controversy was the fact that the proposed landfill would radically transform the tidal flats area where the snipe and plover flew to spend the winter. The area was an internationally recognized Japanese winter harbor for these birds.

While something like a "use rate" might seem to be an objective kind of measurement, as it turned out there was a huge difference between the use rates calculated by the promoters of the project, on the one hand, and by an independent NGO that conducted its own investigation, on the other. The city assessment calculated the rate at somewhere between 0.0% and 10.7%. The NGO, on the other hand, calculated the rate at between 31% and 96%. This discrepancy followed directly from differences in defining how the use rate was determined. For those promoting the project, the use rate was defined as the result of ascertaining "the percentage of birds using the proposed area during the day, regardless of whether the land was submerged at the time or not." In contrast, the definition employed by the NGO was: "what percentage of the birds were feeding during the time when the area of the proposed project was not submerged under water." The city criticized the NGO's definition of use rate on the grounds that "an investigation conducted under the circumstances most amenable for birds to use the land simply observes one aspect of the birds' daily activity."

The project's promoters conducted their investigation and collected data on four days in 1994: February 15th, May 12th, May 19th, and September 6th. May 19th was the day of the neap tide, when the difference between high and low tide was at its smallest. The other three were days of flood tide, when the difference between high and low tides was at its greatest. These days were selected in order to come up with the mean value for the year. The investigation counted the number of birds in certain designated areas every hour from sunrise to sundown. In other words, in calculating the mean value for the day, this investigation used the hours between sunrise and sundown regardless of whether the land was submerged or not. This meant that the final calculation was based on the "percentage of the total number of birds in the proposed

[58] **Local residents were strongly opposed to the project:** local residents は「その地域の住民」。local が「田舎の」の意味ではないことに注意 (e.g. a *local* paper「地元紙」/ cf. a *local* (general) anesthetic「局所(全身)麻酔」)。be opposed to ... は「…に反対している」という意味の決まった言い方のひとつ (cf. Are you *for* or *against* my proposal?)。

[59] **flatly disagreed with ... :**「…に真っ向から反対した」。flatly「断固として(…に反対する, …を否定する, …を拒絶する)」という場合によく使う副詞 (e.g. He *flatly denied* any wrongdoing.)。

[63] **the data intended to ... :** (be) intended to ... は前出の (be) designed to ... と同様「…するためのものである」「…することを目的としている」という意味でよく用いられる表現型。

[64] **the area targeted by the proposed project:**「提案されたプロジェクトの対象となる地域」。target は「目標」「ねらい」という名詞が「…を目標にする」「…にねらいを定める」という動詞として使われたもの (e.g. This product is designed to *target* baby boomers. / cf. This product is *targeted* at baby boomers. / Our *target* audience is women and men in their forties.)

[64] **At the heart of the controversy was ... :**「論争の中心にあったのは…であった」。このように英語でも主語が新たに導入される話題である場合には倒置構文がしばしば用いられる (3 章 [4, 11, 186], 13 章 [208]) (e.g. *Underlying her argument is* the assumption that democracy can be made to work.)。

[70] **as it turned out ... :**「実際には(…であった)」。

[72] **NGO:** *n*on*g*overnmental *o*rganization「非政府組織」。

[73] **The city assessment calculated the rate at ... :** calculate A at B で「A を計算して B であるという答えを出す」。at はこのように算出された値を表示することがよくある (e.g. The authorities estimated the number of demonstrators *at* 15,000. / The car is priced *at* 3,500,000 yen)。

[76] **defining how the use rate was determined:** この議論の詳細については, 日野明日香, 佐藤仁,「環境アセスメントにおける「客観性」: 藤前干潟埋め立て事業を事例として」『環境情報科学論文集』15 (2001 年): 101–106 を参照。

[78] **ascertaining:** finding out (e.g. We need to *ascertain* whether she is willing to cooperate.)

[79] **was submerged:** be submerged は「水没している」。

[84] **on the grounds that ... :**「…ということを根拠にして」。

[84] **the circumstances most amenable for birds to use the land:**「鳥がその土地をもっとも使いやすい状況」。amenable: suitable.

[89] **neap tide:**（上弦時または下弦時の）「小潮」。

[91] **flood tide:**「上げ潮」あるいは「差し潮」。

[93] **come up with the mean value for the year:**「年間の平均値を算出する」。come up with ...（1 章 [31], 2 章 [50]）はここでは後出の produce と同じ「算出する」。ここでの mean は形容詞で「平均の」。

landfill area out of the total number of the birds counted in all the designated areas between sunrise and sunset."

The NGO, on the other hand, conducted their investigation and collected data on four different days in 1994: February 27th, March 27th, April 24th, and May 8th. These days were selected in order to allow the NGO to make the bird count on the days when the tidal flats area was most likely to be used by the birds. The NGO's investigators counted the number of birds in the designated areas every hour from three hours before low tide to three hours after low tide. This method concentrated on the hours when the land would be most heavily used by the birds. By using these days and this method the NGO defined the use rate as "the percentage of birds feeding in the Fujimae tidal flats area, during the time when it was least submerged, out of the total number of birds in all the designated areas." It is this difference in the selection of dates and the definition of use rate that produced such a gap in the numbers.

So, which use rate should have been used in determining whether or not to go ahead with the Nagoya city project to fill in the tidal flats area? The promoters of the project used random sampling and claimed that this should be taken as an "objective figure." The NGO side insisted that the correct use rate should be the representative figure taken from the periods when the area was most heavily used.

At the heart of the dispute between the project's promoters and the NGO was the question of how to define use rate, how to approximate it, and what kind of sample should be used as data. The two investigations differed not only in the timing of their measurements (when they collected data) but also in the actual methodology of their measurements. These differences sprang from their different positions on how best to approximate use rate and what should be emphasized in the approximation: in other words, what could be ignored and what had to be considered essential — in short, there was a disagreement over S/N ratio. The promoters of the project believed that the use rate should be approximated by random sampling, that is, by establishing the mean throughout the year and then throughout one day. That was the basis of their decision to collect their data during those particular time periods and in that particular way. On the other hand, the NGO approximated the use rate by focusing on the time period when the birds were most concentrated in the target area. Which of these two methods of approximation should have been used in assessing the impact of the proposed landfill?

The NGO's use rate figure was designed to reflect local knowl-

[105] **allow the NGO to . . . :** ここでの allow A to B は make it possible for A to B の意味で enable と同義と考えてよい（4 章 [176]）。

[105] **when the tidal flats area was most likely to be used by the birds:**「干潟を鳥が一番使いそうな時に」。be likely to . . . は「…という可能性が高い」という意味を表す助動詞的な表現型。このように most などの副詞を伴うことも多い (e.g. Can you think of a situation where one of these expressions *is more likely to* be used than the others?)。

[116] **whether or not to go ahead with . . . :**「…を推進するかどうか」。go ahead with . . . は「…（計画していたこと，許可を求めていたこと）を始める」(e.g. We've finally received permission to *go ahead with* the expansion program./cf. The steering committee has finally given us the *go-ahead*.)。

[120] **the representative figure:**「代表的な数字」。

[133] **by establishing the mean throughout the year:**「1 年を通しての平均を確定することによって」。

[141] **local knowledge that it had gained on site:**「現場で得たその地域の知識」。ローカルノレッジとは，科学技術社会論ではよく使われる用語。人々がそれぞれの生活や仕事，その他の日常的実践や身の回りの環境についてもっている知識のことを指す。特定の地域や実践の現場の文脈に固有のものであり，①文脈を越えた一般性をもたず，②文脈を共有しない外部の者には通常知られていない，という二重の意味で局在的（local）な知識である。生活知，現場知ともいわれる。例えば漁師が，その労働環境である海の潮の流れや水温，魚の生態，天候について熟知していることを指す。元来は文化人類学の術語。cf. an *on-site* report「現地レポート」。

Fujimae tidal flats

edge that it had gained on site. The figure produced by the promoters of the project, on the other hand, was understood to be a mean that could even be used for engineering planning and regarded as a figure fit for an ideal engineering system. But in this idealized calculation, based on a scientifically random sampling, the difference between low tide and high tide was ignored. A different kind of science, based more on detailed local knowledge, would nonetheless see this tidal difference as something essential that should not be ignored. This is a good example of differences in S/N ratio as produced within an ideal system on the one hand and a realistic system on the other.

The fundamental problem at the heart of the Nagoya dispute was that differences in approximation and in the definition of calculation methods were debated in terms of "which is more scientific." The project's promoters argued that a random sampling that could be used in planning any engineering project was "the objective figure." The promoters associated science with approximated assessment and did not recognize that the process of assessment always incorporates certain value judgments. Because they were unable to recognize the limitations of their scientific method, they could not respond to the different kind of objectivity that the NGO was asking for, which would have included the need to come up with a figure that corresponded to the realities of the actual local situation. The promoters were unable to understand that estimated assessments always include approximations and that approximation always includes value judgments about relative importance: what is significant and what can be ignored. They failed to understand that this kind of value judgment on the part of those involved in the preparation of any so-called objective data will inevitably affect the methodology by which that data is gathered, and thus the nature of the data itself.

[145] **a figure fit for an ideal engineering system:**（be）fit for ... は「…に適している」という意味でよく使われるフレーズ（e.g. I'm afraid your essay is not *fit for* publication./cf. His room wasn't *fit* to be seen.）。

[150] **as produced:** as の後に they (= differences in S/N ratio) are が省略されていると考えればよい（cf. Japan *as* we know it.）。

[156] **The project's promoters argued that . . . :**「プロジェクト推進派は…と主張した」。この場合の argue は「主張する」で，このように that 節が主張内容を表す。argue for/against ... と言えば「…に賛成／反対の主張をする」という意味（cf. Her *argument against* the project was quite convincing.）。

[160] **value judgments:**「価値判断」。事実ではなく，自分の意見に基づいて物事の善し悪しを決めること。ネガティブな意味合いを伴うこともある（e.g. Be careful not to allow *value judgments* to creep into your ideas.）。ここでは，アメリカの批評家スーザン・ソンタグ（Susan Sontag）が『写真論』(*On Photography*) などで示したように，一見「事実」と見えることの裏に価値判断が入り込んでいる可能性を示唆している。

「藤前干潟を守る会」のホームページより

Fujimae, a tidal flat area left untouched in the middle of the industrial zone of Nagoya Port, is one of Japan's largest stopovers for migratory birds. On the tidal flat live large numbers of crabs, lugworms and small fish that form the diet of the birds. The tidal flat is a vital resting area for migratory birds to get needed nourishment after their long flights. The city of Nagoya was planning to use Fujimae as the site of a garbage landfill, but after many years of conservation efforts by local citizens, the plan was cancelled. This was the impetus for Nagoya to launch its unprecedented garbage reduction campaign.　　（**www.fujimae.org**）

6

SUBJECTIVITY

Introduction
Junichi Murata

When we say we know what "Prussian Blue" is, what is it that we think we know?

If you open an encyclopedia, you can easily find a relatively detailed account of this particular color. Probably you will find that it was discovered in 1704 almost simultaneously in Germany and France, and that it is an inorganic pigment made of the blue sediment accidentally obtained when a potassium salt made of an animal's blood or liver was heated and iron (II) sulfate was added. You will also find many other incidents and explanations related to this color which will help you to understand, for example, why this particular blue is called "Prussian."

In this way, you will be able to get a lot of information about the color "Prussian Blue." Does this mean that you now know what the color is? To be sure, you can now answer various questions about it, and in this sense we can say you now have some "professional" knowledge of the color. But what if you have never seen the color before, and there is no actual representation of it in the explanation you read? You'll probably feel that you have not yet grasped the essential character of the color, as you still have no idea what it looks like. Indeed, if you were shown several shades of blue, you would still not be able to identify the Prussian Blue among them.

The well-known proverb "seeing is believing" really fits this situation. According to this proverb, knowledge gained by direct experience is essentially different from and sometimes more important than knowledge gained by indirect report and description. There are some kinds of things and events which the proverb seems to fit very well. Colors are one of the most typical cases of this kind, but we can also find a similar situation in the case of sensations and

[4] **this particular color:**「この特定の色」。このように particular は（「特別な」ではなく）「特定の」という意味で用いられることが多いことにも注意（e.g. *particular* languages, such as English and Japanese)。

[6] **an inorganic pigment made of the blue sediment:** an inorganic pigment は「無機顔料［色素］」。sediment は「沈殿物」。

[7] **a potassium salt:**「一種のナトリウム塩」。

[8] **iron (II) sulfate:**「硫酸（第一）鉄」。

[14] **To be sure ...:**「確かに…」は，it is true that ... と同様に，後に出てくる but などの逆説の接続詞と呼応して用いられることが多い表現（3 章 [176], 9 章 [80]）。

[17] **there is no actual representation of it:** representation は「表象」「表示」の意だが，ここでは Prussian Blue の実例のこと。

[20] **shades of blue:**「濃淡の異なる青」。

[21] **identify:** 日本語に翻訳しにくい動詞だが，このように「これだと特定する」「ある特定のものが（他のものではなく）そのものであるとわかる」と言う場合によく用いられる。

also in the case of various kinds of emotion.

For example, what does it mean to know what lumbago is like? More than ten years ago I suddenly developed a severe back pain and started to have difficulty moving around. Before this experience, I had thought I understood what it meant when someone said she had lumbago and I thought I could sympathize with her. However, after having experienced it myself, my sympathetic understanding of persons suffering from lumbago clearly became deepened. At least, so it seems to me.

Or, what does it mean to know what sorrow is like, for example, the sorrow which a parent feels on losing a child? Even though we sympathize deeply with their situation, there seems to be an essential element in their sorrow which we cannot experience, and in this sense our understanding and our knowledge about their sorrow has an essential limit which is impossible to overcome, no matter how much information we might have about their situation.

We often describe these kinds of situations in the following way: there are things and events in the world which we can understand only from "inside." This place of "inside" is usually called the place of mind or soul, and the problem concerning the relationship between this "inside" and "outside" has been called the "mind-body problem" by philosophers. The fundamental problem is that we cannot reach this "inside" in the same way that we can reach the inside of a room; we cannot open it as we open a closed bag and find what is inside. The inner aspect of pain and sorrow cannot be dealt with in the same way as the outer (physical or physiological) aspect can be, and the knowledge of mind and of body are essentially different.

Perhaps you have already noticed that the implication of these examples is a little ambiguous. On the one hand, these examples demonstrate that inside knowledge is important for deepening and enhancing our understanding of other people and that it contributes to strengthening interpersonal relationships. On the other hand, they could be interpreted in the opposite direction. They could indicate that there is always an essential limitation to our understanding of and knowledge of the experiences of other people, as my situation and that of others cannot be the same in the strict sense of the word.

This ambiguity is revealed in an extreme sense in the following example. Everyone knows that all individuals will die at some point, and that one must die one's own death. I know that I cannot avoid my death and that nobody can die in my place, substituting for me.

- [30] **lumbago** [lʌmbéɪgoʊ]:「腰痛」(cf. He's suffering from a severe lower back pain.)。
- [49] **the "mind-body problem":** 日本語でも「心身問題」と呼ばれている。
- [57] **the implication of . . . :**「…の含意」とは「…から出てくる(暗黙の)結論」「…に暗に含まれる意味」のこと(12 章 [69])。
- [58] **ambiguous:**「あいまいな」と訳されるが，(vague とは異なり)ひとつの表現などが二通り以上の解釈を許容すること (cf. ambiguity)。
- [65] **in the strict sense of the word:**「厳密な意味で(は)」。このような場合，日本語では word に相当する語は用いられないが，英語ではよく用いられることに注意 (cf. literature *in the strict* [*broad*] *sense of the term*)。
- [70] **nobody can die in my place:**「誰も私の代わりに死ぬことはできない」。in someone's place または in place of someone は「…の代わりに」と言う場合の決まった表現(10 章 [37])。

In this sense, my death is the most private and intimate event I will encounter in my life. However, can I say that I know what it is like to die my own death? Can I say that I know it better than anyone else? Obviously I can't, as I have never experienced my own death, and, once I have experienced it, I will be already dead and therefore not in a position to have any kind of knowledge about it. In this sense, it is logically impossible for me to have any genuine knowledge about the most basic and private event of my own life. To be sure, I can and do have considerable knowledge about my own death from biological, sociological and psychological points of view. However, these various kinds of knowledge belong to the sphere of knowledge from the outside, and they cannot contribute to my acquiring knowledge from the inside. This would be one way of interpreting the apparently innocent proverb "seeing is believing."

Does this consequence sound a little odd to you? Surely it must. If this consequence sounds strange, we must once again, from the beginning, reconsider and revise the story we have followed up to this point. Such an attempt would be an attempt to search for a new story about knowledge, in which I would hope that we could acquire genuine knowledge in order to understand more adequately the question of what it is like to die our own death.

Dying a Death

Allan Kellehear

There are several books on the market describing what death is like. They make grim reading. None of them spares you any of the gruesome details. Breathlessness is breathlessly described. Nausea is explained *ad nauseam*. Pain and convulsions are sketched in agonizing detail. Every little bit, and then some. You can see what I mean by reading the following example of a young doctor's account of his open chest resuscitation attempt on a dying man:

"I had read that the sensation imparted by a fibrillating heart is like holding in one's palm a wet, jellylike bagful of hyperactive worms, and that is exactly the way it was. I could tell by its rapidly

[84]　**the apparently innocent proverb:**「一見どうということはない諺」。この場合の innocent は「悪意のない」「無害な」という感じ（cf. innocuous）。

[93]　**make grim reading:** reading は「読み物」（cf. Her latest novel was a really good *read*.）。この場合の make ... は「…になる」に相当するが，主語に来る物や人が「…（を作るため）の素材になる」「…の素質を持っている」という場合に用いられる（e.g. I'm sure she'll *make* an excellent teacher./cf. I wonder what *makes* her such an excellent teacher.）。

[93]　**None of them spares you ... :** *Spare* me the (gruesome) details.「（そんなぞっとすることについて）詳しいことは聞きたくありません」「具体的な話は結構です」というよく用いられる表現をもじった言い方。

[94]　**Breathlessness is ... :** この文とそれに続く二文で死の gruesome details の典型的な語られ方が例示されている。いずれの文でも語り方そのものが語られる対象を思わせるものであることが巧みに表現されていることに注意。nausea は「むかつき」「吐き気」。*ad nauseam* は「吐き気がするほど」。convulsions は（このようにしばしば複数形で）「痙攣」「ひきつけ」。in agonizing detail は「苦痛になるほど詳しく」。

[96]　**Every little bit, and then some:**「あらゆる細部について述べ，その上さらにいろいろ」。

[98]　**his open chest resuscitation attempt on a dying man:** resuscitation ＜ resuscitate:「蘇生させる」（cf. open-heart surgery/*an attempt* on his life「彼を暗殺する企て」）。

[100]　**I had read ... :** impart は「（情報や知識などを）与える」。fibrillate は「（心臓が）細動する」（cf. defibrillator「細動除去器」）。hyperactive は「過度に活動的な」（e.g. *hyperactive* syndrome「多動症候群」）だが，ここでは「さかんにうごめく」といった感じ。

[102]　**I could tell ... :** この場合の can tell は「わかる」だが，このように五感を通してわかる場合に用いられる（13 章 [95]）（e.g. I *could tell* from the tone of her voice that she was quite upset.）。

decreasing resistance to the pressure of my squeezes that the heart was not filling with blood, and so my efforts to force something out of it were useless, especially since the lungs were not being oxygenated. But I still kept at it. And suddenly, something stupefying in its horror took place — the dead McCarty, whose soul was by that time totally departed, threw back his head once more and, staring toward the ceiling with the glassy, unseeing gaze of open dead eyes, roared out to the distant heavens a dreadful rasping whoop that sounded like the hounds of hell were barking. Only later did I realize that what I had heard was McCarty's version of a death rattle, a sound made by spasm in the muscles of the voice box, caused by the increased acidity in the blood of a newly dead man. It was his way, it seemed, of telling me to desist — my efforts to bring him back to life could only be in vain."[1]

A little too much detail do you think? Indeed, these kinds of books are the roller-coaster rides of death and dying. You open the book, strap yourself in, read the first chapter, brace yourself and then, weeeeee — chariot ride through a set of anatomical images that make the Marquis de Sade look like he needs assertiveness training.

But are we any better off? Do these books tell us what death is really like? At best, these graphic accounts of dying are testimonies to how the experience of dying seems to onlookers or the clinical professions attending these events. And they are described as events or as carer's experiences. These stories tell us little about what dying might be like for the person at the centre of the experience.

What is the experience of dying like for dying people? We can gain a valuable measure of insight from other related everyday experiences.

When I was seventeen, I was involved in a car accident. Three of us decided to go out to get burgers at midnight one Saturday. We got as far as four blocks from the house when a car, driven by a woman rushing home to her children, hit us. A man walking his dog saw the accident. He said that her car hit ours on the passenger side. She was speeding. Our car rolled once and then the tires peeled off as the wheel rims dug into the asphalt. As the rims gouged the road, the car flipped into the air and sailed into a telegraph pole. It wrapped itself around the pole and slid to the ground with a resounding crash. The engine of the woman's car was ejected by the impact of the collision and lay several metres away from the crash site.

What happened inside our car?

- [105] **oxygenated:** oxygenate [άksɪdʒəneɪt] は「酸素を与える」。
- [106] **I still kept at it:** keep at it は「困難にもかかわらず諦めずに(仕事などを)続ける」。
- [106] **stupefying:**「呆然とさせるような」(cf. I *was* completely *stupefied* by his remark.)。
- [109] **glassy:**「(目が)生気のない」「うつろな」(cf. glassy-eyed)。
- [110] **rasping whoop:**「しわがれた叫び声」(cf. a *raspy* voice)。
- [111] **Only later did I realize . . . :** 否定的な意味をもつ only later「後になってはじめて」が強調のために文頭に出たのに伴って倒置が起こっていることに注意(3章 [105], 8章 [184]) (cf. *Never in my wildest dreams did I* expect her to help me out.)。a death rattle は「臨終の喉声」。spasm は「痙攣」。voice box は「喉頭」(専門用語では larynx)。acidity (< acid) は「酸度」。a newly dead man は「死んだばかりの男」(cf. newlyweds)。
- [115] **desist:**「やめる」「断念する」という意味の文語的な動詞。
- [117] **Indeed, these kinds of books . . . :** indeed は「全くその通り」。roller coaster は日本語の「ジェットコースター」に当たるが, roller-coaster ride はこのように「波瀾万丈の物語」という意味で比喩的に用いることも多い。
- [118] **You open the book . . . :** strap yourself in「(乗り物の中で)シートベルトを着用する」, brace yourself「衝撃などに備える」などは前文の roller-coaster rides を受けた表現。the Marquis de Sade「サド侯爵」はフランスの作家 (1740–1814)。ここで話題になっている本に見られる描写と比べれば、サディズム (sadism) という語の由来となっているこの人物でさえ自信をもって自己主張ができるようになるための訓練 assertiveness training を受ける必要があると思えてくる、と言っている。assertiveness training は,「自己主張訓練」「アサーティブネス・トレーニング」と訳される。消極的な人に自信をもたせるようにするトレーニングのこと。
- [123] **are we any better off?:**「よりましになっているだろうか」とは, こうした本を読むことで以前よりも死がどういうものかがよくわかるようになっただろうか、ということ。
- [124] **At best . . . :** at best は「せいぜいよくても」(cf. at worst「最悪の場合には」「最悪の場合でも」)。graphic は「なまなましい」「どぎつい」。testimony は to . . . を伴って「…を証言するもの」(cf. His latest book *testifies to* his talent.)。onlooker は「傍観者」(cf. a non-participating observer)。clinical professions は「(患者と関わる医者や看護婦などの)臨床的な職業(に従事する人々)」。
- [130] **a valuable measure of insight:**「貴重な洞察」(cf. achieve *a measure of* success「ある程度の成功を収める」)。
- [135] **A man walking his dog:** walk a dog は「犬を散歩させる」と言う場合の決まった表現。
- [138] **As the rims gouged the road . . . :** gouge は「えぐる」。flip は「はじけ飛ぶ」(cf. *flip* a coin)。sail は「素早く滑らかに移動する」。
- [140] **slid to the ground with a resounding** [rɪzáʊndɪŋ] **crash:**「大音響とともに地面に滑り落ちた」「地面に滑り落ちて大きな音を立てた」(cf. a *resounding* victory)。
- [141] **was ejected:**「はじき出された」。

When the other car hit us, we were talking, but I don't remember the topic. I caught a glimpse of headlights. There was a bang, which stopped the conversation. We turned upside down. I raised my arm above my head to protect myself against my fall on the car's ceiling as we rolled. I smelt dust in my nostrils. There was another loud explosion, and I felt jerked about and dropped. Dust and glass went everywhere. As the car stopped, I turned to the friend who was driving and remarked that this meant hamburgers were out of the question. The accident gave me a broken pelvis.

To onlookers, the incident looked far worse than my recollection of it. To me, it was much like rolling down a hill in a potato sack with someone making violent banging noises as I went. I would have been more scared if I had been the witness walking his dog.

The sports commentator at a racetrack can describe a fall or a crash in the way the crowds see it but not as the driver or rider suffers it.

My experience of the crash was no fun, let me tell you, but it was a long way from the dramatic eyewitness account I heard later. Both were "true" accounts, but they came from different perspectives. The witness's account reported what our crash was like for onlookers. My account told how it felt for me, an insider.

At a dinner party one night, my mother's chair collapsed, for no apparent reason. We rushed to her side, but she was unconscious. Slowly she came around and asked what had happened. To us, she was there one minute and gone the next, in a jerky set of movements that ended with a crashing noise on the floor. It was dramatic and scary. Everyone was shocked and distressed.

When my mother had recovered sufficiently, she recalled the conversation, a sudden inexplicable movement to one side and then blackness. Even in this murkiness, however, she recalled feelings of comfort and peace, as if she were having a good sleep. She was better off than her panicking hosts and guests.

When doctors describe someone fainting, their descriptions will be about the effects of heat, or standing too long, or cardiac insufficiency, or fluid dynamics, or the psychosomatics of threat and shock. Ask someone who has fainted what it was like, and their account will sound like a page out of *Alice in Wonderland*, or my mother's story of a dark and velvet place of peace.

When it comes to death, remember that few people know what dying is really like, least of all those who have not done it. Very old people often say that they feel middle-aged or younger. People who have been resuscitated consistently report pleasant feelings. Those

- [150] **I felt jerked about:** jerk は「突然ぐいと動かす」。about は「あちこちに」。
- [152] **remarked that this meant hamburgers were out of the question:**「これじゃあハンバーガーはとても食べられないね，と言った」。
- [153] **The accident gave me a broken pelvis:**「その事故のせいで骨盤を骨折した」。英語らしい表現法 (cf. How did you *get that bloody nose*? / He *gave me a black eye*.)。
- [159] **the driver or rider suffers it:** suffer はこのように「よくないことを経験する」という意味の他動詞としてよく用いられる (e.g. *suffer* financial losses)。
- [161] **was no fun:**「決して楽しくなんかなかった」。wasn't fun よりも否定の意味が強い (cf. He's *no* fool.)。
- [161] **let me tell you:**「実際の話」。
- [168] **she came around:**「意識をとり戻す」。
- [174] **murkiness:** < murky「(水が)濁っていて中がよく見えない」という意味から「はっきりしない」「よくわからない」。
- [178] **cardiac insufficiency:**「心臓の機能不全」(cf. suffer cardiac arrest)。
- [179] **fluid dynamics:**「流体力学」の意味だが，ここでは身体の中の水分の動きのこと。
- [179] **psychosomatics:**「心身症」の意味だが，ここでは脅威とショックに対する心身的な反応。
- [183] **When it comes to death:** when it comes to . . . は「…ということになると」(4 章 [73])。
- [184] **least of all:** 否定の文脈 (この場合は few people know「ほとんど誰も知らない」) で用いて，「中でも[とりわけ]…はそうである」という意味を表している (e.g. No one was happy with the results, *least of all* our teacher.)。

who recover from a coma often report dreamy or dreamless sleepy states. The worst rumours about death seem to come from people with the least first-hand experience. Isn't that always the way?

---

[1] Sherwin Nuland, *How We Die*, London: Chatto & Windus, 1993, p. 7.

[189] **Isn't that always the way?**:「いつだってそういうものじゃないですか?」という感じ。

7

VOICE

Introduction
Jun Ishibashi

Karaoke — like *manga*, *anime* and character goods of the "Hello Kitty" variety — is a globally popular form of entertainment with a Japanese origin. In the case of *karaoke*, in my opinion, it was the Chinese diaspora that really brought about its worldwide diffusion. Nowadays, a party without *karaoke* might be almost unimaginable for any Chinese community anywhere in the world.

This fact really came home to me personally in 1996, my last year of working for a Japanese electronics company. At that time I was supporting the company's South East Asian business network while based in Japan. On one occasion, I visited the Regional Headquarters in Singapore to give a products seminar for South East Asian customers from neighboring countries, 90 percent of whom were of Chinese origin. The closing event of the seminar was a cruise around Singapore Bay. We joined the cruise ship at Clifford Pier and enjoyed glasses of champagne, marvelous sunset views, a special Cantonese buffet, a gorgeous night-time panorama. In other words, we followed the normal program for this kind of event.

When the ship reached the middle of the beautiful bay, a voice from a loudspeaker invited us inside, where we found that the main cabin had been converted into a *karaoke* room with a huge screen for the video projection system at the front. Suddenly the cruise liner exploded into a singing party. As the only visitor from Japan, I was almost immediately expected to sing a song, while still not fully recovered from my surprise at finding that everyone there seemed to prefer singing to enjoying the incomparable night view from the ship.

For me the problem was how to select my number, as the songs were all listed in either Mandarin or Cantonese (both of which I

[1] *Karaoke*: a form of entertainment in which people sing popular songs over pre-recorded backing tracks. Origin 1970s: from Japanese, lit., 'empty orchestra' (*Concise Oxford English Dictionary*, 10th ed., 1999). このように karaoke という言葉は英語として受け入れられている。したがってイントロダクションでは外国語として斜体字になっているが，本文ではそのまま用いられている。

[3] **the Chinese diaspora:** 本来 Diaspora [daɪǽspərə] は，紀元前597年および586年のバビロン捕囚以後，多数のユダヤ人がパレスチナから離散したことをさす。普通名詞化した diaspora は「(民族の)集団移住，離散」「(家族の)離散」のこと。

[4] **its worldwide diffusion:**「カラオケが世界中に広まること」。diffusion < diffuse「拡散する」。

[7] **This fact really came home to me:** A comes home to B (人) は「A を B が痛感する」(cf. Her remarks *brought home to us* the seriousness of the trouble we'd gotten ourselves into.)。

[9] **while based in Japan:** while I was based in Japan の I was が省略されている。このように時や条件を表す従属節の主語は，主節の主語と一致する場合には be 動詞とともに省略されることがよくある (e.g. If (you are) in doubt, turn to a specialist for advice.)。be based in ... は「…にいる」「…に駐在している」(cf. 9章 [149])。

[10] **Headquarters:**「本部」「本社」。この意味での headquarters は (動詞との一致などの点では単数扱いであっても) 常に最後に s がつくことに注意 (9章 [143])。

[12] **neighboring countries:**「近隣の国々」(neighboring は「近隣の」という意味の限定用法の形容詞)。

[19] **the main cabin had been converted into ...:** convert A into B は「A を B に転換する」(cf. change [transform/turn] A into B)。

[22] **exploded into a singing party:**「突然大音響の歌唱パーティーになった」(cf. burst into tears [laughter])。

[25] **the incomparable night view from the ship:**「船からのこの上なく美しい夜景」。incomparable [ɪnkʌ́mpərəbl] は「比類のない」。

[27] **my number:**「自分が歌うべき曲」。

[28] **Mandarin or Cantonese:** Mandarin [mǽndərən] は「普通話」すなわち標準中国語のこと。中国語の最有力の方言である北方語を基礎にして作られたが，北方語は役所での公用語であったことから，かつて「官話」と呼ばれていた。そのことから，17世紀に渡来した宣教師がそれを Mandarin と名づけた (小文字で mandarin は中国清朝時代の官吏のこと)。Cantonese は広東語。

hardly understand). Then a melody came into my mind and I scatted it to a colleague beside me. "— Ah, it's 'Hua Xin'!" He helped me identify the title and the music started. It was "Hana" by Kina Shokichi, completely subtitled in Cantonese. I sang the original Japanese lyrics from memory, and when the music came to the refrain "*nakinasai, warainasai*," the whole audience responded in Cantonese.

Six months later, I was again with some of the members who had participated in the Singapore seminar, this time accompanying them on a Japan tour. I took them to our factory in Tochigi and also sightseeing in Nikko. At night, in the famous Japanese *ryokan* where we were staying, my guests, dressed in *yukata* and *tanzen*, got together in a *tatami* party room and enjoyed a traditional Japanese dinner served on individual *ozen*. But here again, *karaoke* singing was indispensable to close the night!

The main readings for this session are extracts taken from a book by Chinese-American anthropologist Casey Man Kong Lum. They offer you yet another story of *karaoke* as it is enjoyed by the Chinese diaspora around the world.

In Search of a Voice

Casey Man Kong Lum

I can vividly remember how I felt the first time I attended a karaoke event. One of the hosts of the party set up the karaoke system in the living room. Before long, he was singing a song by the Beatles in front of the rest of the group. I felt the video was kind of ridiculous but my mind was so overwhelmed by the anticipation that the hosts might ask me to sing that I cannot even remember which Beatles song it was.

Only three from the party were active in singing that evening. The hosts passed the wireless microphone to us every so often — between songs, or even between two verses — but the rest of us avoided it as if it would burn us. I offered all kinds of excuses, both publicly and in my own mind, to stay away from the fearsome-looking microphone. "I'm still digesting my food," I found myself saying at one point. In my weakest moment of the evening, I even

- [29] **I scatted it:** scat は「メロディーを口ずさむ」という感じ。
- [30] **Hua Xin:**「花心」。沖縄出身の歌手，喜納昌吉の「花」のこと。
- [32] **completely subtitled in Cantonese:**「すべて広東語の字幕つきで」。subtitle [sʌ́btàɪtl] は「字幕」という意味の名詞としても（subtitles と複数形で）よく用いられる（e.g. a Japanese movie with Italian *subtitles*）。

- [47] **vividly remember:**「鮮明に[ありありと]憶えている」と言う場合によく用いられる組み合わせ（cf. I have *vivid* memories of our trip to Egypt in 2000.）。
- [49] **Before long:** soon; in a short time.
- [50] **in front of the rest of the group:**「(他の)みんなの前で」。the rest of ... は「…の残り」だが，この日本語の直訳表現よりもはるかに広く用いられることに注意（e.g. He may well spend *the rest of his life* in jail. / This book is sure to help *the rest of the world* to understand Japanese culture better.）。
- [50] **kind of ridiculous:** kind of は口語ではこのように「ちょっと」「何となく」といった副詞的な意味でしばしば用いられる（cf. I *sort of* like him）。
- [51] **my mind was so overwhelmed by . . . :** cf. I felt an *overwhelming* desire to tell her the truth.
- [57] **as if it would burn us:**「まるでマイクに触れると火傷をしてしまうかのように」(cf. My hand was *burned* as soon as I reached into the fire. / He was being treated for severe *burns*.）。
- [60] **I even gave myself the shameless excuse of "I'm doing research here":** do research は「研究する」という場合の決まった表現のひとつ(8 章 [99])。「研究活動の一環としてここで観察しているので自分が歌うわけにはいかない」という，自分でもよくもぬけぬけとそんなことが言えたものだと思う言い訳をしてしまった，ということ。

Chinatown, New York, NY

gave myself the shameless excuse of "I'm doing research here."

Halfway through the evening, however, I began to notice a gradual change in my reaction to the event. Although the fear of making a fool of myself stood between me and the microphone, the intensity of my hesitation subsided. Meanwhile, the hosts were becoming indifferent to the few of us who were not singing. They did not ask us to sing as often as before. I began to develop a sense of unease, feeling a bit out of place. "I hope they are not upset with me," I thought.

My "moment" finally came when the Beatles' "Hey Jude" was finishing with those long "la . . . la . . . la . . . la la la la, la la la la, hey Jude" phrases. The hosts were crooning along, and I, almost imperceptibly, eased into the chorus. "La . . . la . . . la . . . la la la la . . . " Feeling no objection from the hosts and seeing no apparent unusual reaction from the others, especially my wife, I began to sing louder and louder.

A few numbers later, I picked Don McLean's "Vincent" for my solo debut — a song that I have always loved to listen to and hum. It took me less than a minute to realize that I really could not sing the song. I was off by a couple of keys. I ran out of breath numerous times. I tended to sing ahead of the lyrics, or, at times, I was chasing after them. By the middle of the song, I began to feel the song was much longer than I had thought.

In the car on the way home, I busily wondered whether everyone at the party had discovered how badly I had sung. But, almost miraculously, my wife told me how surprised she was that I could sing so well. "So well?!" I thought. I was puzzled by my wife's compliment because I knew she actually meant what she said. Nonetheless, I began to feel better about my singing.

For several days afterward, I could not help but think about the

[62] **Halfway through . . . :**「…の途中で」(cf. The lecture was so boring that I decided to leave *halfway through*.)。

[63] **making a fool of myself:** make a fool (out) of oneself は「(ばかなまねをして)笑いものになる」と言う場合の決まり文句 (cf. Every time he gets drunk, he *makes a spectacle* [*an exhibition*] *of himself*.「恥さらしなまねをする」)。笑いものになってしまうのではないかという不安のためにマイクをもつ気になかなかなれなかった，ということ。

[65] **subsided:** subside は「(感情や天候が)静まる」(e.g. It took hours before the torrential rain finally *subsided*.)。

[66] **indifferent to . . . :**「…に無関心の」「…などどうでもいいという態度の」。

[68] **feeling a bit out of place:** 分詞構文が主節の内容を言い換えている。out of place はこのように形容詞的に「場違いの」「その場にふさわしくない」という意味でよく用いられる。

[72] **The hosts were crooning along:** croon は「小さな声でくちずさむ」。ここでは「低音でセンチメンタルに歌う」という感じ。along は「誰か(ここではこの歌を選んで歌っている人)に合わせて一緒に」という意味を加えている (cf. Feel free to *sing along* if you know the lyrics.)。

[73] **eased into . . . :** ease into . . . は「…に徐々に入っていく」だが，ここでは比喩的に用いられている。直前の almost imperceptibly と意味がうまく調和していることに注意。

[77] **A few numbers later:** この場合の numbers は「曲目」。「その数曲後に」ということ。

[77] **Don McLean's "Vincent":** ドン・マクリーンは，1945年ニューヨーク生まれのシンガー・ソング・ライター。「ヴィンセント」は1972年の彼のヒット曲で，画家ゴッホ (Vincent van Gogh) に捧げられた曲。

[77] **for my solo debut** [déɪbjuː, ‑ ‑́]: カラオケを初めて，それも一人だけで (all by myself) 歌ったので「ソロデビュー」ということになる。

[80] **I was off by a couple of keys:**「少々音程が外れていた」。この場合の key は「調べ」「音程」(cf. She sounded slightly *off-key*. / His singing was perfectly *in tune*.)。

[80] **I ran out of breath:** run out of breath は「息が切れる」という意味の決まった言い方。

[87] **I was puzzled by my wife's compliment:** be puzzled by . . . は「(理解できないために)…に当惑する」「…に考え込んでしまう」(cf. I often find his remarks *puzzling*.)。compliment は「お世辞」と違って「本心ではない」という意味合いは必ずしも伴わないことに注意 (e.g. Thank you for the *compliment*. / cf. I *complimented* her on her flawless command of Japanese.)。

[88] **I knew she actually meant what she said:**「妻が本気で言っていることがわかっていたので」。mean what one says は「(冗談や誇張ではなく)本気で言う」という意味の決まった言い方 (cf. Surely you don't *mean* that, do you?「まさか本気じゃないよね」)。

[90] **I could not help but . . . :** cannot help but + 原形動詞または cannot help . . . ing は「…しないではいられない」という意味を表す定型表現で，動詞は (feel, think, wonder など)思考や感情を表すものであることが多い (cf. I'm sorry I laughed but I just *couldn't help myself*.)。

various emotions I had experienced that evening: from the anxiety to the longing to be part of the group, and from the positive approval of a mediocre performance to the willful acceptance of such a compliment. Also, I thought about how casual and invisible karaoke as a form of entertainment and popular culture had already become to my hosts of that evening, as well as to millions of people like them in various parts of Asia, in overseas Asian immigrant communities, and, increasingly, around the world. I wanted to know more.

Karaoke in Three Chinese American Communities

Karaoke encapsulates certain cultural practices of amateur participatory singing whereby social reality can be created, maintained, and transformed. How karaoke is ultimately used and the social consequences of such usage are determined by the past experiences, needs, and expectations of the people who use it, as well as by the interactional performance making use of it, hence the concept of the interpretive communities of karaoke.

In my study of karaoke in three Chinese American communities, I focused on the karaoke experiences of three interpretive communities of first-generation Chinese American immigrants in the greater New York-New Jersey metropolitan area. The focus of my analysis was on how these interpretive communities use karaoke as a forum for the construction of their respective social identities. Based on original data I gathered from field research, I developed three distinct themes to describe the different uses and significances of karaoke to the three communities: karaoke as cultural connection and translation, karaoke as status symbol, and karaoke as escape.

The first interpretive community consists of mostly lower middle to middle-class Cantonese people from Hong Kong and its vicinities in southern China. Members of this group are socially active in New York's Chinatown on the Lower East Side of Manhattan. Although their main interest is in singing Cantonese opera songs, these people use karaoke as an alternative medium for Cantonese opera singing for themselves and for providing cultural service to the elderly in their ethnic community. The second interpretive community I studied consists mostly of Taiwanese immigrants. Coming from affluent backgrounds, members of this community are highly educated professionals living in exclusive neighborhoods in New Jersey. They adopt an interpretive frame of reference that views karaoke as a status symbol. I examined how karaoke is used by people in this affluent interpretive community as a means to express their wealth and social class and, to a certain extent, their

[92] **the longing to be ...**: longing は動詞 long「切望する」「思い焦がれる」に対応する名詞で，動詞の場合と同じく，後に続く for（または after）の後の名詞句または to 不定詞句が切望の対象を表す (cf. She *longed to see* him again soon. / We all *long for* peace.)。

[93] **mediocre**:「良くも悪くもない」「並の」などと訳されることが多いが，ほぼ確実に（「二流の」「凡庸な」など）否定的な意味合いを伴う (e.g. I found his latest book rather *mediocre*. / cf. mediocrity)。

[93] **the willful acceptance of such a compliment**: 普通なら（"You've got to be kidding" などと言って）受け流すようなほめことばを，過大であることを知っていながら受け入れたこと。willful は「本来はそうすべきではないとわかっていながら（…する）」という感じ。

[94] **casual and invisible**: casual は「さり気ない」「何気ない」，invisible は「目につかない」「目立たない」といった感じで，カラオケが多くの人々の生活の自然な一部になっていることを表すために用いられている。

[100] **Karaoke encapsulates ...**: encapsulate (< capsule)は「圧縮して簡潔に表現する」。amateur participatory singing はカラオケの歌い方をうまく要約している。amateur [ˈæmətər, ˈæmətʃʊər] (cf. professional)。participatory [pɑːrˈtɪsɪpətɔ̀ːri] は「（全員）参加型の」。

[105] **hence the concept of ...**: hence「このため」は直前の内容を理由とする帰結を導入する機能を果たすが，hence 以下ではこのように文相当の内容（「このために interpretive communities of karaoke という概念が生じる」）が名詞句で表現されることも多い。interpretive < interpret:「解釈する」。interpretive community というのは，元来，文学批評家 Stanley Fish の作った用語で，「解釈共同体」と訳される。ある読者があるテクストを解釈する場合，その解釈は，その読者がどのような「解釈共同体」の中に所属し，どのような文化的諸前提を受け入れているかに左右されるが，フィッシュは，テクストの解釈を左右するそのような「解釈共同体」の機能に着目したのである。ここでは How karaoke is ultimately used の内容がカラオケの解釈の仕方に相当し，そうした解釈をそれぞれに独自の仕方で決定する共同体が interpretive communities。

[109] **the greater New York-New Jersey metropolitan area**: ニューヨーク市およびその周辺にあるニューヨーク州南部，ニュージャージー州北東部に広がる大都市域。人口約 2000 万。

[118] **Hong Kong and its vicinities**:「香港とその近郊諸地域」。

[120] **New York's Chinatown on the Lower East Side of Manhattan**: ニューヨーク市は，マンハッタン，ブルックリン，クィーンズ，ブロンクス，スタテンアイランドの 5 区からなる。マンハッタン区の東南部ロウワー・イースト・サイド地区は，かつてはユダヤ人をはじめとする東ヨーロッパからの移民が居住していたが，現在は多数の中国系が住み，全米最大規模のチャイナタウンがある。

[121] **Cantonese opera songs**:「広東オペラ」。

[125] **Coming from affluent backgrounds**: affluent は「裕福な」。from ... backgrounds はよくある組み合わせ (e.g. This class includes people *from* different cultural *backgrounds*.)。

[127] **exclusive neighborhoods**: exclusive は「限られた人たち限定の」「高級な」(e.g. an *exclusive* hotel)。neighborhood は（日本語の「近所」より意味が広く）この場合「地域」「地区」(e.g. I live in a quiet residential *neighborhood*.)。

[128] **an interpretive frame of reference**: frame of reference は「理解や判断の基準となる枠組み」（10 章 [236]）。「基準系」「準拠枠」などと訳される。

[128] **views karaoke as ...**: view A as B は「A を B と見なす」という意味の頻出表現型 (cf. Most of his colleagues *saw* him *as* a visionary.)。

[131] **their individual competitive drive**:「彼ら個人個人の競争心」。drive は「衝動」「意欲」。

individual competitive drive. The members of the third interpretive community I studied are mostly Malaysians of Chinese descent living in the Flushing area of Queens in New York City. Many of these people are undocumented immigrants and therefore confined to the economic underground. To many members of this community, karaoke serves as a temporary form of escape.

Karaoke as Escape

Ah Maa turned 55 in the summer, and almost everybody she knew at the time showed up at her karaoke birthday party. The majority of Ah Maa's friends are Malaysians of Chinese ancestry, living in the multiethnic working class neighborhood of Flushing. Ah Maa and her friends mostly come from humble social, educational, and economic backgrounds. At a very young age, for example, Ah Maa was taken to Malaysia by her parents from her birthplace in southern China after Japan began its invasion of China and before World War II was over. Ah Maa never had enough education to develop the ability to read or write Chinese (or any language) at a functional level, an inadequacy she now regrets enormously, in part because she cannot "read those words on the television to sing karaoke."

Since marrying her husband, "a quiet and simple man," Ah Maa has spent most of her life working menial jobs to help raise their seven children. The last long-term job she had in Malaysia was as a cleaning lady for a Japanese company in the city of Kuala Lumpur. On Saturdays she would moonlight as a *daaikamje*, a woman hired to accompany a bride on her traditional Chinese wedding day until the evening banquet is over. One day in 1986, after speaking to friends returning from the United States, Ah Maa told her husband that she wanted to travel to America on a pleasure trip. What Ah Maa really had in mind, however, was to come to the United States to work, make "a lot of American dollars," and then "go home to live my last years with my *lougung* and my youngest daughter. Buy a house for sure." (*Lougung* is a colloquial way of addressing one's husband in Cantonese.)

Not unlike many early European and Asian immigrants to the United States a century or so ago as well as some of her Malaysian contemporaries, Ah Maa came to the United States as a migrant worker who had no intention of putting down roots in the country. Ah Maa and an undetermined number of her karaoke friends are undocumented immigrants. In the early 1990s, she was a housekeeper and a nanny for a couple from Hong Kong. The couple were business people and had a large piece of property in an expensive

[133] **Malaysians of Chinese descent:** of ... descent は「…系の」と言う場合の決まった表現のひとつ。後出の of Chinese ancestry も同じ意味 (cf. people *of* Asian *origin*)。

[134] **the Flushing area of Queens:** クィーンズ区にあるフラッシング地区は近年中国系の移民が増え，非常に大きなチャイナタウンができた。

[134] **Many of these people are undocumented immigrants ...:** undocumented immigrants が指している人々は illegal immigrants のこと (undocumented は「公的書類に記載されていない」)。

[135] **confined to:** be confined to ... は本来「…に閉じ込められている」だが，ここでは比喩的に用いられている。

[139] **Ah Maa turned 55:**「…歳になる」と言う場合にもっとも普通に用いられる動詞は turn。

[140] **showed up:** show up は「(会合などに)顔を出す，やって来る」(cf. Three of the applicants were *no-shows*.)。

[143] **humble:**「(社会的)地位，階級などが低い」。

[149] **an inadequacy:** inadequacy (< inadequate「不十分な」「妥当でない」) は「不十分さ」「欠点」。

[149] **in part because ...:**「…という理由もあって」。他にも理由があることを含意する決まった表現のひとつ (cf. partly because ... /mainly because ...)。

[152] **menial** [míːniəl] **jobs:**「特別な能力を要さない単純でつまらない仕事(普通賃金も低い)」(cf. low-skilled and low-paying jobs)。

[155] **moonlight:**「(正規の仕事の他に)アルバイト[副業]をする」(夜間にすることが多いことから)。「アルバイトをする」に相当する普通の表現としては do a part-time job, work part-time などがある。

[163] **a colloquial way of ...:** colloquial [kəlóʊkwiəl] は「口語的な」(cf. colloquialism(s) 口語表現)。address one's husband「自分の夫に話しかける」(address が他動詞であることに注意。cf. an opening address「開会のスピーチ」/a public-address (PA) system「(劇場などのマイクや拡声器を利用した)拡声[音響]装置」)。

[165] **Not unlike ...:**「…と似ている」という意味の決まった言い方のひとつ (cf. In this day and age, it is *not uncommon* for a seven-year-old to know a lot more about the Internet than her parents.)。

[167] **a migrant worker who had no intention of ...:** have no intention of ... ing は「…するつもりが全くない」と言う場合によく用いられる表現 (cf. I *have every intention of* repaying you for everything you've done for me.)。

[171] **a nanny:**「乳母」。

neighborhood overlooking the Long Island Sound. They gave Ah Maa a small room in the house and paid her under the table with no benefits. During the day, Ah Maa was all by herself doing household chores, cleaning the garden, preparing meals for her employers and their young children, and for some extra money washing her employers' pleasure boat at their private dock at the end of the large backyard, where the couple's tennis court was located.

The fact that Ah Maa had no choice but to stay on Long Island six days a week gave her a desperate sense of isolation and loneliness. "I'm trapped here, you see," Ah Maa often said to me during interviews, as if the enormous house were nothing but a large cage. The words "trapped," "bored" and "lonely" were always present in her consciousness during the many times over two years that I spoke with her at work. In fact, it was her enormously desperate sense of isolation and loneliness that drove her to karaoke.

Ah Maa first came into contact with karaoke at a friend's birthday party at a club late in 1992. Ah Maa was very taken by the fact that in the club "all these people were so happy singing." She was a bit afraid of going up onto the stage area because it was all so new to her; it was so unlike singing (or humming) "those old songs I know" on her cassette player all by herself while doing her chores. She did not quite know what to do at first when her friends suggested that she take the microphone. Ah Maa excused herself by saying, "I like to listen to you sing." On the inside, however, she acknowledged to me that she wished she could sing as well as everybody else at the club.

This first karaoke birthday party introduced Ah Maa to a community. It is the association with this community of karaoke enthusiasts that gives Ah Maa the sense of self and social identity that she longs for six days a week. Like many of her friends from Malaysia, Ah Maa loves to sing, even though she really cannot sing well. "I have a male goose's voice," she once told me. But singing serves an important and explicit function for Ah Maa:

> I've liked to sing all my life. I like to sing even when I work. Especially when I'm upset. I can forget my troubles. I concentrate on the lyrics and not on other things. It's a relief. Try not to remember unhappy things.

Singing karaoke has become a means for Ah Maa and many of her compatriots to escape the humdrum routine of everyday life, a life that is as alienating as it is confusing. "I don't know why I'm doing this — except I want to buy a house back home so I won't

[173] **the Long Island Sound:**「ロングアイランド海峡」。この場合の sound は「海峡」「入り江」「河口」の意味。

[174] **paid her under the table with no benefits:** under the table は「（金銭の授受を）不法にこっそりと（行う）」。日本語の「袖の下」に近い発想の表現。benefits は「（病気，失業などに際して給料以外に支給される）手当」（個々の「…手当」という場合は allowance が使われる。e.g. a travel allowance「出張手当」/ a transportation allowance「通勤手当」/ a family allowance「扶養手当」）。with no benefits で「保険等が一切出ない」ということ。

[175] **Ah Maa was all by herself . . . :**「一人っきりで…していた」。do household chores は「家庭内の雑用［家事］をする」。

[180] **had no choice but to . . . :**「…するより他ない」という，選択の余地のないことを表す頻出表現型（e.g. We *had no choice but to* fire him for dereliction of duty.）。

[189] **Ah Maa was very taken by . . . :** be taken by . . . は「…に魅力を感じる」（cf. be attracted by . . . /be taken by surprise「不意をつかれる」）。

[196] **On the inside:**「内心では」（cf. They may appear to hate each other's guts, but *deep down* they are madly in love.）。

[200] **this community of karaoke enthusiasts:** . . . enthusiast はこのように「…愛好家」「…好きの人」という意味で用いることの多い表現（e.g. Quite a few colleagues of mine are soccer *enthusiasts*.）。

[211] **her compatriots:** compatriot [kəmpǽtriət] は「同国人」。

[211] **the humdrum routine of everyday life:**「日常生活の退屈で決まり切った仕事」。humdrum: always the same and boring.

[211] **a life that is as alienating as it is confusing:** as A（形容詞）as it is B（形容詞）は「A である程度と B である程度が同じ」（e.g. The insect is *as long as it is wide*. / cf. This table is *twice as long as it is wide*.）が基本的な意味であるが，このように「B であると同時に A である」という場合にも用いられる（e.g. a novel *as moving as it is funny*.）。日本語の「哀しくも美しい」などと同じ発想。

have to live in a government housing project."

Summary Analysis

People in this interpretive community construct karaoke scenes as a temporary social and symbolic haven where they can escape from a sense of entrapment, the everyday repetition and humdrum routine, and the reality of being in isolation. Singing karaoke is more than just entertainment to them. They use karaoke to create certain social spaces to keep in touch with people who share similar life histories, through either vocal or silent participation. These are spaces where people in the community, even in the most adverse of social and economic conditions, can have a voice of their own, a voice of self-assurance and connection. The use of karaoke here speaks to people's need to have an escape, or therapeutic mechanism, that gives them access to a way of life otherwise absent from their everyday existence, even if the escape can only be temporary.

[222] **either vocal or silent participation:** vocal は(カラオケで)歌うことを，silent は(他人が歌うのを)聞いていることを，それぞれ表す。

[225] **The use of karaoke here speaks to . . . :** この場合の speak to . . . は「(欲求など)に応える」という感じ。

[226] **therapeutic mechanism:** therapeutic [θèrəpjúːtɪk] < therapy [θérəpi].

8

GENDER

Introduction
Ai Tanji

There certainly do appear to be a variety of differences between men and women, differences which — whether they are most fundamentally physiological, physical or mental — clearly have significant social effects. But these effects are realised in very complex ways. When you look around the Komaba campus do you ever question why there are significantly fewer women than men at the University of Tokyo? Or have you ever considered closely the reasons why there have been so many fewer female Nobel prize laureates than male?

If you had asked people living some 140 years ago in Victorian Britain about the different social positions held by men and women, almost all of them would have looked for the reasons behind that "natural" difference in inherent biological differences. We can find the most representative example of this style of thinking in Charles Darwin's *The Descent of Man* (1871).

Darwin perceives "a decided pre-eminence" of men over women not only in physical power but also in mental power, and he argues that this difference is a biologically inherited one which has been slowly formed over the course of the long, long evolutionary process of the "struggle for existence" and "natural selection."

> We may conclude that the greater size, strength, courage, pugnacity, and energy of man, in comparison with woman, were acquired during primeval times, and have subsequently been augmented, chiefly through the contests of rival males for the possession of the females. The greater intellectual vigour and power of invention in man is probably due to natural selection, combined with the inherited effects of habit, for the most able men will have succeeded best

[5] **do you ever . . .**: ever は「…することがありますか」という意味を付け加えるために疑問文でよく用いられる。

[6] **significantly fewer women:** significantly はこの場合 considerably とほぼ同じ意味。

[8] **so many fewer female Nobel prize laureates:** many fewer は many more の反対で数がずっと少ないという意味 (cf. We have about *twenty fewer* applicants this year than last year.)。Nobel prize laureates [lɔ́ːriəts] は「ノーベル賞受賞者」。

[10] **some 140 years ago:**「およそ 140 年前」。

[13] **inherent biological differences:** inherent は人や物の属性などについて「生まれつき備わった」(「後天的」ではない),「本来備わった」「本質的な」(「偶然的」「偶有的」ではない) という意味を表す (e.g. This may well be a problem *inherent in* a project like ours.)。

[15] *The Descent of Man*: ダーウィンは,『種の起源』においては,おそらくは宗教的な理由のゆえに人間の進化の問題を避けていたが,『人間の由来』において,それを真正面から論じることになった。

[16] **"a decided pre-eminence" of men over women:** 引用符は Darwin 自身の用いた表現であることを示す。「…より優れた[優位の]」という意味を表すのに over が用いられるのは非常に一般的 (cf. Her years of experience gives her *a definite advantage over* the other candidates./You'd be surprised to know how much power you have *over* every important decision I make.)。

[19] **over the course of . . .**: over the course of . . . は during とほぼ同じ意味を表す決まった言い方。

[20] **the "struggle for existence" and "natural selection":** the struggle for existence は, the struggle for life とともに,「生存闘争」を, natural selection は「自然選択」を意味する。ちなみに,『種の起源』の正確なタイトルは,『自然選択,すなわち生存闘争における有利な品種の保存による種の起源について』(*On the Origin of Species by Means of Natural Selection, or the Preservation of Favoured Races in the Struggle for Life*)。

[21] **pugnacity** [pʌgnǽsəti]: < pugnacious「喧嘩好きな」「喧嘩っ早い」。

[23] **primeval** [praɪmíːvəl] **times:**「原始時代」。

[23] **and have subsequently** [sʌ́bsəkwèntli] **been augmented** [ɔːgméntɪd]:「そしてその後さらに強化された」。

[25] ***The greater intellectual vigour and . . .***: vigour (アメリカ英語では vigor) は「肉体的,精神的な力強さ」(cf. If you want to lose weight, I suggest you take *vigorous* exercise on a regular basis.)。be due to . . . は「…が原因である」という意味でよく用いられる言い回し (e.g. death *due to* overwork「過労死」)。provide for . . . は「…を扶養する」(cf. Language *provides for* the symbolization of ideas.)。offspring が単複同形であることにも注意。

in defending and providing for themselves and for their wives and offspring. (chap. 20)

Darwin's understanding of the difference between women and men as biologically or evolutionarily determined was widely accepted in Victorian society, and sustained an ideology that justified the normative structures of daily life in Britain after the Industrial Revolution. This was a society in which societal roles had been increasingly divided between men, who went out to work, and women, who took care of the home and of children.

In contrast to Darwin's view, John Stuart Mill, a feminist in the age when there was no such word as "feminism," argues in *The Subjection of Women* (1869) for the diametrically opposed idea that gender differences are socially constructed:

If men had ever been found in society without women, or women without men, or if there had been a society of men and women in which the women were not under the control of the men, something might have been positively known about the mental and moral differences which may be inherent in the nature of each. What is now called the nature of women is an eminently artificial thing — the result of forced repression in some directions, unnatural stimulation in others. (chap. 1)

As we can see here, Mill thinks of most of the differences between the two genders as the result of "artificial" construction rather than of any essential characteristics "inherent in the nature of each." The apparent differences, for Mill, are the result of "education or external circumstances" rather than inheritance or biological determinism. In short, Mill attributes the differences to nurture rather than nature.

Twentieth-century feminism has an evident tendency to deny Darwin's biological or evolutionary determinism and to favor Mill's social constructionism. For example, Virginia Woolf, a British feminist writer, reveals her constructionist position in *A Room of One's Own* (1929) when she remarks that "Women have had less intellectual freedom than the sons of Athenian slaves. Women, then, have not had a dog's chance of writing poetry. That is why I have laid so much stress on money and a room of one's own." She is followed along this constructionist line by Simone de Beauvoir, a French feminist thinker, who writes in *The Second Sex* (1949), "One is not born a woman, but becomes one."

While constructionism can be said to have advanced our under-

[31] **biologically or evolutionarily determined:**「生物学的または進化論的に決定されている」とは「(男女の性差が)生物として本来備わったもの，または進化の過程で(自然選択によって)形成されたものである」ということ (cf. Most linguists believe that some universal features of human languages are *genetically determined*.)。

[33] **the normative structures of daily life:** たとえば男性が外に仕事に出かけ，女性が家で家事と育児を行う，というような「日常生活の規範的な構造」。19 世紀後半のミドルクラスの規範的な男女の役割分担は，産業革命で仕事の場が家から工場に移っていく過程の中で形成ないし強化されていった。

[34] **societal roles:** societal [səsáɪətl] は society の形容詞形のひとつだが，social がもつ「社交の」「社交的な」などの意味を避けて，「社会の」という中立的な意味を表したい時に(特に学問的な文脈で)よく用いられる。

[37] **In contrast to . . . :**「…とは対照的に」。

[37] **John Stuart Mill:** ミル(1806–73)はイギリスの思想家，経済学者で，主著は『論理学体系』『経済学原理』『女性の隷従』。ヴィクトリア朝を代表するフェミニストであった彼は，下院議員であった 1866 年に婦人参政権の請願を下院に提出してもいる。

[38] **there was no such word as . . . :**「…などということばはなかった」。これとよく似た there is no such thing as . . . は「…などというものはない」と何かの存在を強く否定する時の決まった言い方として覚えておきたい (e.g. *There's no such thing as* a free lunch.)。ちなみに，女性の権利擁護の運動を意味する feminism という言葉が英語で用いられるようになったのは 1895 年以降のこと。

[39] **diametrically opposed** [dàɪəmétrɪkəli əpóʊzd]:「正反対の」と言う場合によく用いる表現。

[50] **as the result of "artificial" construction . . . :** artificial と inherent，construction と nature が，それぞれ意味上ゆるやかに対立していることに注意。A rather than B は(「B というよりはむしろ A」という煮え切らない意味ではなく)「B ではなく A」という意味になるのが普通。

[54] **nurture rather than nature:** nature と nurture は(頭韻と脚韻の両方を含んでいて口調がよいせいか)対として非常によく用いられる表現で，行動特性や性格について，その決定要因が生まれつきの素質(遺伝)か育った環境か，先天的か後天的か，等の二項対立的な考え方，問いの立て方を意味する(日本語の「氏か育ちか」に相当する場合もある)。現代ではそうした二分法の妥当性自体が疑問視されている。

[57] **Mill's social constructionism:**「ミルの社会構築主義」。社会構築主義は文化構築主義 (cultural constructionism) とも呼ばれ，「われわれが自然だと思っているものの多くは実は社会の中で構築された (socially constructed) 人為的なものである」というような考え方。

[58] **Virginia Woolf:** イギリスの女性小説家，批評家 (1882–1941)。代表作は，『ダロウェイ夫人』(*Mrs. Dalloway*, 1925)，『灯台へ』(*To the Lighthouse*, 1927)。評論『自分だけの部屋』は，20 世紀のフェミニズムの先駆的著作。「女性が詩を書くほんのわずかな見込み (a dog's chance) ももってこなかった」のは，「アテネの奴隷の息子よりも少ない知的自由(= 知識を求める自由)しかあたえられこなかった」からだと考えるウルフは，本書の別の個所で，「女性がものを書くようになれるためには，年に 500 ポンドのお金とドアに鍵のかかる部屋が必要なのだ」とも述べている。女性がなかなか作家になれなかったのは，女性の生来的能力の欠如のせいではなく，女性を取り巻いてきた社会的文化的環境に由来すると主張しているのである。

[64] **Simone de Beauvoir:** ボーヴォワール(1908–86)はフランスの女性小説家，思想家。サルトルの事実上の妻として，実存主義に加担するとともに，女性解放のための活動を精力的に展開した。

Caricatures of Charles Darwin, as an exponent of the descent of man from apes, and J. S. Mill, as "the Ladies' Advocate," printed in nineteenth-century English magazines.

standing of the differences between the sexes, it cannot be said to have answered all of our questions about these differences. The reading for this session, made up of three extracts from a research paper published in *Psychological Review* (2000, 107: 3, 411–29), suggests that these differences — their source as well as their nature — remain one of our hottest topics today.

Biobehavioral Responses to Stress in Females

Shelley E. Taylor, Laura Cousino Klein, Brian P. Lewis, Tara L. Gruenewald, Regan A. R. Gurung, and John A. Updegraff

The first extract comes from the introduction to the paper. Here the authors outline the academic background to their study and reveal the key question that set their research in motion.

The fight-or-flight response is generally regarded as the prototypic human response to stress. First described by Walter Cannon in

Biobehavioral:「生物行動学的な」。生物行動学とは，人間をふくんだ動物の行動を，生物学的生理学的観点から研究する学問。

[77] **The fight-or-flight response:** fight-or-flight は「戦うか逃げるか」「闘争か逃走か」。fight と flight（対応する動詞は flee）は語頭の母音が同じ，つまり頭韻（alliteration）になっている上に，-ight も [aɪt] で同じ発音，つまり脚韻（rhyme）にもなっていて，口調が非常によい。

[78] **stress:** もともとは「圧力によるひずみ」を意味する機械工学的用語だったが，1936 年セリエ（Hans Selye）がストレス学説を提唱して以来，現在われわれが普通に用いる意味で用いられるようになった。セリエは，「生体が外傷，中毒，寒冷，伝染病のような異なった種類の刺激にさらされた際，刺激の性格のいかんにかかわらず，ある種の一様な反応が生じる事実に注目し」，この反応を，「脳下垂体−副腎皮質系の内分泌系統が関与して成立するもので，もともと生体の防衛あるいは環境の変動に対する適応的な反応」と考えた（『平凡社大百科事典』）。

[78] **Walter Cannon:** アメリカの生理学者（1871–1945）。*The Wisdom of the Body*（1932）において，生体の恒常性維持（homeostasis ホメオスタシス）という概念を確立。

1932, the fight-or-flight response is characterized physiologically by sympathetic nervous system activation that innervates the adrenal medulla, producing a hormonal cascade. In addition to its physiological concomitants, fight-or-flight has been adopted as a metaphor for human behavioral responses to stress, and whether a human (or an animal) fights or flees in response to sympathetic arousal is thought to depend on the nature of the stressor. If the organism sizes up a threat or predator and determines that it has a realistic chance of overcoming the predator, then attack is likely. In circumstances in which the threat is perceived to be more formidable, flight is more probable.

A coordinated biobehavioral stress response is believed to be at the core of reactions to threats of all kinds, including attacks by predators; assaults by members of the same species; dangerous conditions such as fire, earthquake, tornado, or flooding; and other threatening events. As such, an appropriate and modulated stress response is at the core of survival. Through principles of natural selection, an organism whose response to stress was successful would likely pass that response on to subsequent generations, and the fight-or-flight response is thought to be such an evolved response.

A little-known fact about the fight-or-flight response is that the preponderance of research exploring its parameters has been conducted on males, especially on male rats. Until recently, the gender distribution in the human literature was inequitable as well. Why have stress studies been heavily based on data from males? The justification for this bias is similar to the rationale for the exclusion, until recently, of females from many clinical trials of drugs, from research on treatments for major chronic diseases, and from animal research on illness vulnerabilities. The rationale has been that, because females have greater cyclical variation in neuroendocrine responses (due to the reproductive cycle), their data present a confusing and often uninterpretable pattern of results. The fight-or-flight response may also be affected by female cycling, and, as a result, evidence concerning a fight-or-flight response in females has been inconsistent. However, what if the equivocal nature of the female data is not due solely to neuroendocrine variation but also to the fact that the female stress response is not exclusively, nor even predominantly, fight-or-flight?

In the the paper's final section, the authors summarize their argument, acknowledge the limitations of their study, and discuss the implications of their conclusions. The second extract comes from the beginning of this section.

[79] **is characterized physiologically by ...:** be characterized by ... は「…によって特徴づけられる」だが，要するに「…という特徴がある」「…を特徴とする」ということ (cf. Japanese society *is* commonly *characterized as* group-oriented.)。

[80] **sympathetic nervous system:**「交感神経系」(cf. parasympathetic nervous system「副交感神経系」)。

[80] **innervates:**「(神経や器官を)刺激する」。

[80] **adrenal medulla:**「副腎髄質」。

[81] **a hormonal cascade:** cascade とは，元来「階段状に連続した滝」の意味だが，ここでは「カスケード」と呼ばれる生化学的な用語。カスケードとは，前段の反応産物によって順次活性化されていく酵素群により触媒される一連の反応であり，最初の刺激応答を増幅する作用をもつ反応のこと。

[82] **concomitants:**「付随して生じること[現象]」。

[84] **sympathetic arousal** [əráuzəl]:「交感神経の興奮」。

[85] **stressor:**「ストレスの原因となるもの」「ストレス因子」。

[86] **sizes up ...:**「…について見極める[判断する]」。

[88] **formidable:**「手強い」。

[90] **A coordinated biobehavioral stress response:** coordinated は「調整される」「協調して行われる」の意味。ストレスへの生物行動学的な反応を構成する一連の動きが，全体の協調をはかりながら調整されつつ行われていること。すぐ後の modulated も同じ意味。

[98] **an evolved response:**「進化の結果として生じた反応」。

[99] **the preponderance of research ...:** preponderance は「大部分，大多数」。conduct research on ... は「…に関する研究を行う」と言う場合の決まった表現のひとつ (7 章 [60]) (cf. A great deal of *research has been done* over the years *on* this mysterious phenomenon.)。parameters はここでは「要因」「特質」。

[102] **the human literature:** この場合の literature は，「文学」ではなく，「(集合的に)研究論文」「文献」。したがって，human literature は，「人間を研究対象とした論文」。

[102] **inequitable** [ɪnékwɪtəbl]:「不公平な」だが，ここでは「偏っている」といった感じ。

[104] **rationale** [ræ̀ʃənǽl]: ここでは justification の言い換え。

[107] **illness vulnerabilities:** cf. be *vulnerable to* illness.

[108] **greater cyclical variation:** この場合に cyclical は「周期的な」の意味。女性の場合，男性よりも，ホルモンの分泌においてより大きな周期的な変動があること。すぐ下の female cycling も同じことをさす。

[113] **the equivocal nature of the female data:** この場合の equivocal [ɪkwívəkl] は「相反する複数の解釈が可能なため理解[説明]するのが難しい」という意味 (cf. He was rather *equivocal* about his role in the steering committee./The answer is an *unequivocal* no)。

[114] **neuroendocrine** [njʊ̀ərouéndəkràɪn]:「神経内分泌(系)の」。

We propose, first, that successful responses to stress have been passed on to subsequent generations through principles of natural selection: Those without successful responses to threat are disproportionately unlikely to reach an age when reproduction is possible. An additional assumption is that, because females have typically borne a greater role in the care of young offspring, responses to threat that were successfully passed on would have been those that protected offspring as well as the self. The female of the species makes a greater investment initially in pregnancy and nursing and typically plays the primary role in activities designed to bring the offspring to maturity. High maternal investment should lead to selection for female stress responses that do not jeopardize the health of the mother and her offspring and that maximize the likelihood that they will survive. "Tending," that is, quieting and caring for offspring and blending into the environment, may be effective for addressing a broad array of threats. In contrast, fight responses on the part of females may put themselves and their offspring in jeopardy, and flight behavior on the part of females may be compromised by pregnancy or the need to care for immature offspring. Thus, alternative behavioral responses are likely to have evolved in females.

The protection of self and offspring is a complex and difficult task in many threatening circumstances, and those who made effective use of the social group would have been more successful against many threats than those who did not. This assumption leads to the prediction that females may selectively affiliate in response to stress, which maximizes the likelihood that multiple group members will protect both them and their offspring. Accordingly, we suggest that the female stress response of tending to offspring and affiliating with a social group is facilitated by the process of "befriending," which is the creation of networks of associations that provide resources and protection for the female and her offspring under conditions of stress.

We propose that the biobehavioral mechanism underlying the tend-and-befriend pattern is the attachment-caregiving system, a stress-related system that has been previously explored largely for its role in maternal bonding and child development. In certain respects, the female tending response under stressful conditions may represent the counterpart of the infant attachment mechanism that appears to be so critical for the development of normal biological regulatory systems in offspring. Numerous investigations have explored the effects of the mother-infant bond on infants' emotional,

- [120] **have been passed on to . . . :** pass A on to B は「A（情報など）を B（他人）に伝達［転送］する」「A（伝統など）を B（次代の人々）に伝える」(e.g. Could you *pass* this message *on to* him?/ a custom *passed* [*handed*] *down* from generation to generation)。
- [122] **are disproportionately unlikely to reach an age . . . :**「(生殖が可能になる)年齢に達する可能性が(ストレスに対する適切な反応のできる個体に比べて)相当低くなる」。
- [128] **a greater investment:** investment は元来「投資」の意味だが，この場合は，女性のほうが男性より妊娠と育児に多くの時間と労力を投じるということ。
- [129] **in activities designed to . . . :** (be) designed to . . . は「…することを目的とする」の意(5 章 [55])。
- [131] **selection for . . . :** < be selected for . . .「(進化の過程で特徴や個体が)選択される」。
- [131] **jeopardize** [dʒépərdàɪz]:「危険にさらす」(cf. put . . . in jeopardy [dʒépərdi]/in danger/at risk)。
- [134] **caring for . . . :** この場合の care は日本語の「ケアする」に相当する動詞だが，「…をケアする」「…の世話をする」と言いたい場合には前置詞が必要であることに注意 (cf. Would you *care for* a cup of tea?/He really *cares about* you.)。
- [134] **blending into:** blend into . . . は「(人やものが)…(周囲)に溶け込む」(e.g. I managed to *blend into* the crowd.)。
- [135] **addressing a broad array of threats:** address は「(問題などに)取り組む，対処する」。a broad array [əréɪ] of threats は「多種多様な脅威」(cf. a broad range [spectrum] of . . .)。
- [138] **may be compromised:** この場合の compromise は「損なう」「危険にさらす」(e.g. That kind of conduct could seriously *compromise* security.)。
- [145] **females may selectively affiliate:**「選択的に連携する」とは，そうする者もおり，そうしない者もいる，ということ。そうするものは，本人も子孫も生き残っていく確率が高くなるので，それもまた自然選択の一例となる。
- [153] **underlying the tend-and-befriend pattern:** underlie は他動詞で「…の根底にある」(cf. One of the *underlying* assumptions of his theory is that . . .)。tend-and-befriend の内容はすぐ上で説明されているが，-end という脚韻を踏んでいることにも注意。
- [154] **the attachment-caregiving system:** 子どもが母親に「愛着」(attachment) を感じ，母親が子どもの「面倒を見る」(caregiving) という母子関係を支えている生理学的なシステム。脅威に直面したとき，男性(オス)が「闘争か逃走」という行動パターンを示しがちであることの背後には交感神経系の活動が関わっているが，同じ状況で女性(メス)が「(子どもの)世話と(他の女性との)連携」という行動パターンを示しがちであることには，交感神経系の活動とは異なるこのような生理学的システム(以下で「神経内分泌系の諸メカニズム」とも呼ばれる)が働いている。
- [159] **critical:** extremely important.

social, and biological development, but less literature has explored the counterpart maternal mechanism, that is, what evokes tending behavior in the mother. We attempt to redress that balance here. In addition, we suggest that the befriending pattern may have piggy-backed onto the attachment-caregiving system and thus may be at least partially regulated by the same biobehavioral systems that regulate tending. From this analysis, it follows that neuroendocrine mechanisms would have evolved to regulate these responses to stress, much as sympathetic activation is thought to provide the physiological basis for the fight-or-flight response.

Before concluding the paper with a discussion of implications for future research, the authors explain their view of the social and political implications of their study.

The issue arises as to whether sex differences in human behavior would be better understood as differences in social roles rather than as evolved biobehavioral responses. For example, given substantial human behavioral flexibility, one can question whether maternal investment in offspring continues to be higher than that of fathers. In response, we note that current differences between men and women in parental investment do not matter as much as differential parental investment during the period of time that stress responses evolved. An evolutionary biobehavioral argument does not constrain current human behavior but neither is it necessarily challenged by current human behavioral flexibility. We also note that, although human social roles vary substantially across cultures and may, in some cases, prescribe behavioral patterns for women similar to the tend-and-befriend pattern, social roles alone are unlikely to account for it. A social role position neither addresses the cross-species similarities we have identified nor accounts for the underlying biological evidence for our position. Nonetheless, it will be important for future research to detail the parts of our biobehavioral model that are sensitive to environmental input.

An analysis that posits biological bases for gender differences in behavior raises important political concerns as well. Many women feel, with some justification, that such models can be used to justify patterns of discrimination and social oppression. To head off any such effort, we emphatically point out that our analysis makes no prescriptive assumptions about the social roles that women occupy. Our analysis should not be construed to imply that women should be mothers, will be good mothers, or will be better parents than

[164] **redress that balance:** redress the balance は「崩れていたバランスを取り戻す」「不均衡を正す」という意味の決まり文句。

[165] **may have piggybacked onto ... :** piggyback は本来「おんぶ」(e.g. Give me a *piggyback*.) だが, 動詞として用いて piggyback on ... とすると「…に便乗する」といった意味になる。

[170] **much as sympathetic activation ... :** much as ... は「…とほぼ同じように」。「交感神経系の活動が fight-or-flight という反応に生理学的な基盤を提供する」というのは, ストレスに対する反応の男女差が男女の社会的役割の違いに由来するとしても, それが単なる後天的な傾向ではなく, 進化の過程を通じて, 生理学的な基盤をもつ反応になってしまっているということ。

[177] **given substantial human behavioral flexibility:**「人間の行動にはかなりの柔軟性があることを考えると」。substantial「実質的な」は, この場合のように「かなりの」「相当な」という(considerable と同じような)意味になることが多い。

[180] **current differences ... :** current「現在の」と the period of time ...「ストレスに対する反応(の仕方)が進化した期間」との対比に注意。

[184] **but neither is it necessarily challenged by ... :**「かといって, 現在の人間の行動が柔軟性をもっていることが必ずしもそれに対する反論になるわけでもない」。challenge は「(理論や信念に対して)異を唱える」「(理論や信念の)妥当性を疑問視する」(11 章 [72])。it は an evolutionary biobehavioral argument を指す。否定の意味の語が文頭に生じたのに伴って倒置になっていることにも注意。

[186] **human social roles vary substantially across cultures:**「人間の社会的役割は文化によって相当異なる」。

[187] **may, in some cases, prescribe ... :** prescribe は「規定する」。tend-and-befriend のパターンに似た行動パターンを取ることを規範として女性に課しているような社会が存在する可能性があるということ。

[189] **cross-species similarities:**「(文化の違いを超えた)人間という種全体に見られる類似性」。

[192] **detail the parts:** detail は「詳述する」という意味の動詞として用いられている (cf. a *detailed* description of the suspect)。

[194] **An analysis that posits ... :**「行動における性差に生物学的な基盤があるとする分析」。posit は「…が事実であると考える」。

[195] **raises important political concerns:** raise は「(話題や問題を)提起する」「取り上げる」。

[196] **with some justification:**「ある程度は無理もない[もっともな]ことであるが」。話題になっている行為に妥当な理由があることを示すためによく用いられる表現。

[197] **To head off any such effort ... :** head off は「(通例よくない事態の発生を)阻止する」「機先を制して防ぐ」。emphatically は「きっぱりと」「明確に」(cf. Her answer was an *emphatic* "Yes.")。makes no prescriptive assumptions about ...「…について規範的な想定は全く立てない」とは「…について(例えば女性は母親になるべきだといった)特定の規範を前提にはしていない」ということ。

[200] **construed:** construe は「解釈する」「…という意味に取る」。

men by virtue of these mechanisms. Similarly, this analysis should not be construed as evidence that women are naturally more social than men or that they should shoulder disproportionate responsibility for the ties and activities that create and maintain the social fabric.

Other political concerns, however, may be based on false assumptions about what biological underpinnings signify. Biological analyses of human behavior are sometimes misconstrued by social scientists as implying inflexibility or inevitability in human behavior or as reductionist efforts that posit behavioral uniformity. These perceptions constitute unwarranted concerns about biological bases of behavior. Biology is not so much destiny as it is a central tendency, but a central tendency that influences and interacts with social, cultural, cognitive, and emotional factors, resulting in substantial behavioral flexibility. The last few decades of biological research have shown that, just as biology affects behavior, so behavior affects biology, in ways ranging from genetic expression to acute responses to stressful circumstances. Rather than viewing social roles and biology as alternative accounts of human behavior, a more productive theoretical and empirical strategy will be to recognize how biology and social roles are inextricably interwoven to account for the remarkable flexibility of human behavior.

- [204] **shoulder:**「(責任などを)引き受ける[負う]」という意味の動詞。
- [205] **the social fabric:** fabric は本来「布地」「織物」だが，このように比喩的に「(社会などの)基本的な構造，骨組み」といった意味で用いることも多い。
- [208] **biological underpinnings:** underpinnings は「基盤」(この意味では通例複数形)。
- [209] **are sometimes misconstrued:** misconstrue (cf. construe) は「誤って解釈する」「誤解する」。
- [211] **reductionist efforts that posit behavioral uniformity:**「(人間の)行動が均質的であると考える還元主義的な試み」。reductionist「還元主義」とは複雑な対象をより基本的な少数の(ここでは生物学的な)原理等に分解することによって理解・説明しようとする立場。
- [211] **These perceptions ...:** この場合の perception は「捉え方」「見方」(e.g. a *perception* gap「見方の違い」「認識のずれ」)。unwarranted concerns は「いわれ[根拠]のない懸念」(cf. This is certainly another topic that *warrants* attention.)。
- [215] **resulting in substantial behavioral flexibility:** 分詞構文が主節の後に用いられた場合，このように主節の内容の結果や帰結を表すことがある(4章[100]) (e.g. Dozens of flights have been delayed or cancelled due to the hurricane, *leaving* a lot of people stranded at the airport.)。
- [218] **ranging from genetic expression to acute responses ...:**「遺伝子発現から，ストレスの多い状況への急性反応までの」。acute は「急性の」(cf. chronic)。
- [220] **alternative accounts:**(あれかこれかという)「二者択一的な説明」(cf. alternate)。
- [221] **empirical strategy:**「経験主義的な戦略」(cf. empiricism)。直前の theoretical (理論的[な戦略])と対をなす。
- [222] **are inextricably interwoven ...:** 複数のものが分ち難く結びついていることを表す場合によく用いられる表現のひとつ(9章[104]) (cf. be *inextricably* bound up [with ...])。

9

COFFEE

Introduction
Ryuichiro Usui

In Ethiopia, where coffee originated, there is a coffee ritual still performed today in which people bite off the tips of unshelled dried coffee beans, roast them in a deep pan, and then boil them in milk and butter. When the coffee is ready, both the dish and the people taking part in the ritual are blessed, and then a prayer is said while a few drops of coffee are sprinkled on to the ground: "May peace last in this world. May people remain healthy."

The name of this ritual might be translated as "slaughtered coffee." The idea of "slaughtering" coffee may sound barbaric, but this ritual has a deep significance. We have to remember that people cannot live without killing other living things. Human eating and drinking is always based on killing, whether the "killing" is slaughtering a cow, crushing grapes to get juice, or piercing the earth to sow crops like rice and wheat. The Ethiopian slaughter ritual shows an awareness that even coffee must be slaughtered. It also demonstrates the need to express gratitude to the earth.

The practice of brewing and drinking coffee has long been woven into the history of human culture. One interpretation of the Arabic word *kahwa* (coffee) is that it originated in a word that meant "modesty." The practice of drinking coffee originally developed in a religious community that refrained from vanity and unnecessary socializing as well as from meaningless gluttony. The way in which coffee drinking spread so rapidly throughout the Islamic world was related to various global movements. In the sixteenth century, as the revolution in world markets was taking place, Arabian merchants who had traditionally been doing well in trade with the eastern world found that they were facing a grave crisis. But then suddenly, at just the right moment, the new commodity of coffee appeared

- [2] **unshelled dried coffee beans:**「殻を剥いていない乾燥したコーヒー豆」。shell は名詞で「殻」だが，動詞では「殻を剥く」。同様な例は dust（「塵」「塵を取り除く」）(e.g. You should *dust* your desk once in a while.)。
- [5] **a prayer is said:**「お祈りを唱える」と言う時にこのように動詞として say が使えることは覚えておきたい。(「祈る人」ではなく)「お祈り」の意味の prayer は発音が [préər] であることにも注意。
- [6] **May peace last in this world:** May + 主語 + 原型動詞は「…でありますように」と祈る場合に用いられるパターン (e.g. *May all your Christmases be* white.)。
- [9] **barbaric** [bɑːrbǽrɪk]:「野蛮な」(cf. barbarism)。
- [17] **brewing and drinking coffee:** brew は「(熱湯を注いでコーヒー，紅茶などを)入れる」(cf. Let me make you some coffee.)。
- [17] **has long been woven into:** be woven into ...「…に織り込まれている」はこのように比喩的に用いられることも多い (cf. Many philosophers believe that language and thought are inextricably *interwoven*.)。
- [21] **vanity:**「虚栄(心)」。
- [21] **unnecessary socializing:**「不必要なつき合い」(cf. He doesn't spend much time *socializing* with his colleagues.)。
- [22] **gluttony:**「大食い」「暴飲暴食」(cf. He is certainly *a glutton for punishment*.)。
- [27] **a grave crisis:**「深刻な危機」(cf. You don't seem to appreciate the *gravity* of the situation.)。

like a gift bestowed on them by Allah. The great merchants of Cairo immediately saw how they could regain their power by producing and marketing this new product. But first, in order to encourage the widespread consumption of coffee, they needed to raise its social prestige. Their approach was to establish gorgeous "coffee houses" in the most prominent areas of large cities.

Cafés, which originated in this way in the Islamic world, went on to play a large role in modern European nations, which imported the idea of the coffee house as well as the actual coffee beans from the Islamic world. But as coffee became a global product, the relationship between coffee and its origins still honored in the Ethiopian coffee slaughtering ritual became increasingly tenuous. Distributors and consumers living in countries where coffee is consumed today are primarily interested in price and quality. They are oblivious to the fact that the coffee on the table in front of them does not just appear out of nowhere but has actually taken its life from the earth, the people, and the water of other parts of the world.

Ever since its first appearance, coffee has continued to throw light upon the ever-changing relationship between human beings and nature. Today, what might we be asking? How is global warming related to the roasting of coffee? How does the process of cleaning coffee beans contribute to soil and water contamination? What is the relationship between the expansion of coffee fields and the destruction of forests?

Coffee is not simply a drink. Coffee houses are not simply buildings. Coffee and coffee houses are threads that weave together a whole range of academic fields from history to sociology, psychology to human language and performance, medicine to business to environmental studies and the analysis of environmental destruction. If you let your eyes follow the fragrant curling threads of steam that rise up from your next cup of coffee, you will start to see new patterns in the mutually influential forces that shape and frame human society.

[29] **a gift bestowed on them by Allah:**「アラー（神）から授けられた贈り物」。bestow A（物）on B（人）というパターンに注意。

[40] **tenuous:**「（関係やつながりが）弱い，希薄な」。

[42] **oblivious to . . . :**「…を意識していない」（cf. I suppose this is just another fad that will quickly fade into *oblivion*.）。

[44] **appear out of nowhere:**「どこからともなく現れる」という意味の決まった言い方(1章[82])（cf. *appear out of* thin air）。

[50] **contribute to soil and water contamination:** contribute to . . . は後ろに望ましくないことが来て「…の一因となる」という意味でも用いられることに注意。soil and water contamination は「土壌と水の汚染」。

Coffee and Globalization

Ryuichiro Usui

You probably wouldn't think much about it if you came across a café called "Kafka" in Prague, or a tea shop called "Victoria" in London. But given that Hans-Dietrich Genscher was the former foreign minister of the Federal Republic of Germany, you might be surprised to find a "Café Genscher" in Zagreb. Still, it turns out that there are quite a few Genscher cafés in Croatia, and for good reason. When Yugoslavia was embroiled in ethnic conflicts in the 1990s, it was the German Hans-Dietrich Genscher who managed to steer Croatia successfully toward independence in the face of widespread opposition. The cafés are an interesting show of appreciation. When I visited Croatia, I even had coffee in one of them.

I am not a specialist in Croatia. All I really knew about the country ahead of time was that it was the place where neckties were invented, and that it had played against Japan in the 2000 soccer World Cup. Aside from the image I had of a war-scarred nation, this was pretty much all I could have told you about Croatia then. But once I visited Zagreb and Dubrovnik, the old capital along the Dalmatian coast, I realized how inadequate my image of the country

Dubrovnik, 2000

[62] **You probably wouldn't think much about it if . . .**:「…しても特に何とも思わないでしょう」。if 以下のことがあっても何も不思議はない，という意味。it は if 以下を漠然と指している (cf. I'd really appreciate *it if* you could keep me informed.)。

[62] **you came across a café:** come across は「偶然誰かに会う」「何かを見かける，見つける」という意味で非常によく使う表現 (e.g. I *came across* an old friend from high school yesterday.)。

[64] **Hans-Dietrich Genscher:** ハンス-ディートリヒ・ゲンシャー (1927–) はドイツの政治家。1974年，ドイツ連邦共和国(西ドイツ)の外相兼副首相となった。ドイツ連邦共和国は，90 年 10 月，ドイツ民主共和国(東ドイツ)を編入するが，ゲンシャーはその後も 92 年まで外相に留まり，「新東方外交」の推進役となった。

[66] **Zagreb:** ザグレブ。1991 年 6 月にユーゴスラヴィアから独立したクロアチア共和国の首都。

[66] **Still, it turns out that . . .**:「しかし，実際には…」。It turns out that . . . はこのように驚くべき(予想に反する)事実を提示する場合にしばしば用いられる。

[67] **and for good reason:**「それにもっともな理由もあるのです」。「十分な理由(根拠)」という意味の good reason はよくある組み合わせ (e.g. I have *good reason* to believe that she's telling the truth.)。また，for good reason/with (good) reason は，このように，その前に述べられたことについて，「それはもっともである」「無理もない」という意味を付け加えるために使うことが多い表現 (e.g. She was upset by the news, and *with good reason.*)。

[68] **When Yugoslavia was embroiled in ethnic conflicts:**「ユーゴスラヴィアが民族対立に巻き込まれていた時」。be embroiled in . . . は「…(困難な事態)に巻き込まれている」という意味の決まった言い方。

[70] **steer:** 本来「船の舵をとる」だが，(方向を表す表現を伴って)比喩的に「人[もの]を…の方向に導く」という意味でもよく使われる (e.g. She managed to *steer* the new organization in the right direction.)。

[70] **in the face of . . .**:「…(困難な事態，問題など)にもかかわらず」という意味で用いることが多い (e.g. He got himself reelected *in the face of* mounting criticism of his foreign policy.)。

[73] **All I really knew about the country ahead of time was that . . .**:「クロアチアについてあらかじめ (ahead of time) ちゃんと知っていたことは…だけだった」。このように，英語の all を含む表現は日本語の「だけ」「さえ」などの限定を表すことばを含む表現としばしば対応する (e.g. Is that *all* you have to tell me? / *All* you have to do is (to) keep up the good work.)。

[75] **it had played against Japan:**「クロアチアが日本と対戦したことがあった」。play against . . . は「(スポーツの試合などで)…と対戦する」(e.g. Who are you *playing against* in tomorrow's match? / cf. England are[is] *playing* Argentina this evening.)。

[76] **Aside from the image I had of a war-scarred nation:**「戦争の傷跡の残る国というイメージを抱いていたことを別にすれば」。aside from は apart from と同じ意味の表現で，ここでは「…は別にして」「…はさておき」(e.g. *Aside from* the corny ending, it was a pretty good movie. / cf. Joking *aside* . . .)。of a war-scarred nation が the image にかかっていることに注意。

[78] **Dubrovnik:** ドゥブロヴニクは，クロアチア南部の都市。アドリア海に面したダルマツィア海岸沿いに位置し，「アドリア海の真珠」とも呼ばれる古都。旧市街は，その正門であるピレ門 (Pile Gate) をはじめ，数多くの歴史的建造物を誇っており，ユネスコ世界遺産にも登録されている。

had been. True, there were some remnants of war damage still visible. But it all seemed very safe and definitely worth visiting. A coastal fort city, Dubrovnik has stood overlooking the Adriatic Sea since the time of the ancient Greeks. It was a dignified city with an air of serenity and peace. And of course it too had its coffee shops. Right next to the fort's Pile Gate, I found a good one. Not a "Café Genscher" this time, but an internet café.

The internet café in Dubrovnik, like the city as a whole, opens itself generously to the world. Sit down at any of the computers and instantly the Windows system ushers you into the virtual spaces of world information. At the same time, the café's windows open onto the waters of the Adriatic, beyond which lie the eastern Mediterranean and Africa . . . and New York. Yes, it was that day, when the eyes of the world were turned toward New York. In one corner of this internet café filled with Hungarian-made computers, a Dutch-made television was showing images of the World Trade Center in New York City. The world seemed rather small that day, and Croatia just another part of the global communications network. Indeed, its national telephone company seemed likely at that time to be sold to Deutsche Telekom.

This is the age of globalization. It's not that the local no longer matters. Human beings still exist very locally. So perhaps it really is, as people say, not an era of "globalization" but an era of "glocalization," in which the extremes of the global and local are inextricably mixed together, at the same time, everywhere. And, no matter how the global economy is doing, it seems that at the local level the economy is depressed everywhere. Only the multinational corporations continue to go from strength to strength in a gloriously world-ranging manner. In comparison, the nation-state has an essentially local existence. The basis of the nation-state is its citizens and its taxes. But the multinational corporation exists in a different kind of space to the nation-state, freely moving its centers of operation around the globe as it seeks out cheaper labor and lower taxes.

Coffee, a world commodity which ranks number two in world trade after oil, demonstrates quite well what globalization is about. Let's go back to Hans-Dietrich Genscher and take coffee in Germany as an example. Suppose 500 grams of coffee sold at a German supermarket costs four euros. That's about 500 yen. Of the four euros, only about 0.8 (100 yen) goes to the producer of the coffee. In contrast, 1.2 euros (150 yen) will go to the German government. It's strange that the country that produces the coffee gets less than the

[80] **True, there were . . . But . . . :** このように，「確かに…ではある」「…であるのは事実である」という意味で true を副詞的に使っておいて，その後に「しかし (But) …である」として，より重要な内容を提示するのはよくある文章構成法 (3 章 [176], 6 章 [14]) (cf. *It's true that* he is a nice man, *but* is he really cut out for the job?)。

[82] **overlooking the Adriatic Sea:** overlook は「(建物などが)…を見下ろす位置に立っている」(e.g. We had dinner at a restaurant *overlooking* the ocean.)。

[83] **with an air of serenity and peace:** an air of . . . は「…の態度，雰囲気，様子」(e.g. She *has an air of* confidence about her.)。

[89] **the Windows system ushers you into . . . :** usher someone into . . . は「人を…の中へと案内する」(cf. The collapse of the Berlin Wall *ushered in* a new era.)。

[95] **the World Trade Center in New York City :** ニューヨークのシンボル的存在だった世界貿易センターは 2001 年 9 月 11 日の航空機テロによって破壊された。

[96] **The world seemed rather small that day, and Croatia just another part of the global communications network:** Croatia の直後に seemed が省略されている。このように同じ動詞を用いた文が連続する時には二つ目以降の文ではその動詞が省略されることが多い (3 章 [113])。communication は，通信[報道]機関や手段を表す場合は，このように(複合語の一部であっても)複数形になることが多い (cf. a *telecommunications* engineer)。

[99] **Deutsche Telekom:** ドイツテレコムは，ドイツのボンに本社をおく，ヨーロッパ最大規模の情報通信会社。

[100] **It's not that the local no longer matters:**「ローカルなことがもはや重要ではないというわけではない」。It's not that . . . (または Not that . . .)は，このように前言から引き出される可能性のある推論を先手を打って否定するために但し書き的に用いる (e.g. He doesn't seem to like me — *not that* I care.)。

[104] **inextricably mixed together:** inextricably は複数のものが分かちがたく結びついていることを表すのによく用いられる副詞 (8 章 [222]) (e.g. be *inextricably* linked [bound up] with . . .)。

[106] **multinational corporations:**「多国籍企業」(cf. foreign affiliated companies「外資系企業」)。multinational 自体をこの意味の名詞として使うこともある。

[107] **go from strength to strength:**「急速に力をつける」。

[108] **the nation-state:** 日本語では「国民国家」と訳される。絶対主義の時代に成立した主権の概念は，君主主権から国民主権へと転換し，その結果近代国民国家が形成されたといわれる。国民国家の成立には国民的自覚を備えた国民の創出が不可欠とされる。

[110] **a different kind of space to the nation-state:** to the nation-state は different にかかっている。「…と異なる」は different from . . . が最も一般的だが，このように(similar to . . . との類比で) different to . . . となることもある (cf. The movie was quite *different than* I had expected.)。

[114] **Coffee . . . demonstrates quite well:** demonstrate は「実証する」(1 章 [3])だが，このように実証するための証拠自体が主語として表現されることも多い (cf. The incident clearly *illustrates* the vital importance of cross-cultural communication.)。

[115] **what globalization is about:** what . . . is about は「…の本質」「…の本来の目的」「…の存在意義」といった意味で用いられることの多い表現で，about の前に all を入れて意味を強めることもある (e.g. This book gives you some idea of *what* linguistics *is all about*.)。A is about B が「A で大事なのは B だ」とか「A の存在意義は B にある」というような意味を表すこともある (e.g. Leadership *is about* making things happen, not *about* maintaining the status quo.)。

country that consumes it, but that's how the world market works. In 1995, the German government earned the equivalent of 1150 million euros through taxes on coffee. In 2003, the government's budget for assisting developing nations was 3500 million euros. In other words, the German government's income from coffee is equal to about a third of its budget for overseas assistance. One of the reasons Germany gives for assisting developing nations is to "eradicate poverty," and some of the coffee growers in Central and South America are certainly suffering terribly from poverty. But the problem here is that the overseas development assistance does not benefit the coffee growers directly.

During the mid-nineteenth century, Germany put a lot of effort into establishing coffee farms in the highlands of Central America, particularly in Guatemala and Costa Rica. The large plantations established in high altitude areas in those countries dealt a devastating blow to indigenous cultures and languages. Then in the late nineteenth century the highly successful German coffee planters moved on to Mexico. This kind of border crossing is the very first step to globalization. Today, Mexico ranks number four in the world in coffee production, and from the area that includes Guatemala and Mexico came the Nauman Coffee Group, which today controls 10% of the world's coffee trade from its headquarters in . . . Hamburg.

The Nauman Enterprise and the German state form an impressive combination. Globally, Germany is second only to the United States in the amount of coffee imported. And because there is a high tariff imposed on beans roasted on-site at the location of production, the overwhelming majority of Germany's coffee imports are raw beans. The Nauman Group based in Hamburg takes care of the roasting process for these beans once they arrive in Germany. If we go back to our example of the bag of coffee that costs four euros, it turns out that more than half of that figure — 2.2 euros (275 yen) — goes to the traders, transporters and roasters, all of which belong to the Nauman Group. So this is a brilliant collaboration between the nation and the company. Furthermore, and even more paradoxically, Germany — where coffee beans cannot be grown — is, as a result of this process, one of the world's largest exporters of roasted coffee beans. The global market certainly triggers some mysterious geographies.

We started at the "Café Genscher" in Zagreb with a famous German and a cup of coffee. We can conclude in Mexico, with an even more famous German and a prediction. Karl Marx once said that the capital which would conquer the world market with its ad-

- [122] **that's how the world market works:** how . . . works は「…の仕組み」に相当することの多い表現(13 章 [60]) (e.g. This book gives us fascinating insights into *how* the human mind *works*.)。

- [133] **Germany put a lot of effort into . . . :** put A into B は「A (努力，時間など)を B (仕事，勉強など)に費やす，注ぎ込む」という意味で用いられている (e.g. She is *putting* a lot of time and effort *into* improving her command of Japanese./cf. It's amazing how much work she's *put in* as captain of the team.)。

- [136] **dealt a devastating blow to indigenous cultures and languages:**「土着の文化と言語に壊滅的な打撃を与えた」。deal a blow to . . . または deal . . . a blow は「…に打撃を与える」という意味の決まった言い方。indigenous [ɪndídʒənəs] は「その土地に固有の」(10 章 [48]) (e.g. Some species *indigenous to* the island are on the verge of extinction.)。

- [143] **headquarters:** (このように語尾に s を伴って)「本社」という意味の名詞で用いられる(7 章 [10])。後出の [177] be headquartered in . . . は「…に本社がある」という意味。

- [146] **there is a high tariff imposed on . . . :**「…には高い関税が課せられている」。

- [147] **on-site:**「現地で(生産地でそのまま)」。

- [149] **based in Hamburg:**「ハンブルクに本拠がある」(cf. His daughter *is based in* London.「彼の娘はロンドンに駐在している」)(7 章 [9])。

- [158] **triggers some mysterious geographies:**「不可思議な地理的状況を生み出す要因になっている」。trigger は本来「(銃の)引き金」であるが，(日本語でも「…の引き金になる」と言うように)「(事態を)引き起こす」「(事態の)誘因になる」という意味の動詞として使われることも多い(2 章 [49]) (e.g. The police are trying to determine what *triggered* the multiple pile-up.)。

vanced machinery and high technology would also undermine the value of the soil and the dignity of human labor. This prediction seems to have had some truth. For no matter how much the names of German coffee plantations in Mexico like "Germania" and "Schwarzwald" carry with them transplanted images of bountiful nature, these coffee plantations cannot be understood in any way as sites which enable human beings to work in harmony with the soil. What was once done by skilled human hands is now being taken over by increasingly advanced machinery. Local people now only provide the kinds of labor that the machines cannot do. Human beings have become work animals with hands. In 1994, a year before the Asian currency crisis, the peso crisis hit Mexico. Mexican coffee farmers in these plantations mounted a rebellion. The locally dominant multinational businesses, headquartered in Europe and elsewhere and registered in Guatemala, where taxes are low, seem to exist in a postmodern and postindustrial future world, but their Mexican laborers are treated as if they are stuck in a premodern, preindustrial world of brute labor. In this sense, when we look at globalization as it's played out in the production of a cup of coffee, we can see how it's not so much a case of "glocalization" as a "grotesqualization," in which the global and the local are collapsed together in such a way that colonialism and postcolonialism, the premodern and the postmodern, have been blended horribly together.

[164] **undermine:**「価値のあるもの(自信，権威，信頼，地位など)を徐々に損なわせる」という意味でよく用いられる (e.g. Don't let yourself be affected by what he says. He's just trying to *undermine* your confidence in your talent.)。

[168] **bountiful nature:**「豊かな自然」。

[175] **the peso crisis hit Mexico:**「(災害，危機などが)襲う」という場合には，このように hit (または strike) が用いられるのが普通 (e.g. Another typhoon is expected to *hit* the area soon./ The church *was struck by* lightning last night)。「ペソ危機」は，1994年末のメキシコ通貨ペソの暴落をさす。これをきっかけに他の中南米やアジアの新興市場にも通貨危機が波及した。

[176] **mounted a rebellion:**「暴動を起こした」。この場合の mount は「(運動，催しなどを)組織する，始める」(e.g. *mount* an aggressive campaign for reelection)。

[180] **they are stuck in . . . :** be stuck は「(望ましくない状況で)身動きが取れない」「(面倒な問題に)ひっかかっている」状態を表すのによく用いられる表現(4章 [58]，12章 [37]) (e.g. We were *stuck in traffic* for over two hours./I'm *stuck*. I don't think I'll ever be able to figure out this problem.)。

[182] **it's played out:** be played out は「(事態が)展開する」。

[183] **we can see how it's not so much . . . as . . . :** このように日本語の「…であることが(わかる)」などに英語の (see) how . . . などが対応することがよくある。このような場合，how の代わりに that を使ってもほとんど意味は変わらない。not so much A as B は「A と言うよりは B と言った方が適切である」という時の決まった言い方 (e.g. I'm *not so much* angry *as* sad about what's happened.)。

[184] **grotesqualization:** glocalization という造語にさらに grotesque という言葉を加えて造った語。グローバルなものとローカルなものがグロテスクに混在している状況を指す。grotesque [ɡroʊtésk] は「奇怪な」「異様な」。

[184] **the global and the local are collapsed together:**「グローバルなものとローカルなものがひとつにまとめられて」。この場合の collapse は「(椅子，自転車などを)折り畳む」という用法に近い (collapsible は「折り畳みの」)。

[185] **postcolonialism:** post は「〜以降の」という意味。したがって，postcolonial という語は，帝国主義時代の列強の植民地支配のあとに独立した国々の政治的・経済的・文化的状況に関して用いられる。postcolonialism は植民地主義から生じた様々な事象や言説を批判的に捉える考え方であり，植民地化を通して「他者」として位置づけられた人々を主体とする視点を重視する。

10

POETRY

Introduction
Masami Nakao

How many Polynesian countries can you name? Probably, when you think of Polynesia, names like Samoa, Tonga, and Fiji spring to mind. But could you point them out on a world map?

Polynesia is roughly defined as a triangle-shaped area of the Pacific, with the Hawaiian islands at the top and New Zealand and the Easter Islands to the west and the east at the bottom. It is thought to be the most recently inhabited region of the earth. People from Melanesia sailed to the Polynesian islands only about 3,000 to 4,000 years ago. When we think about the fact that they had originally moved from Asia to Melanesia nearly 50,000 years before that, we can see that it took them a very long time to make the next step. The development of marine technology is considered to have been the main factor enabling this second move. When they moved to Melanesia, the surface of the sea was much lower than it is today, so it was not a daring adventure to move from one Melanesian island to another. The Polynesian islands, on the other hand, were too distant to be visible to the naked eye.

It is now agreed among scholars that these voyages among islands were often two-way. Once the mariners found a new island, they shuttled back and forth between it and their home island, using the newly found land as a base. They were people always facing towards the wide ocean, seeing it as their connection to a thousand other islands. As a result, each island in Polynesia has its own culture, but also shares much with other islands.

The world map most familiar to Europeans is centred on longitude zero degrees, running through Greenwich, London, and this means that Oceania, where these islands are located, has to be split apart and positioned at the far left and right of the map. Traditional

- [2] **Polynesia** [pùləníːʒə]: 太平洋の島々のうち，北はハワイ，西はニュージーランド，東はイースター島を結ぶ巨大な三角形に含まれる島々の総称。ポリネシアという言葉は，元来ギリシア語で「多数の島々」を意味する。これに対して，「黒い島々」を意味する Melanesia [mèləníːʒə] は，南太平洋の島々のうち，ほぼ180度の経線以西の島々の総称。さらに，「小さい島々」を意味する Micronesia [màɪkrəníːʒə] は，西太平洋，赤道のほぼ北，南緯3度〜北緯20度，東経130度〜180度の海域に散在する島々の総称（地図参照）。
- [2] **spring to mind:**「すぐに頭に浮かんでくる」（cf. come to mind / flash through one's mind）。
- [7] **the most recently inhabited region of the earth:**「世界でもっとも最近になって人が住むようになった地域」（cf. an uninhabited island「無人島」）。
- [15] **a daring adventure:** この場合の daring は「危険を伴う」「勇気のいる」。
- [17] **visible to the naked** [néɪkɪd] **eye:**「裸眼で見える」と言う場合の決まった表現。
- [19] **mariners:**「船員」「水夫」。ここでは「海の民」というような感じ。
- [25] **longitude zero degrees:** longitude [lúndʒətjùːd] は「経度」（cf. latitude「緯度」）。

European maps showed monsters and gigantic waterfalls in those apparently distant regions, to signify their wildness. Even after it became accepted that the world was a sphere rather than a plane, this area remained the other or 'reverse' side of the earth for Europeans, and this must have been what made it possible to set the international dateline, a geographical necessity invented to 'make the ends meet', in this area.

Europeans first explored this region while searching for sea routes and natural resources, later looking for land to settle or exploit in place of the recently independent United States of America. For European colonisers, Polynesia represented a resource to be utilised, an untrodden paradise to be yearned for, an immoral barbarian habitat — or all of the above. But of one thing they were certain: the arrival of messengers from the civilised world would benefit the people that were waiting for them as well as they themselves.

For the Polynesians, the arrival of people all the way from the 'other' side of the globe was anything but eagerly awaited. And, as the European population in Polynesia increased, society in areas colonised by English-speakers became predominantly white and English-speaking. The indigenous population experienced an unprecedented change in their life-styles, often being forced to assimilate to the culture and the language of the settlers, so that finally

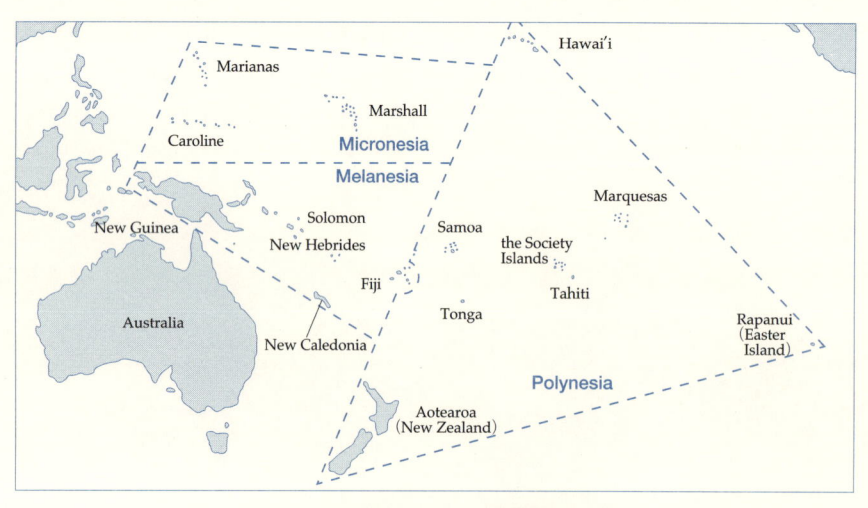

Polynesia, Melanesia, and Micronesia

[33] **the international dateline:**「国際日付変更線」。

[34] **make the ends meet:**「(家計の)帳尻を合わせる」という意味のイディオム make ends meet をもじった表現。

[37] **in place of . . . :**「…の代りに」(6章[70])。

[40] **an untrodden paradise to be yearned for:**「人跡未踏の憧れの楽園」(cf. a *yearning for* a quiet life)。

[45] **anything but eagerly awaited:**「決して待ち望まれてなどいなかった」。anything but . . . は(「…以外の何でも(ありうる)」から)「…では断じてない」という意味でよく用いられる表現。

[48] **The indigenous population . . . :** indigenous [ɪndídʒənəs] は「土着の(外からやって来たのではない)」(9章[136])。unprecedented [ʌnprésədentɪd] は「前例のない」(cf. set a *precedent* for . . .)。assimilate to . . . は「…に同化する」。

there appeared a generation whose first language was English. The self-image of modern Polynesians as a result is very complex, especially when they express it in English.

Polynesian poetry in English is obviously very different from poems expressed in the native languages of the region. Traditional Polynesian literature was handed down orally with no written records. Sometimes it was chanted in rituals; at others, it expressed more intimate emotions; or, it even functioned as a historical record to preserve important knowledge such as tribal myths, histories or genealogies. Some of the poems in English try to incorporate the traditional life-style and culture. Others describe contemporary urban life. Undoubtedly, both are indispensable parts of contemporary Polynesian life.

Robert Sullivan's poem, 'Honda Waka', weaves these two strands together. Sullivan is a young Maori poet and one of the co-editors of the anthology of Polynesian poetry whose introduction is the main text for this session. A waka is a Maori vessel hollowed from one huge Kauri tree and designed to accommodate as many as 50 or more people. It is part of Maori myth that the ancestors of the whole Maori population sailed to New Zealand from their legendary homeland, Hawaiki, in seven wakas. It is also said that any present-day Maori can trace his or her genealogy back to one of them, each of which is named. A waka, therefore, not only relates an individual Maori's origin and family history but also represents the whole of Maori identity as a seafaring people.

The combination of a Japanese car and a waka looks incongruous at first sight. Though Japanese cars are a familiar component of contemporary cityscapes in New Zealand, they have nothing to do with its indigenous culture. And still, the poet calls his second-hand Honda his waka. The dilapidated car saw the poet experience all the important events and engagements of life: his father's death, his son's birth, his career as a librarian, and, more than anything else, the creation of his poetry. The Honda waka is at once within Maori tradition and the poet's own.

It is more than 200 years since Europeans settled in Polynesia, and now it is not easy to untangle the complexly integrated workings of indigenous and imported cultures in the area. Moreover, Polynesians themselves have sometimes utilised the stereotyped images which Europeans have attached to the region. Only by listening to individual voices can we reach in to find some sort of reality behind the facade.

[56] **was handed down orally:** hand down は「(慣習，伝統などを)若い世代に伝える」という意味の表現で，このように受身形で用いることが多い。orally は「口承で」。
[57] **it was chanted:** chant はこの場合「(詩歌などを)詠唱する」。
[60] **genealogies:**「家系」「系譜」「系統」。
[64] **Robert Sullivan's poem, 'Honda Waka':** Robert Sullivan (1967–) は，ニュージーランドのマオリ詩人。オークランド大学図書館司書として勤務しながら，作品を発表している。'Honda Waka' を含む詩集 *Star Waka* は，100篇の詩を100艘のワカ(マオリの手漕ぎ舟)の船団にみたてた詩集。口絵［Poetry］参照。
[65] **Maori:** マオリはニュージーランドの先住民で，ポリネシア系に属する。マイノリティではあるが，政治的経済的文化的政策によって人口は回復傾向にあり，現在，約50万人，総人口の約15%を占める。(マオリ語で Maori とは「人間」を意味)。
[67] **hollowed from . . . :**「…をくりぬいて作った」。
[68] **Kauri tree:**「カウリマツ」。ニュージーランド北島の北部に分布するナンヨウスギ科の常緑の高木。良質の木材になる。
[75] **a seafaring people:**「船乗りの民族」「海洋民族」。
[76] **incongruous** [ɪnkáŋɡruəs]:「釣り合わない」「調和しない」(cf. incongruity)。
[80] **The dilapidated car saw . . . :** dilapidated は「(建物や乗り物が)老朽化した」「ガタガタの」。文全体は感覚動詞 see が目的語と to のない不定詞句 (experience 以下) を取る構文になっているが，主語が見た人ではないところが特殊。see は目的語 (+ to のない不定詞句) の表す出来事の起こった空間や時間を主語にして，その空間や時間でその出来事が起こったという意味を表すことがある (e.g. Tuesday *saw* yet another startling development./The early 1990s *saw* the economic bubble burst.)。
[88] **stereotyped images:**「ステレオタイプ化したイメージ」という意味でよく用いられる組み合わせ。本文 [126] では名詞として用いられている stereotype は「特定のタイプの人やものに関する固定観念」のことで，「不当である」「事実に反する」という意味合いを伴うことが多い。

Honda Waka

Today I surrendered the life
of my Honda City
to a wrecker in Penrose for $30.

I bought it seven years ago for $6000.
It has rust in the lower sills,
rust around the side windows —
on the WOF inspection sheet it says:
'this car has bad and a lot of rust . . . '

That car took me to Uncle Pat's tangi in Bluff.
We stopped and gazed at Moeraki,
the dream sky, on the way.

A friend followed us in it on the way
to National Women's for Temuera's birth
(we were in her huge Citroën).

We went to Otaki, and Wellington,
in the Honda to visit family.

The Honda took me to Library School
perched next to Victoria Uni.

I drove Granddad across the creek in the Honda
at night after the family reunion bash.

Temuera's first car seat was in the Honda.
That Honda has seen a high percentage

of my poetry.
Now I have left it behind.

Robert Sullivan

[94] **Honda City:** ホンダ・シティ。1981〜94 年に本田技研から発売された乗用車のシリーズ。日本車はニュージーランドでは人気があり，中古車も多く輸入されている。

[95] **Penrose:** ニュージーランド，オークランド市南部の，中古車販売業者，自動車解体業者の並ぶ地域。

[99] **WOF:** Warranty of Fitness. ニュージーランドの車検証。

[101] **tangi:** マオリ語で「葬儀」。

[101] **Bluff:** ニュージーランド南島南端の町。

[102] **Moeraki:** ニュージーランド南島中部西側の地名。北島在住の詩人が，Bluff に至る道すがら通過した。

[105] **National Women's:** National Women's Hospital. オークランド市にある，国立産婦人科病院。

[106] **Citroën:** フランス，シトロエン社製の乗用車。

[107] **Otaki:** ニュージーランド北島，ウェリントン市の北にある町。

[110] **Victoria Uni:** ウェリントン市にあるヴィクトリア大学。uni は university の俗称。

[112] **bash:** 「パーティ」「宴会」。

Whetu Moana, Ocean of Stars

Albert Wendt, Reina Whaitiri and Robert Sullivan

Polynesia, the very word is polymorphic. It conjures up multiple images: warm tropical seas, palm fringed lagoons, grass huts, semi-naked dusky maidens, portraits of Captains Cook and Bligh, even Kevin Costner and Elvis Presley. While the area known as Polynesia is indeed incredibly beautiful, it is also home to many thousands of people who have learned over the centuries to survive extraordinary hardships. The romantic ideas and images held by outsiders about the Pacific have plagued our people since first contact; and breaking away from rest-and-recreation stereotypes has been a major issue for Polynesian writers, artists, scholars and politicians ever since.

Polynesia, Melanesia and Micronesia are the cultural regions of the Pacific. The Melanesians and Micronesians settled the Pacific starting about 50,000 years ago. Our Polynesian ancestors settled about 3,000 or 4,000 years ago, and they named the ocean, Te Moana Nui a Kiwa. The names for the three regions and the distinctions between them were established over the last 200 years, mostly by outsiders, sometimes by ourselves. The distinctions are not marked and outsiders may find it difficult to distinguish Tongan from Samoan or Niuean from Maori, for example, but we respect the differences between our cultures and take great pleasure in drawing attention to them.

When Polynesians first came into the region, they couldn't have known much about the Pacific's boundaries; they acquired that knowledge as they explored and settled the islands that stretched across the vast sea. The sky and the sea must have seemed both boundless and eternal to the early Polynesians, for how the people lived and connected with one another was determined by how well they understood and could control these two elements. This immense space of sea and sky was, and continues to be, the known

[117] **polymorphic:** 本来は「多形の」だが，ここでは(すぐ後で述べられるように)この単語が（poly「多くの」と nesia「島」という構成になっていることとも関係して）多様なイメージを喚起することを指している。

[117] **conjures up:** conjure up は「(イメージや考えを)喚起する」。

[119] **semi-naked dusky maidens:**「半裸で肌の浅黒い少女」(cf. dusk「夕暮れ」「たそがれ」)。

[119] **Captains Cook and Bligh:** キャプテン・クックこと，ジェイムズ・クック (James Cook, 1728–79) は既出 (3 章)。Bligh は，ウィリアム・ブライ (William Bligh, 1754–1817)。イギリスの海軍提督。クックの第 2 回航海に参加したのち，バウンティ (Bounty) 号の艦長になり，「バウンティ号の反乱」(1789) と呼ばれる船員たちの反乱に遭遇した。

[120] **Kevin Costner:** アメリカの俳優 (1955–　)。1995 年に彼が主演した映画 *Waterworld* はハワイでロケが行われた。

[120] **Elvis Presley:** 1950 年代から 60 年代にかけて一世を風靡したアメリカの歌手・俳優 (1935–1977)。*Blue Hawaii* (1961) や *Paradise, Hawaiian Style* (1966) などハワイを舞台にした映画に主演。

[121] **it is also home to . . . :** be home to . . . は「…の故郷である」。

[124] **plagued:** plague は「(plague「疫病」のように)長期間苦しませる[悩ませる]」。

[125] **breaking away from . . . :** break away from . . . は「(政治的に)…から分離独立する」(cf. a *breakaway* republic) という意味でよく用いられるが，ここでは「…から脱却する」という感じ。

[131] **Te Moana Nui a Kiwa:** マオリ語で「太平洋」を意味する。ポリネシアは Moutere o Te Moana nui ā Kiwa と言う。Moana は「海」を意味する。本章のもととなっている詩集のタイトル *Whetu* (星) *Moana* は「星の海」という意味になる。

[136] **Niuean:** ニウエ人。彼らが住むニウエ島は，トンガ諸島の東に位置する珊瑚礁の島で，ニュージーランドに属する自治領。

[137] **take great pleasure in . . . :** take pleasure in . . . は「…(すること)に喜びを感じる」「喜んで…する」という意味の決まった言い方 (cf. take pride in . . .)。

world of the Polynesian. Our view of the world is unique, it is as broad and deep as it is high, and unlike those who come from continents or large bodies of land, we see a world with few limits. The people of Polynesia carefully and meticulously recorded their whakapapa, or lineage, thus establishing and strengthening their links with the earth, the sky, the gods and each other. Polynesians also believe that when we die we become the stars that help to guide the living across that huge body of water Te Moana Nui a Kiwa. The people learned how to read and work with their world, they learned about reading the ocean currents, the winds and stars, using that knowledge to sail and navigate their lives by. That is why we have called this anthology *Whetu Moana, Ocean of Stars*, which incorporates the concepts of sea, sky and stars. The title also suggests the variety of poets and poetry in the anthology, and their roots in Te Moana Nui a Kiwa and in their various cultures.

Polynesia extends from Hawai'i (to the north-east) across to Rapanui (Easter Island) and down to Aotearoa/New Zealand in the south-west. Within that triangle are Tonga, Samoa, the Cook Islands, Niue, Tokelau, and the Society Islands. There are also Polynesian enclaves, like Rotuma, within Melanesia. These countries range from high volcanic islands to atolls, from snow-capped peaks to blue lagoons. This anthology is confined to poetry from most of the countries mentioned because they are English-speaking but because of an accident of history, it is forced to exclude work from French-speaking Polynesia.

Over the last 200 years, under the influences of colonialism first from Europe, then America and Asia, our cultures have changed rapidly. Religion, diet, transport, housing, communication, every facet of life has been influenced by the colonial influx. As well, many of our people now include other ancestry, such as European and Asian, in their whakapapa. The peoples of the Pacific have always intermarried with other island groups, including Melanesia and Micronesia.

Since the 1950s decolonisation has taken place, and while most of our nations are again politically independent some, such as Aotearoa, Hawai'i and the Society Islands, remain colonised. Polynesian people within these countries are now minorities striving for their political independence and are intent on saving and developing their cultures. Literature and the arts are part of the decolonisation process and help define new cultures as they emerge from colonial influences as free and independent nations.

Polynesia was written into existence by outsiders and that litera-

[150] **meticulously** [mətíkjələsli]:「細部にまで気を配って」。

[151] **lineage** [líniɪdʒ]:「血統」「系統」。

[157] **using that knowledge to sail and navigate their lives by:**「(海や空を)航行する」という意味の navigate が(広大な海が重要な役割を果たす)彼らの生活様式の特徴を表すのに有効に用いられていることに注意。

[163] **Aotearoa:** アオテアロアは,ニュージーランドのマオリ語名。「白く長い雲のたなびく地」という意味。

[164] **the Cook Islands:** 南太平洋上に位置するニュージーランドの自由連合国。諸島名の由来は言うまでもなく,1770 年代に 3 度来航したキャプテン・クック。

[165] **Tokelau:**「トケラウ諸島」。南太平洋,サモアの北方に位置するニュージーランド領の珊瑚礁島群。

[165] **the Society Islands:**「ソシエテ諸島」(フランス領なので,日本語では「ソシエテ」となる)。中部南太平洋に位置する諸島で,そのなかで最大の島がタヒチ (Tahiti) である。この諸島の名前の由来は,1769 年にタヒチ島を訪れたキャプテン・クックが,航海のスポンサーであるイギリス王立協会 (Royal Society) にちなんで命名したためと言われている。

[166] **enclaves** [énkleɪvz]:「飛び地」。例えば Rotuma は,地理的にはメラネシアの中にあるが,文化的にはポリネシアに属するのでポリネシアの「飛び地」ということになる。

[167] **atolls** [ǽtɔːlz; éɪtɔːlz]:「環状珊瑚島」「環礁」。

[175] **influx:**「流入」「人やものが大量に入り込むこと」(cf. in (a state of) *flux*)。

[180] **decolonisation:**「脱植民地化」とは植民地が宗主国の政治的経済的文化的な支配を脱して独立すること (cf. decentralise, decaffeinate)。

[184] **are intent on saving:** be intent on … ing は「…しようと心に決めている」。

[188] **Polynesia was written into existence:** write … into existence (= bring … into existence by writing about it) は「著作によって生み出す」(cf. *write* a person *out of* one's will「遺言を書き換えて人が遺産を相続できないようにする」)。

ture has created many myths about our region. From about 1950 Polynesians have been writing back, presenting our view of the world and placing our people and places at the centre. All these changes are evident in the poetry we have selected, which reveals an interconnected web of worldviews. There is a commonality in our bubbling polyglot Polynesian diversity, the commonality of the ocean, of a shared vocabulary, of our communal cultures and values, and our colonial experience. These are the forces that draw our poetries together.

There are many western myths surrounding our region, ranging from Mead's fascination with the sexual, to the cardboard, plastic culture of the tourist trade and the myths surrounding Captain Cook. We hope this anthology succeeds in shifting the western gaze from current and historical myths onto the expressive reality of the poets included here.

Being Polynesians who love poetry, we wanted to look at the poetry that has developed in our region over the last two decades, and through that poetry to look at what has happened and is happening to ourselves and our cultures. Poetry is one of our most ancient art forms and is still respected and loved by our peoples. How are those ancient poetic traditions manifested in the new poetry? We wanted to create a collection that makes it possible to examine this.

But why have we focused only on poetry in English? There are over forty indigenous languages plus English, French, Portuguese, Spanish, Japanese and others in Polynesia. It is simply impossible to anthologise all those languages. English is more than 200 years old in our region, and is now one of the major languages of communication. English has become a Pacific language. In fact, it has become many Englishes in Polynesia, with each Polynesian country indigenising it for its own use. So now we have Maori English, Samoan English, Hawaiian English and so forth. Many pidgins have emerged too, such as Hawaiian Creole English. The languages of the colonisers have been, and continue to be, enriched and revitalised with the introduction of Polynesian words and concepts.

The content of this anthology reflects that rich diversity in English and pidgin. Many of our poets are bilingual but have chosen to write mainly in English; others are not fluent in their indigenous languages and so write only in English. We have arranged the poets by alphabetical order of surname in *Whetu Moana* rather than by countries. Our purpose is to juxtapose the poetries of the Pacific to generate views of culture that are both common and strange, to see

[193] **There is a commonality ...:** bubbling は(「泡立つ」から)「活気のある」。polyglot は「いくつもの言語を話す」(「数カ国語に通じた人」という名詞としても用いられる)。communal は community の形容詞形。values は「価値観」という意味ではこのように常に複数形(3 章 [49])。

[196] **draw our poetries together:** draw ... together は「…をひとつにまとめる」。poetry は通例集合不可算名詞(2 章 [19])(e.g. I love *poetry*.)だが,ここでは多種多様であることを強調するために複数形で用いられている。

[199] **Mead:** Margaret Mead (1901–78) はアメリカの文化人類学者。南太平洋のサモアをフィールドにして人間の成長に関する研究を行った *Coming of Age in Samoa* (1928; 邦訳『サモアの思春期』)において,ミードは,性が解放されているがゆえにストレスや葛藤から自由なサモアの思春期についての「神話」をつくりあげた。

[199] **the cardboard, plastic culture of the tourist trade:** cardboard は本来「厚紙,ボール紙(でできた)」だが,ここでは比喩的に「真実性に欠ける」「実質のない」,plastic は「合成された」「にせものの」という意味。

[201] **the western gaze:** 「西洋のまなざし」。「まなざし」「視線」を意味する gaze はポストコロニアル理論のキーワードのひとつ。権力を有する征服者・植民者が,被征服者を自らの視座のもとにおき,都合の良い解釈を付与することを指す際に用いられることが多い。

[214] **It is simply impossible to anthologise:** simply は「全く」といった感じで,発言内容を強調するために用いられている。anthologise は「アンソロジーに入れる」。

[217] **In fact, it has become ...:** many Englishes の内容は with 以下で説明されている。indigenise は「土着化させる」。

[220] **Many pidgins have emerged too ...:** ここでは pidgin [pídʒən] の一種が creole [kríːòʊl] であるかのような書き方になっているが,厳密には,母語を異にする人々が交易などに用いるために発達し,文法や語彙が単純化されていて母語話者のいない混成語が pidgin。pidgin が文法や語彙を精緻化させて母語話者をもつようになったものが creole。

[229] **juxtapose:** 「隣同士に並べる」「並置する」。

Polynesian poetry through a prism creating many coloured bands: age, language, place, polity and gender are some that leap out. We anticipate that the poetry of Polynesia will continue to develop in new unexpected directions twenty years from now, just as our own history has developed. We sincerely hope that this anthology is a true reflection of Polynesian poetry today, that it will serve as a reference point for the future, and will be a useful teaching resource at all educational levels.

Homecoming

He was just a child,
Your eldest,
When he was stolen
By blackbirders
Carried away
To the Great Southern Land.
You cried and cried
Sorry for a parent's scolding,
Even sent someone
In search of him
But where do you start looking
In the big red country?
150 years later he has returned
In the blue-eyed blonde
Who sits on the urūatete
Where you used to sit
Waiting for him to return
The trade winds are
Your welcoming embrace,
The kuriri sing
Your song of turou
As they fly past.

Jean Tekura Mason
Whetu Moana, p. 135.

[232] **polity:**「統治組織の形態」「政治形態」（a specific form of political organisation, a form of government）.

[236] **a reference point:**「参照点」。frame of reference「準拠枠」とも言い,「何かを理解したり評価したりする際に基準となる考え方（の枠組み）や視点」のこと（7 章 [128]）。

[239] **Homecoming:** Jean Tekura Mason（1964– ）はクック諸島出身の女性詩人。母親はクック諸島マオリで, 父親はイギリス生まれ, 後にニュージーランドに帰化した。クック諸島はニュージーランド北東に位置し, 同国と自由連合関係にある国。クック諸島マオリは, ニュージーランド・マオリと親近性はあるが, 独自の民族であり, 独自の言語をもつ。'Homecoming' は, 1854 年に 11 歳でオーストラリアに誘拐されたクック諸島の少年 Taura についての詩。彼は, オーストラリアでカトリック司祭に育てられ, 同地で結婚して多くの子孫を残した。

[243] **blackbirders:** blackbird は, ポリネシアから誘拐されてオーストラリアの農園で働かされた奴隷の俗称。blackbirder はその業者や船。

[245] **the Great Southern Land:** オーストラリアのこと。本文 [251] の the big red country も同じ。

[254] **urūatete:** クック諸島マオリ語で「崖」。

[259] **kuriri:** クック諸島マオリ語で「キアシシギ（シギ科の海鳥）」。

[260] **turou:** クック諸島マオリ語で「歓迎」。

over PONSONBY / over PONSONBY

Last night just before dawn while the cold foraged thru' our backyard, the BLACK STAR hovered above PONSONBY right over our house. Yeah, it was like CLOSE ENCOUNTERS OF THE THIRD KIND + I opened my window to It, Sam sd. Yeah and opened my PORES to ITS converting LIGHT + deep scent of SPACE-travel, oceans without-end, + GOD. But you don't believe in God, I sd NOW I do, he smiled

Albert Wendt
Whetu Moana, p. 252.

Over Ponsonby: Albert Wendt (1939–) は，サモア出身の詩人・小説家で，オークランド大学英文学部教授でもある。'Over Ponsonby' は，*The Book of the Black Star* (2002) 所収。この詩集の中の詩はすべてモノクロームの手描きのペン画のような表現になっている。このように視覚的要素を表現の一部として組み込む詩を視覚詩（visual poetry）と呼ぶが，ポリネシアの英語詩では，しばしばこのジャンルの作品が書かれており，画家と詩人のコラボレーションも活発に行われている。この詩は，詩人自身を思わせる語り手と若い詩人 Sam の対話の体裁をとっている。

thru': through の省略形(口語的)。

the BLACK STAR: 表題と 1 行目の間に小さく記されたサモア語 le fetu uliuli の英語訳。詩集全体をとおして繰り返し現れるこのモチーフは，宇宙の起源や人間の生命，そして詩作にも関わるエネルギーのようなものを表象しているようであるが，その意味は明示されない。

Ponsonby: ニュージーランド，オークランド市中心部の地域。

CLOSE ENCOUNTERS of THE THIRD KIND: スティーヴン・スピルバーグ監督の SF 映画 (1977) のタイトル。邦題は，『未知との遭遇』。宇宙生物との交信と接近遭遇を叙情的に描く。

Sam: この詩集に含まれる他の詩群によれば，Sam はサモア出身の若い詩人で，ウェントの創作講座に出席していたが，21 歳の誕生日(ニュージーランドではこの日が成人になる節目)の前夜，麻薬の過量摂取で死亡したとある。夢の中で Black Star を見たと語っていた。

sd: said の省略形(口語的)。

converting: "to change from one form to another"; (他動詞として) "to persuade someone to change their religious faith or other belief."

11

VIEW

Introduction
Shigeki Noya

What happens if you look at a single object from different angles? Try it out with something commonplace like a coffee mug. Regardless of how you hold it, or how you tilt your head, it still looks like the same coffee mug, doesn't it? It would be quite weird if it looked like a mug from one angle, and an apple or a pencil from another. Your mug looks like a mug no matter how you orient your point of view. Whether you look at it from above, from one side, from a distance, or in close-up, it's still the same mug. Our experience with things like coffee mugs might easily lead us to assume that an object is invariable regardless of the way we view it. But actually, it's not that simple.

Some time ago, there was a fad among young women in Japan for wearing shoes and sandals with platform soles more than 10 centimeters thick. This was certainly rather unstable footwear and no doubt not a few young women stumbled a few times or even fell over. But the women were nonetheless happy to wear these extreme platform shoes. In my opinion, they were not simply looking for a different style but also for a change in the landscape around them — a change that was generated by the experience of wearing such shoes. In the same way, you used to see people squatting down in the middle of the street. Some people still do. Maybe you should try it. The things you see will probably look rather different, a bit changed. If you tilt your body or lie flat on the ground, the landscape and the objects around you will change even more. What has changed? As we learned with the coffee mug just now, the significance of the objects does not seem to vary. People still look like people, mugs like mugs, and trees like trees. But something changes for sure.

[2] **Try it out with something commonplace:** try ... out は「…(方法や装置など)を(うまく機能するかどうか確認するために)試してみる」。commonplace は「ごく普通の」「何の変哲もない」。

[4] **weird** [wíərd]:「奇妙な」「風変わりな」で口語的な用法。

[6] **no matter how you orient your point of view:** no matter + 疑問詞で始まる節は自分でも使えるようにしておきたい重要なパターン (e.g. *No matter what* you say, I'll never change my mind.)。orient (イギリス英語では orientate を使うこともある。cf. 12 章 [173] reorientate) は「ある方向に向ける」。

[8] **in close-up:**「すぐ近くから」という意味の決まった言い方。日本語の「クローズアップ」に相当する英語の close-up の発音が [klóusʌp] であることに注意 (cf. a *close-up* (photo) of her face)。

[10] **invariable** [ɪnvéəriəbl]:「一定不変の」(cf. His answer is *invariably* "Beats me.")。

[12] **a fad:** fad は「一過性の流行」(cf. It's just one of those *fads* that come and go.)。

[13] **platform soles:**「台のような厚い靴底」。こういう靴は「厚底靴」と呼ばれていたが, すぐ後で出てくるように英語で言えば platform shoes。

[20] **see people squatting down:** squat down は「しゃがみ込む」。

Objects change their meanings when our relationships with them change. A coffee mug retains its meaning as long as we understand it to be an object to pour coffee into and to drink coffee from. However, if we turn it upside down — and of course this expression itself shows how our relationship with the mug has been standardized — and dangle a piece of string downwards from the center with a piece of metal attached at one end, and if then we hang it like that under the eaves, and if that becomes the standard way to treat this object — well, then it will come to be regarded as a wind chime. When I sit at a table and look at a coffee mug, it looks as if I can hold it when I reach for it. It is telling me that it is a kind of vessel. Or if I stand in front of a door, the door looks like an object to be opened or shut. We are trained to see the door that way. So if a door is installed crookedly, or if we see a door that looks just like a front entrance but is sitting right in the middle of a road, we cannot help but feel baffled. If we look around us with this kind of awareness, we notice that objects actually limit our views much more than we realize, because they encourage us to relate to them in very particular ways. That is why the act of destabilizing our standard perspective shifts our relationship with the objects around us and this, in turn, shifts the very meaning of the object.

But of course shifting the meaning of an object is not that easy. If we suddenly happen to see some familiar object from a different perspective, we will no doubt feel a sort of unstable curiosity. But as long as this is merely a chance occurrence, our perspective will very quickly stabilize itself and return to normal. That is why simply turning a coffee mug upside down does not really change its meaning as a coffee mug at all. In order to really destabilize its meaning, we have to change the position of the "normal" state or reorient the standard perspective. When what we currently call "upside down" becomes the standard — and when what we used to think was the normal way of putting the mug on the table becomes upside down — then *that* is the moment when the object ceases to be a coffee mug. We have to change not only the way we look at the object but also the very relationship we have with it.

Photographs, in that regard, show the photographer's relationship with the objects. The photographs reproduced for this session are not taken by someone who just happened to fall or someone who is trying to make an artificial composition. They are taken by a person for whom stumbling and falling down is a part of daily life. So the power of these photographs does not simply stem from their performance as images but also from the body that takes them. The

- [33] **has been standardized:** standardize は「標準化する」。turn ... upside down「上下を逆さまにする」と言えるということは…に来るものの上下が決まっている(= 標準化されている)ことを示す。
- [37] **a wind chime:**「風鈴」。
- [39] **vessel:**「容器」(cf. a container, a receptacle)。
- [42] **crookedly** [krúkɪdli]:「(まっすぐでないという意味で)ねじれて」。
- [43] **sitting right in the middle of a road:**「道のど真ん中に置いてある」。このように sit は(人や動物が「座っている」という場合のみならず)「ものがある場所にある」と言う場合にも普通に用いられる (cf. I saw an ambulance *sitting* right outside his house.)。
- [43] **cannot help but feel baffled:**「(わけがわからなくて)戸惑わないではいられない」。cannot help feeling baffled と言ってもよい。
- [53] **a chance occurrence:**「偶然の出来事」(4章[60]) (cf. It can't have happened *by chance*.)。
- [54] **return to normal:**「正常にもどる」「もとどおり普通になる」という意味の決まった言い方 (cf. Things are expected to be *back to normal* soon.)。
- [69] **stem from ... :**「…に由来する」。因果関係を表す時によく用いられる言い方のひとつ。

upside-down photos are accompanied by an overturned body. The perspective of that fallen body challenges the standardized perspective. As long as we see these photographs within the rigid framework of our normative everyday perspective, we cannot fully grasp the new meaning generated within them. Nevertheless, even within those limitations, I believe we will still be able to feel that they contain a power that is destabilizing and transforming *something*.

The Fall Guy

Samantha Ellis

Martin Bruch falls over. A lot. And every time he falls he takes a photograph from the perspective of his landing. So far he's got 366, a chronicle-in-pictures of the multiple sclerosis that makes him fall. His skewed shots have been shown in Austria and at the Venice Biennale, and next week they come to London.

Bruch is an obsessive man. He photographs everyone he meets, while in his day job as a sound archivist he is busy collating door noises. "Every door you can imagine, opening and closing. There's a door in a hallway, a wood door, a metal door . . . " He's also got a photographic project on the go at work, photographing everyone who sits on a certain red sofa. Another series is called Trunks. "When I go on the street I photograph open car boots. It's a never-ending story because there are millions of cars."

Born in Hall, Tirol, in 1961, the son of an abstract artist, Bruch cites his favourite artists as snowball-melter Andy Goldsworthy, cathedral-wrapping duo Christo and Jeanne-Claude and fat-and-felt merchant Joseph Beuys. His first camera was a gift — a Lomo, one of the clunky cameras, made in Russia's Leningrad Optical Mechanical Organisation factory, which sparked an art craze in the 1990s. The Soviet-era cameras are absurdly low-tech, but devotees learn to love the blur. Bruch loved his Lomo, but became disenchanted after taking 1,250 pictures and finding only 50 salvageable.

Then his balance started failing, as a result of his multiple sclero-

[72] **challenges the standardized perspective:** challenge ... は「…に異を唱える」「…を疑問視する」(8 章 [184])。

[74] **our normative everyday perspective:**「われわれが規範として常日頃用いている視点」。

The Fall Guy: 文字どおりの意味(転ぶ男)に加えて,「貧乏くじを引かされる人」の意味もある。

[81] **a chronicle-in-pictures of the multiple sclerosis:** chronicle は「出来事を起こった順番に記録した文書」だが,この場合には文書ではなく写真で構成されているので chronicle-in-pictures。multiple sclerosis [skləróʊsɪs] は「多発性硬化症」。

[82] **His skewed shots:** skewed は「ゆがんだ」「ねじれた」。

[83] **Venice Biennale:** biennale は「隔年行事」を意味するイタリア語(英語の biennial に対応)。Venice Biennale (ベネチア・ビエンナーレ) は,偶数年にベネチアで開催される現代絵画・彫刻の国際展覧会。1895 年創設。1 年おきに開催される現代美術展としてのビエンナーレとしては,ほかにサン・パウロ・ビエンナーレ,パリ青年ビエンナーレなどがある。

[85] **an obsessive man:** obsessive は「執着心のある」「こだわりのある」(cf. He's *obsessed by* [*with*] fitness.)。

[86] **a sound archivist:** archivist [á:kɪvɪst] < archives [á:kaɪvz]: 本来「歴史的文書や記録の保管所」「そこに保管された書類」。

[88] **He's also got ... on the go:** have (got) ... on the go は「…(プロジェクトなどを)抱えている」。

[91] **open car boots:**「車の開いたトランク」。boot はトランク (trunk) のイギリス英語。

[93] **Tirol:** チロルは,アルプス山脈の東部に位置し,標高 3,000 m 前後の山々からなる山岳地帯。地理的には北,東,南の 3 つに分かれ,北部と東部はオーストリアのチロル州を構成し,南部は第一次大戦の結果イタリア領となっている。

[94] **snowball-melter Andy Goldsworthy:** イギリスの「環境芸術家」(environmental artist)。1956 年生まれ。自然環境に存在する素材を使った芸術で知られる。snowball-melter は彼が大きな雪玉を真夏のロンドンの道に持ち込んだことに由来する。

[95] **cathedral-wrapping duo Christo and Jeanne-Claude:** Christo Vladimirov Javacheff (1935–) と Jeanne-Claude Denat de Guillebon (1935–)。アメリカを拠点に活動する芸術家夫婦。1960 年代から共作している彼らは,とくに物を「包む」(wrap) アートで知られている。包む対象は小さいものばかりでなく,ここで述べられているように建造物や海岸にまでいたる。

[95] **fat-and-felt merchant Joseph Beuys:** ドイツの前衛芸術家 (1921–86)。フェルトや動物の脂肪を用いた彫刻で知られる。

[96] **a Lomo, one of the clunky cameras:** clunky は「重くて不細工な」。Lomo という名称は「レニングラード光学器械」というロシアのカメラ会社の名前の略。そしてロモといえば,同社の代表的製品であるコンパクト・カメラ,LomoLC-A のこと。

[98] **sparked an art craze:** spark は「突然生じさせる」。an art craze は「熱狂的な芸術ブーム」(cf. be crazy about art)。

[99] **devotees learn to love the blur:** devotees [dèvətí:z] は「熱狂的なファン」。blur は(カメラがローテクなために)「(写真が)不鮮明なこと」。

[100] **disenchanted:**「幻滅した」。

[101] **salvageable:**「何とか使い物になる」(< salvage「沈没船を引き揚げる」)。

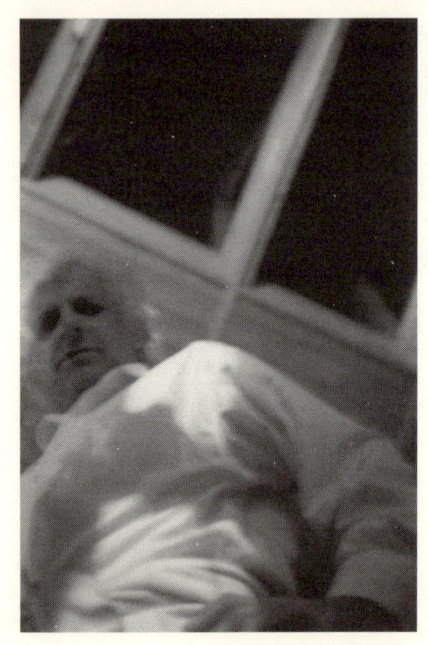

"Hall in Tirol," 1999, by Martin Bruch

sis, and he started to fall. "One day I fell down and saw that this was a perspective that no one had photographed before. I loved it and I knew that I had to photograph it. Most photographers don't lie on the floor and take photographs." So in May 1996, he started photographing his falls, or, strictly speaking, his landings. His surname means "break" or "crash," hence the name *Bruchlandungen* ("crashlandings").

Technical prowess doesn't interest him. "I always use a Kodak FunFlash. It's a very simple camera, it's 99.9% recyclable, and if I fall on it, it won't break." He has other rules: he always uses a flash, he takes landscape shots ("because we see horizontally, we wear our glasses horizontally") and he exhibits them small. "People always say 'slow up, blow up,' but I think all you need to do is get closer to the photograph and then you have it blown up."

They are almost snapshots in their lack of guile, and his photographs offer a glimpse into a topsy-turvy world of woozy landscapes. Stairs loom up, buildings veer away, roads flip up vertically. Sometimes a capsized chair indicates how he must have fallen. His scooter gleams in the corner of some photographs; later images are dominated by his wheelchair's shiny spokes. "The photographs are a chronology of my disease getting worse," he says. Not all sufferers of MS fall this often, but then many don't take the risks he does. "It's wild. It's risky. Other people sit in a wheelchair and get pushed."

[109] **crashlandings:** crash landing は「緊急事態のために機体の破損を覚悟の上で不時着すること」。

[110] **Technical prowess:** prowess [práʊəs] は「優れた腕前」。

[115] **slow up, blow up:** slow up は「ゆっくりやる」。blow up は「(写真を)引き伸ばす」(= enlarge)。

[117] **in their lack of guile** [gaɪl]:「狡猾さ (guile) のない点で」。ここでは「計算されていない」という感じ。

[118] **a topsy-turvy world of woozy landscapes:** topsy-turvy は「逆さまの」(cf. upside-down)。woozy は「クラクラする」。

[119] **Stairs loom up ... :** stairs は「階段」全体をさす場合には常に複数形 (cf. staircase)。loom up は「(大きくてぼんやりと見えるものが)突然立ちふさがる」。veer away は「向きを変えて遠ざかる」。flip up vertically は「跳ね上がる」(cf. I had a bit too much to drink last night and while I was walking home the road jumped up and hit me.)。

[120] **His scooter gleams:** gleam は「ほのかに輝く」。

[123] **Not all sufferers of MS ... :** MS は multiple sclerosis [81] の略。but then は(直前で述べられたことに対して)それは確かにそうであるが,一方でこういうこともあると言いたい場合に用いられる導入表現。

The people in the images are amused, bewildered, shocked. In one image, pensioner twins in green velvet look as quizzical as the queens in Alice's Wonderland. If people rush to help, or if a fall is too devastating for him to whip out his camera, he makes a black photograph recording the place, date and time of the fall. One black photograph records a fall backwards down an escalator. "At least I know I am six escalator steps long," he says.

He photographs car boots because "it's an intimate zone in a public space," and there's nothing more wrenchingly intimate than falling over in public. It's not just the exposure, it's the way strangers feel like they know you. By recording people's reactions, he turns the tables and makes them the subject of his observation.

For his next project, *Handbike Movie*, he attaches a camera to his head and speeds along the open road, cars zooming past, filming the traffic from his three-wheeler wheelchair. But he's not sure about the noise. He turns it up so loud I can barely hear him shouting over the sturm und drang of Vienna's Ringstrasse. "This is what I wanted to convey," he yells. "The noise. And there's a sense of silence in the noise, don't you think?" An irate driver sounds his horn. "That was not because of me," says Bruch. So far he's filmed in Paris and Vienna. Next stop, London. "I'm addicted." He's also still making crashlanding photographs.

Other photographers have played with the idea that, unlike the paintbrush, the camera is almost part of the body, an extra eye. Susan Sontag wrote: "A photograph is not only an image, an interpretation of the real; it is also a trace, something directly stencilled off the real, like a footprint or a death mask." In Bruch's work, the pictures are almost like X-rays in their capacity to record the sensation of falling, and the downward spiral of a disease. *Bruchlandungen* is as much a record of his astonishing positivity as of his struggle with MS. The photographs serve another function too: "You can't be frightened to make a photograph," he says. "There's not time to wallow when you've got to point and shoot." For him the photographs are not bad memories but a testament to survival. "I have had 366 falls with photographs," he says. "A lot more without. But I am alive."

[126] **In one image . . . :** pensioner twins は「双子の年金生活者」。in green velvet は「緑のビロードの服を着た」(cf. men *in black*)。quizzical は「不思議そうな顔をした」。

[128] **Alice's Wonderland:** Lewis Carroll (1832–98) の *Alice's Adventures in Wonderland* への言及。

[129] **whip out his camera:**「カメラをさっと取り出す」(cf. *whip up* a snack)。

[133] **an intimate zone in a public space:** この場合の intimate は「個人的な」という public と対立する意味で用いられている。

[134] **there's nothing more wrenchingly intimate than . . . :** wrenchingly < wrench「ひどく辛い思いをさせる」(e.g. a *wrenching* experience)。ここでは「人前で転ぶことほど，個人的・私的なことはない」という感じ。

[135] **It's not just the exposure:** exposure「人目にさらされること」とは，ここでは転んだところを他人に見られてしまうこと。

[136] **he turns the tables:**「形勢[立場]を逆転させる」(cf. *The tables are turned.*)。

[141] **I can barely hear him shouting over . . . :** over . . . は「…よりも大きな声で」という感じ (e.g. I couldn't hear what he was saying *over* the cacophony of a roomful of people.)。the sturm und drang はドイツ語で文字通りには「嵐と衝動」の意味だが，ここではひっきりなしに行き交う車の騒音を指している。また，Sturm und Drang は，1760 年代終りから 80 年代半ばにかけてのドイツの文学運動を指し，その場合は「疾風怒濤」と訳されるのが普通。この時代の劇作家クリンガー (Klinger) の同名の劇に由来する。Ringstrasse は 19 世紀後半に建設されたウィーン旧市街を囲む幅 57m の環状道路。

[144] **An irate driver sounds his horn:** irate [aɪréɪt] は「ひどく怒った」。sound his horn は「クラクションを鳴らす」(cf. honk his horn)。

[146] **I'm addicted:** cf. Bruch is an obsessive man.

[150] **Susan Sontag:** アメリカの批評家（1933–2004）。*Against Interpretation*（『反解釈』）(1966) 以後，*On Photography*（『写真論』）(1977)，*Illness as Metaphor*（『隠喩としての病』）(1978) などの評論によって，芸術と思想の諸分野にわたって前衛的な批評活動を展開した。

[151] **something directly stencilled off the real:** stencil は同形の名詞「ステンシル（刷り込み型）」から派生した動詞で普通は「ステンシルで刷り出す」という意味だが，ここでは全体で「本物から直接写し取った」という感じ。

[153] **X-rays:**「レントゲン写真」(cf. take an *X-ray* (photograph) of . . . /have one's chest *X-rayed*)。

[154] **the downward spiral of a disease:**「病気がどんどん悪化すること」。spiral [spáɪərəl]「らせん（形）」はこのように「(通例望ましくない事態の)加速度的な進行」という意味で比喩的に用いられることも多い (cf. Land prices are *spiralling* out of control.)。upward や downward との結びつきも一般的。

[155] **positivity:**「積極性」「前向きな考え方」(cf. a *positive* attitude)。

[156] **The photographs serve another function:** serve a function「機能を果たす」はよくある組み合わせ (cf. *serve* a useful purpose)。

[158] **wallow:**「（自己憐憫などの感情に）浸る」(cf. *wallow in* despair)。

[159] **a testament to survival:**「生きている証」。a testament to . . . で「…の証」(cf. a remarkable *testimony to* her resourcefulness)。

12

SPACE

Introduction
Sheila Hones

In her book *For Space*, Doreen Massey argues that the ways in which we imagine and understand space are intimately connected to our views of the world, our attitudes towards other people, and our politics. Of course it's difficult to think creatively about something that seems as obvious and normal as 'space'. Most of the time we are just living in space, taking it for granted, assuming we know what it is. Even so, we do need to stop and think about it, Massey says, because the ways in which we understand and produce space are crucial to the ways in which we live in the world and experience our own lives in relation to other lives and other histories.

So, how do we live in space? Do we live *inside* it, like tiny goldfish in a huge cosmic fishtank? Do we move *through* it, like dolphins weaving their way through water? Or do we live *on* it? Perhaps the most familiar version of global space is the map projection that divides the world into neatly separated oceans and nations. Are we just living on top of that kind of space, like ants walking around on the surface of a really, really big jigsaw puzzle?

Of course we can imagine space as a really big jigsaw puzzle or a really, really big fishtank, and we often do — because those ways of imagining space are ways of organising it, making it comprehensible, and even controlling it. But as Massey tells us, these are just ways of imagining space; they don't define it. We organise space in order to deal with it, to feel in control. But giving up control and accepting complexity isn't necessarily such a bad thing. Rethinking what we mean by something as basic as 'space' can be scary; but it can also be liberating and productive.

Massey wants us to think about space as a sphere of interrelations, possibilities, and mutual recognitions. "What space gives us",

[5] **Most of the time . . . :** most of the time は「普段は」「大抵の場合」。usually と同じような意味。take for granted と assume はいずれも「当然であると考える」「前提とする」。

[9] **are crucial to . . . :** be crucial to . . . は「…にとって決定的に重要な」(cf. be of *crucial* [*critical*] importance)。

[12] **a huge cosmic fishtank:**「巨大な宇宙という水槽」。cosmic < cosmos [kάzməs]:「(the cosmos という形で)宇宙」。

[12] **like dolphins weaving their way through water:** weave one's way through . . . は「(障害物を避けるために)向きを変え続けながら…を通って進む」。[移動の手段・様態を表す動詞 + one's way + 移動の経路を表す前置詞句・副詞句]は非常に一般的な表現のパターン (e.g. Bill *danced* [*laughed*] *his way into* the office. / I saw her *pushing* [*elbowing*] *her way through* the crowd. / He managed to *talk his way across* the border.)。いずれも [make one's way + 移動の経路を表す前置詞句・副詞句](努力や苦労しながら進む)に基づく表現(動詞は「道の作り方」を表している)。

[15] **neatly separated:**「きれいに分かれた」で，neatly divided とともによくある組み合わせ (cf. a *neat* classification)。

[20] **ways of organising it:** organise は「組織化[整理]する」(cf. It's time we started to *get organised* if we are to finish our project in time.)。

she says, "is simultaneous heterogeneity". Taking up this idea, we could imagine space as a totality of all the things and stories and creatures and relationships that are happening at the same time but in different dimensions and locations.

For Space

Doreen Massey

In this first passage from For Space *Doreen Massey writes about the very common experience of 'going home'. Massey opens her reflections on 'going home' with an important point about how easy it is to define 'now' as well as 'here' by reference to our own present moments. Other people, living in other places, can easily seem to have got stuck, somehow, in the past.*

'The West,' in its voyages and in its anthropology, and in its current imaginings of the geography of globalisation, has so often imagined itself going out and finding, not contemporary stories, but the past. We do this in our daily lives, too. I am a northerner who presently lives 'down south' and I have often thought about this in the context of 'going home.' When the train passes Cloud Hill beyond Congleton we're nearly there. I put away my books, the hills get higher, the people get smaller, and I know that when I get off the train I will meet again the constant cheery back-chat which is south Lancashire. I'm 'home,' and I love it, and part of what I love is my richer set of connections here, precisely its familiarity.

And what is wrong with that? This kind of longing, for instance of the migrant, for a 'home' they used to know? Perhaps the point is that when nostalgia articulates space and time in such a way that it robs others of their histories (their stories), then we need to rework nostalgia. My point is that the imagination of going home so frequently means going 'back' in both space and time. Back to the old familiar things, to the way things used to be.

One moment haunts me in this regard. My sister and I had gone 'back home' and were sitting with our parents in the front room having tea. The treat on such occasions was the chocolate cake. It

[29] **simultaneous heterogeneity:**「同時的な異種混在性」。この直前の Massey wants us to think about space as a sphere of interrelations, possibilities, and mutual recognitions を Massey 自身の言葉を使って言い換えるとこうなる。heterogeneity [hètərədʒəníːəti]/heterogeneous [hètərədʒíːniəs] は homogeneity [hùmədʒəníːəti]/homogeneous [hùmədʒíːniəs] の反意語。

[37] **have got stuck, somehow, in the past:** get stuck in ... は「…（望ましくない状況など）にずっと留まることになる」「…の中で身動きがとれなくなる」（4 章 [58], 9 章 [180]）（e.g. Looks like we're *stuck in* traffic.)。

[40] **current imaginings of the geography of globalisation:** current way of understanding globalisation as a spatial process.

[43] **who presently lives 'down south':** presently はこの場合は「今」「現在」（now, currently）を意味するが，「間もなく」の意味で用いられることもあるので注意が必要。down south が引用符に入っているのは著者を含む北部出身者が南部をこう呼ぶことがあることを示すため（cf. down under [（ヨーロッパから見て）地球の正反対（真裏）の土地（the antipodes）；オーストラリア，ニュージーランド]）。

[45] **Congleton:** イングランド北西部に位置する Cheshire 州の町。

[47] **the constant cheery back-chat:**「絶え間ない軽口の応酬」。

[48] **Lancashire:** イングランド北西部の州。Cheshire 州の北に位置する。列車は北にむかっていたのである。

[52] **nostalgia articulates space and time in such a way that ... :**「ノスタルジアによって空間と時間が…というように組織化されてしまう」。articulate [ɑːrtíkjəlèːt] は「はっきり発音する」「明晰に表現する」という意味で用いられるのが普通 (14 章 [64]) だが，ここでは「分節する」という前出の organise と同じような意味。rework nostalgia は「ノスタルジアに手を加える」。

[54] **My point is ... :** so frequently は（going home にではなく）means にかかっていることに注意。

[57] **One moment haunts me:** この場合の haunt は「（主語で表されるものや出来事が目的語で表される人に）どうしても忘れられない」(cf. a *haunting* experience)。

[59] **It was a speciality:** speciality（アメリカ英語では通例 specialty）はこの場合「特定の場所の特産品」(cf. My *speciality* is cognitive psychology.)。

was a speciality: heavy and with some kind of mixture of butter, syrup and cocoa powder in the middle. I loved it. On this occasion though, Mum went out to the kitchen and came back holding a chocolate cake that was altogether different. All light-textured and fluffy, and a paler brown. Not the good old stodgy sweetness that we loved so well. She was so pleased; a new recipe she'd found. But with one voice my sister and I sent up a wail of complaint — 'Oh *Mum* . . . but we like the *old* chocolate cake.'

I've often re-lived and regretted that moment, though I think she understood. For me, without thinking then of its implications, part of the point of going home was to do things as we'd always done them. Going home, in the way I was carrying it at that moment, did not mean joining up with ongoing lives. Certainly it was time travel as well as space travel, but I lived it in that moment as a journey to the past. But places change; they go on without you. Mother invents new recipes. A nostalgia which denies that, is certainly in need of reworking.

For the truth is that you can never simply 'go back,' to home or to anywhere else. When you get 'there' the place will have moved on just as you yourself will have changed. And this of course is the point. For to open up 'space' to this kind of imagination means thinking time and space as mutually imbricated and thinking both of them as the product of interrelations. You can't go back in space-time. To think that you can is to deprive others of their ongoing independent stories. It may be 'going back home,' or imagining regions and countries as backward, as needing to catch up, or just taking that holiday in some 'unspoilt, timeless' spot. The point is the same. You can't go back. You can't hold places still. What you *can* do is meet up with others, catch up with where another's history has got to 'now,' but where that 'now' (more rigorously, that 'here and now') is itself constituted by nothing more than — precisely — that meeting-up (again).

This idea of space and time as interconnected and as the product of interrelations has obvious implications not just for people 'going home' but also for people who explore and 'discover' (or 'are explored and discovered'). Elsewhere, Massey applies the same range of ideas to the history of the place called both Tenochtitlán and Mexico City. She opens her discussion with a description of how the Aztec inhabitants of Tenochtitlán, living then at the centre of a powerful Aztec empire led by Moctezuma, anticipated the arrival of the European explorers led by Hernán Cortés:

- [62] **a chocolate cake that was altogether different:**「全然違うチョコレートケーキ」。altogether different は「全く異なる」と言う場合によく用いられる組み合わせ（cf. completely [totally/entirely] different）。
- [63] **All light-textured and fluffy:** light-textured は「軽い感触の」。fluffy は「ふわふわした」。
- [64] **Not the good old stodgy sweetness:** good old は「（よい意味で）昔ながらの」「なつかしい」（e.g. *good old* days）。stodgy は「こってりした」「胃にもたれる」で，すぐ前の light-textured and fluffy の反対。
- [66] **with one voice:**「声をそろえて」「異口同音に」。
- [66] **sent up a wail of complaint:**「不満の嘆き声をあげた」。
- [69] **implications:**「含意」だが，このように「発言，行動などがもつ意味合い」「言動などが与える影響」という意味で用いることが多い(6 章 [57])（e.g. The outcome of the upcoming general election will *have* profound *implications for* the future of this country.）。
- [71] **in the way I was carrying it:** in the way I was doing it. この場合の it は going home.
- [72] **joining up with . . . :**「（行動をともにするために）…と会う，集まる，合流する」。
- [80] **open up 'space' to this kind of imagination:**「『空間』をこのような想像力に対して開放する」とは，「『空間』を（従来の考え方にとらわれずに）このようなものとして想像し直してみる」ということ。
- [81] **thinking time and space as mutually imbricated:** imbricated は「瓦状に重なった」。全体で「時間と空間が（独立に存在しているわけではなく）連動していると考えること」。すぐ後の space-time はその考え方を反映した表現。
- [85] **catch up:** ここでは catch up with the rest of the world という感じ。
- [86] **some 'unspoilt, timeless' spot:** unspoilt は「昔のままの姿が損なわれていない」「昔と同じ」，timeless は「時の流れに影響されない」。両者ともに前出の good old と同じような意味を表す。
- [87] **You can't hold places still:**「場所を変わらぬままにしておくことなどできない」（cf. We stood *still*, watching the plane go out of sight.）。hold の基本的な意味のひとつは，このように「ある状態のまま保持する」（e.g. *Hold* the elevator, will you? / cf. *Hold* the onions.「タマネギは抜いてください」［食堂などで注文する時に］）。
- [88] **meet up with others:** meet up with . . . はすぐ上の joining up with . . . と同じ意味。
- [89] **that 'now' (more rigorously, that 'here and now') is . . . :**「『現在』（より厳密に言えば「ここと現在」）自体が，まさに出会いそのものによって（再び）構成されているのだ」。here and now は日本語の「今ここ」に相当する決まった組み合わせだが，語順が異なることに注意。meeting-up は同時的異種混交の出会いという感じ。
- [96] **Tenochtitlán:** アステカ王国の首都テノチティトラン。14 世紀半ばにテスココ湖上の島に建設され，スペイン人によって征服される 1521 年まで栄えた。その後，湖は縮小し，現在のメキシコ市の中心部がその位置にあたる。
- [98] **Moctezuma . . . Hernán Cortés:** エルナン・コルテス（1485?–1547）は，スペインの軍人，コンキスタドール（後出 [142] 参照）。1511 年にキューバ島征服に参加した後，18 年にメキシコ遠征隊の隊長に任じられ，約 600 人の部下を率いてアステカ王国の首都テノチティトランに進軍し，王モクテズマ（Moctezuma）を幽閉。21 年に首都を陥落させ，アステカ王国を滅亡させた。

Tenochtitlán — Aztec depiction (The Bodleian Library)

The armies were approaching the city from the quarter named the reed or crocodile — the direction in which the sun rises. Much was known about them already. Tales had come back from outlying provinces. Tax gatherers from the city, collecting tribute from conquered territories, had met up with them. Envoys had been despatched to engage in talks, to find out more. And now neighbouring groups, chafing against their long subordination to the Aztec city, had thrown in their lot with the strange invaders. Yet in spite of these prior contacts, the constant flow of messages, rumours, interpretations reaching the city, the approaching army was still a mystery. And they were arriving from the geographical direction which, in these time-spaces, was held to be that of authority.

It was also the Year One Reed, a year of both historical and cosmological significance: a particular point in the cycle of years. Over past cycles the city had been mightily successful. It was now the biggest city in the world. Its empire stretched, through conquest and continual violent subordination, to the ocean in two directions.

Thus far the Aztecs had conquered all before them. But these

- [100] **the quarter named the reed or crocodile:** アステカの暦日名は，葦，ワニ，家，ウサギなど20の名前から成っており，なかには方位も表すものもあった。
- [101] **the direction in which the sun rises:**「…の方向に，方向へ」と言う場合の direction と結びつく前置詞が in であることに注意 (cf. *in* all directions / Everybody knows the sun rises *in* the east.)。
- [102] **outlying provinces:**「(首都から)遠く離れた(領土内の)地域」(cf. Some *low-lying* areas have been submerged by flood water.)。
- [103] **collecting tribute from conquered territories:** この場合の tribute は「貢ぎ物」。
- [104] **Envoys had been despatched . . . :** envoy [énvɔɪ] は「(外交)使節」。despatch (dispatch とも綴る)は「(特別な任務のために)派遣する」。engage in talks は「会談[協議]を行う」。「(正式な)会談」という意味の talks は常にこのように複数形 (e.g. the next round of arms *talks*)。
- [105] **And now neighbouring groups . . . :** chafe against . . . は「…に苛立つ」(cf. These new shoes are *chafing* my feet.)。throw in one's lot with . . . は「…と運命をともにする」という意味の決まった言い方(この場合の lot は「運命」)。
- [108] **rumours, interpretations reaching the city . . . :** rumours, interpretations の間に and が省略されていると考えるとわかりやすい。
- [112] **the Year One Reed:**「一の葦の年」。アステカの暦では，「一の葦の年」は不規則な間隔で巡ってくる不吉な年とされ，西暦で言えば1363年，1467年，1519年がそれにあたっていた。少し後に，the Year of Our Lord 1519 (「西暦1519年」)という表現が出てくるが，これは，アステカにとって運命的な年だったのである。

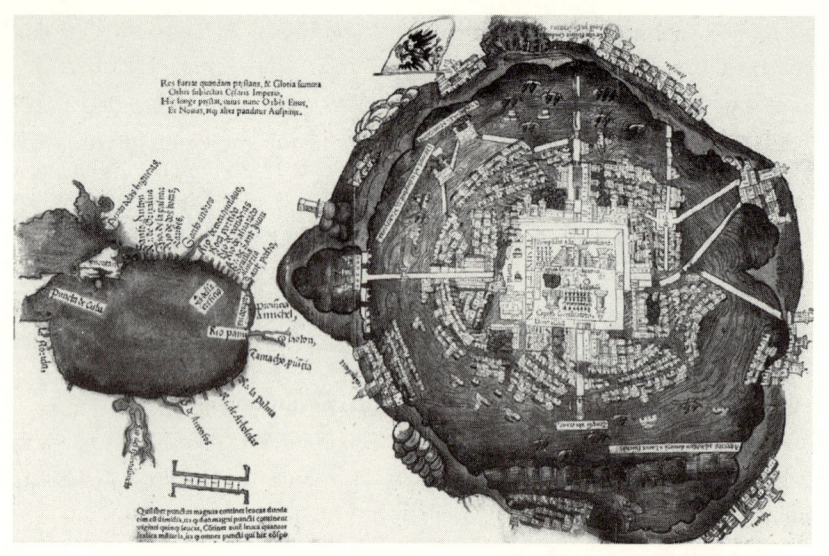

Tenochtitlán — Spanish depiction (The Newberry Library)

armies approaching now are ominous. Empires do not last for ever. Only recently Azcapotzalco, on the edge of the lake, had been brought down after a brief blaze of glory. And Tula, seat of the revered Toltecs, now lies deserted, as do the ruins of Teotihuacan. All these are reminders of previous splendours, and of their fragility. And now these strange invaders are coming from the direction of acatl; and it is the Year One Reed.

Such things are important. Coincidences of events form the structures of time-space.

Then, Massey turns to think about the explorers and how they experienced the encounter with an unfamiliar time-space:

The men in the approaching army could hardly believe their eyes when they first looked down upon the city. They had heard that it was splendid but this was five times the size of Madrid, in the changing Europe which they had left behind just a few years ago. It was now the Year of Our Lord 1519. This small army, with Hernán Cortés at its head and its few horses and its armour, had sailed from what their leaders had decided to call Cuba at the beginning of the year, and now it was November. The journey from the coast had been hard and violent, with battles and the making of alliances. Finally, now, they had heaved to the top of this pass between two

[118] **ominous** [ɑ́mɪnəs]:「不吉な」。関連する名詞の omen [óʊmən]（「兆し」「前触れ」）は，a good [bad] omen というように，中立的な意味であることに注意。

[119] **Azcapotzalco:** アツカポツァルコは，テスココ湖西岸で 15 世紀に栄えた都市国家。この段落では，メキシコ中央部を中心とするメソアメリカ文化（スペイン時代以前の中米の古代文化圏）の担い手を，アステカから，アツカポツァルコ，トルテカ（Toltecs, 6 世紀〜10 世紀），テオティワカン（Teotihuacan, 前 2 世紀〜6 世紀）へと，時代を遡って挙げている。

[120] **Tula, seat of the revered Toltecs:** seat は「（行政などの）中心地」。revere [rɪvíər] は「大いに尊敬する」。トゥーラは「都市」を意味し，トルテカ文化の遺跡。ただし，ここにトルテカ帝国の都があったという通説については異論が多い。

[121] **the ruins of Teotihuacan:** ruin は（しばしばこのように複数形で）「廃墟」。

[121] **All these are reminders of . . . :** reminder of . . . は「…を思い出させるもの」（cf. Oh, that *reminds* me.）。splendours は（このように複数形で用いて）「（とりわけ場所の）壮麗な様子」。fragility [frədʒíləti] < fragile [frǽdʒaɪl]:「壊れやすい」「はかない」（荷物の表示で使うと「こわれもの」）。

[123] **from the direction of acatl:**「葦」（Reed）を意味する acatl は，アステカの 20 ある暦日名の 13 番目。不吉な兆しを意味し，方位では東を表す。コルテス率いるスペイン軍は，東の方向からアステカの首都へ向かっていた。

[137] **the making of alliances:** make alliances [əláɪənsɪz] は「同盟関係を結ぶ」。

[138] **they had heaved to the top of this pass:** heave は「あえぐ」(to draw in the breath with effort; to pant, gasp)。この場合は，「あえぎながら進む」「苦労して登る」。pass は「山道」（cf. an overpass/underpass）。

snow-capped volcanoes. To Cortés' left and high above him, Popocatepetl steamed endlessly. And below him, in the distance, lay this incredible city, like nothing he had ever seen before.

There were to be two years of duplicitous negotiation, bloodshed, rout, retreat, and readvance before Hernán Cortés, Spanish conquistador, conquered the city of the Aztecs, Tenochtitlán, which today we call la ciudad de México, Mexico City, Distrito Federal.

Massey concludes the double telling of this encounter of different people and different ways of imagining and living space by asking, what would happen if we opened ourselves to new ways of thinking about space? Specifically, she asks, what would happen if we started to think of space as the product of interrelations, as always under construction, and as "a simultaneity of stories-so-far"?

The way, today, we often tell that story, or any of the tales of 'voyages of discovery,' is in terms of crossing and conquering space. Cortés voyaged across space, found Tenochtitlán, and took it. 'Space,' in this way of telling things, is an expanse we travel across. It seems perhaps all very obvious.

But the way we imagine space has effects — as it did, each in different ways, for Moctezuma and Cortés. Conceiving of space as in the voyages of discovery, as something to be crossed and maybe conquered, has particular ramifications. Implicitly, it equates space with the land and sea, with the earth which stretches out around us. It also makes space seem like a surface; continuous and given. It differentiates: Hernán, active, a maker of history, journeys across this space and finds Tenochtitlán upon it. It is an unthought cosmology, but it carries with it social and political effects. So easily this way of imagining space can lead us to conceive of other places, peoples, cultures simply as phenomena 'on' this surface. It is not an innocent manoeuvre, for by this means they are deprived of histories. Immobilised, they await Cortés' (or our, our global capital's) arrival. They lie there, on space, in place, without their own trajectories. Such a space makes it more difficult to see in our mind's eye the histories the Aztecs too have been living and producing. What might it mean to reorientate this imagination, to question that habit of thinking of space as a surface? If, instead, we conceive of a meeting-up of histories, what happens to our implicit imaginations of space and time?

- [140] **Popocatepetl:** ポポカテペトル山。メキシコ中央部にある，雪を頂いた円錐形の火山（標高 5,452 m）。山頂の火口から噴煙を上げていることから，ナワトル語で「煙の山」を意味する。アステカの首都へ向かうコルテス軍の前にそびえていた 2 つの秀峰のひとつ。
- [142] **There were to be . . . :** duplicitous [djuːplísɪtəs] は「二枚舌を使う」「不誠実な」。bloodshed は「流血の惨事」「殺戮」。rout [raʊt] は「完敗」。conquistador [kɑnkíːstədɔ̀ːr] はスペイン語で，「征服者」(conqueror)，なかでも特に「16 世紀前葉にメキシコとペルーを征服したスペインの軍人」を意味する。la ciudad de México もスペイン語で，the city of Mexico という意味。Distrito Federal は，同様に Federal District。
- [148] **if we opened ourselves to new ways of thinking about space:** 注 [80] を参照。
- [150] **"a simultaneity of stories-so-far":** simultaneity [sàɪməltəníːəti]「同時性」（< simultaneous）「これまでの経過をとりあえず現在までたどれる（未完結の）物語がいくつも同時的に存在していること」。
- [153] **in terms of . . . :**「…という語り方で」「…という観点から」「…という見方で」という感じ（1 章 [14]）。「語り方」と「考え方，見方」が表裏一体であることがよくわかる表現（cf. Let's think about the problem *in strict mathematical terms.*）。
- [158] **Conceiving of space as . . . :** conceive of A as B は「A を B として捉える」という意味の重要な表現パターン。conceive（cf. concept, conception）は「（概念として）頭に思い描く」(form an idea in one's mind) という意味の動詞。ramifications は（通例このように複数形で用いて）「行動や決定から派生する（しばしば予期しない）さまざまな帰結［意味合い］」で，このように have (. . .) ramifications (for . . .) という形で用いられることが多い（cf. Smoking *has long-term implications for* your health.）。ここではすぐ上の effects の言い換えと考えてよい。
- [160] **Implicitly:**「暗黙のうちに」(cf. explicitly)。
- [164] **an unthought cosmology:**「しっかりと考え抜かれていない宇宙論」。
- [167] **simply as phenomena 'on' this surface:**「単なる表面上の現象として」。この文の後にも説明されているように，空間を表面的なものとしてのみ捉えることは，そこに時間的な重層性を認めない姿勢であると著者は指摘している。
- [167] **an innocent manoeuvre** [mənúːvər]：「罪のない操作」。この場合の innocent は「他人に害を及ぼさない」という感じ。
- [170] **without their own trajectories:** すぐ上の deprived of histories, immobilised と意味的に関連する表現。trajectory [trədʒéktəri] は「軌道」「軌跡」。
- [173] **reorientate this imagination:** つまり，新たな方向で考えるということ。

13

SONG

Introduction

Eijiro Tsuboi

One of the defining features of human language is its structural complexity. Although language as broadly defined is not unique to human beings, animal language generally lacks an elaborate structure comparable to that of human language. To take a simple example, you may see a cat meow to another cat to convey some message, but it is not the case that the "m" sound carries part of the message and the "eow" sound the rest. The message is one indivisible whole, and has no internal structure. Except in fantasy fictions like *Doctor Dolittle*, animal communication is based on words, as it were, rather than sentences. It is true that our own human utterances may sometimes be made up of a single word (such as "fire!") and the proverbial taciturn Japanese husband really may say nothing at home beyond *"furo," "meshi,"* and *"neru,"* but such examples are really only the exceptions which prove the rule, and we can readily employ intricately structured sentences to express exquisitely composed messages. The gap between the simple vocalizations of other animals and our highly structured human language is huge.

How did human language develop into what it is now? When we think about the evolution of language, one tacit assumption would often be that we developed complex ways to compose words into structured sentences, i.e., grammar, in order to express the complex meanings we had in mind. In this view, grammar and meaning developed hand in hand, in an intertwined way, and the driving force for the development was the need for a more sophisticated communication device. However, the well-developed grammatical structure of finch songs, which has been revealed to exist by the author of this session, does not convey any complex meaning; the

- [1] **One of the defining features of ... :**「…の定義の一部となるような［…の本質を決定する］特徴のひとつ」（cf. distinctive/distinguishing features [characteristics]）。
- [2] **language as broadly defined:**「広義の言語」（cf. language in the strict [proper] sense of the term）。
- [2] **is not unique to ... :**「…に特有というわけではない」（cf. This is not a problem *peculiar to* Japan.）。
- [9] ***Doctor Dolittle*:**『ドリトル先生物語』。作者はイギリス生まれのアメリカの児童文学者ロフティング（Hugh Lofting, 1886–1947）。全12巻。1920–53年刊。主人公のジョン・ドリトルはオウムに動物語を教わった医者・博物学者という設定。
- [9] **as it were:**「いわば」。このようにある表現が文字通りにではなく比喩的に用いられていることを示す（cf. She has been, *so to speak*, the center of gravity in this project since it started.）。
- [12] **the proverbial taciturn Japanese husband:** proverbial (< proverb) は（「諺の一部になっている」という原義から）「かの有名な」。taciturn [tǽsətərn] は「（つき合いがよくないと思われるほど）無口な」。
- [14] **the exceptions which prove the rule:**「原則が成り立つことをかえって証明する例外」。"The exception proves the rule" という諺は，原義は「例外は原則を試す」だが，現在は通例「例外の存在は原則の正しさを証明する」という意味で用いられる（cf. ... is the exception rather than the rule.）。
- [15] **exquisitely composed messages:**「精緻に構成されたメッセージ（表現される内容）」。
- [20] **one tacit assumption:** a tacit assumption は「暗黙の前提」という意味の決まった言い回し（cf. an underlying [implicit] *assumption*/*tacit* knowledge）。
- [23] **grammar and meaning developed hand in hand ... :** hand in hand は「手に手を取って」だが，このように「密接に関連し合って」「連携して」という比喩的な意味で（とりわけ go hand in hand という形で）用いられることも多い（cf. Wealth and power often go *hand in hand*.）。in an intertwined way は「密接に関連し合って」で，ここでは hand in hand の意味をさらに強めるために用いられている（cf. Most linguists believe that grammar is closely *intertwined with* meaning.）。
- [24] **the driving force for ... :**「…の推進力」はこのように「（仕組みの成立，組織の運営などにおいて）重要な役割を果たす人やもの」の意味でよく用いられる表現（4章 [75], 14章 [37]）（cf. He was the *driving force behind* the curriculum change.）。
- [27] **finch:** ここでは「ジュウシマツ」。

songs just mean "Be my love!" like the simple mating calls of other ordinary birds. So why did finches bother to develop complex "song grammar"? It is not enough just to refer to the pleasing quality of complex songs to answer this question, since that will only invite the further question of why complex songs sound attractive. It is also to be noted that complex songs are more likely to attract the attention of predators, which seems to make them even more problematic in evolutionary terms.

In this session, the author, a neuro-behavioral scientist researching the acoustic abilities of birds, provides a stimulating evolutionary account for the development of finch songs, and concludes the session with the hypothesis that a similar account can be given for the evolution of human language. Since there are no tangible clues, like fossils, that provide us with any definite hints, theories on the origin of human language have largely remained in the realm of speculation. Some people suggest that it is a kind of mutation, a freak of nature, a phenomenon which lies beyond an evolutionary explanation, but the author's hypothesis offers a new approach to the age-old question of the genesis of human language from an evolutionary perspective. According to his hypothesis, grammar developed under the pressure of sexual selection, despite its uselessness for survival. This allows us to understand human language within the context of evolution, but not in a way which views it as a logical consequence of some functional requirements. The natural world is far too complex, and the dynamic interactions of individually functional motivations may sometimes result in an enigmatic appearance of dysfunctionality.

Finchsong

Kazuo Okanoya

Human language consists of words combined in various ways. The words have relatively fixed meanings, and the process of combining them follows set rules. In other words, what makes human language possible is the combination of meaning and grammar. The chirping of small birds works rather differently. In-

[30] **bother to . . .**:「わざわざ…する」で，このように疑問文または否定文で用いられるのが普通。ここでは「そんなことをする必要などないはずなのになぜ」という感じを表現するために用いられている（cf. He did*n't* even *bother to* respond to my urgent request.）。

[33] **It is also to be noted that . . .**: It is to be noted that . . .「…ということに注目すべきである」は重要性を主張する際によく用いられる表現形式（cf . . . . is worth noting.）。even more problematic in evolutionary terms は「進化という観点からはますます問題のある[理解し難い]」（1章 [14]，12 章 [153]）。

[41] **tangible:**（「触知可能な」から）「明確な」（e.g. *tangible* evidence）。

[44] **a freak of nature:**「造化のいたずら」は「きわめてまれな自然現象」を表す決まった言い方（cf. I wonder if that was really just a *freak* accident.）。

[47] **the age-old question of the genesis** [dʒénəsɪs] **of human language:**「人間の言語の起源という昔からの問題」。

[49] **sexual selection:**「性選択」「雌雄淘汰」。ある自然環境のなかでより生存に適した資質をもった個体が生き残っていくことが自然選択だとすれば，メスによるオスの選択をとおしてある種の資質（たとえば美しい羽根，美しい声）をもった個体がより高い確率で子孫を残していくことが性選択。

[53] **the dynamic interactions of . . .**: 言語の進化の要因の一つ一つは（例えばコミュニケーション上の）機能に動機づけられていても，それらが複雑に絡み合うことによって，何かの機能を果たしているとは思えない謎めいた（enigmatic < enigma）特徴が結果的に生じる場合がある，ということ。

[57] **The words have relatively fixed meanings:**「単語には比較的固定した意味がある」。「比較的（relatively）」と言っているのはコンテクストによる変動などがあって完全に固定しているわけではないため。

[58] **follows set rules:**「決まった規則に従っている」。（動詞 set の過去分詞が形容詞化した）set は前出の fixed と同じ意味で用いられている。

[59] **the combination of meaning and grammar:**「意味と文法の組み合わせ」。意味を持った単語とその組み合わせの規則としての文法，という考え方。文法がそれ自体何らかの意味を表すとは著者が考えていないことを示唆する。

[60] **The chirping of small birds works rather differently:**「小鳥の鳴き声の仕組みはこれとは随分異なる」。chirping は通例「さえずり」に対応するが，すぐ後でわかるように，ここでは chirping を「さえずり」と「地鳴き」に分けていることに注意。動詞 work はこのように日本語の「仕組み」に対応することが多い（9 章 [122]）（cf. *the workings of* the human mind）。

stead of being made up of meaningful words combined according to grammatical rules, bird chirping consists of two different kinds of sounds. The first, *jinaki* is a single sound, while the second, *saezuri*, is a sequence of several sound elements. *Jinaki* can be compared to words that have meanings. But the meaning of a *saezuri* sequence cannot be broken down into separate meaningful elements: it works as a whole. In other words, while the sounds of *jinaki* are equivalent to words that have individual meanings, birds do not compose sentences by combining those sounds. *Saezuri* does have a grammar, and the sound elements are combined in certain ways, but because those elements do not have any separate individual meaning, the grammar cannot be manipulated to produce variant meanings. So, the chirping of birds proceeds according to patterns quite different to those of human language. Nonetheless, by investigating the chirping of birds — in which the communication functions of words and of grammar are quite separate — we may be able to get some clues about the origin of human language.

In the chirping of small birds, *saezuri* (songs) do not have any explicit meaning in themselves and are intended merely to sound attractive to female birds, while *jinaki* (calls) do have specific meanings and each call is used for a different purpose. Let's look at *jinaki* first. The most frequently used *jinaki* is the contact call. This call functions just like saying "hello!" and it is exchanged every now and then among birds in a group. Most researchers think that this contact call is used by a bird just to show that it has no feelings of animosity, and is in a friendly mood. Then there is also what is called the distant call, which is used when a bird can't see any of its fellows. It's like asking, "where are you?" The sound is similar to the contact call but louder. Finches, of course, have two ears, one on each side of their heads. So, depending on the time lapse between the moment the sound reaches one ear and the moment it reaches the other, they are able to judge the direction from which the "where are you?" call is coming. Interestingly, among finches the sound quality of the distant call differs not only among individual birds, which makes it possible to tell exactly which bird in a group is chirping, but also more generally between the sexes. The male finch chirps in a clear voice but the female voice is less clear.

A third important type of *jinaki* call is the alarm call. For most small birds, hawks and eagles are a huge threat. So when predators like these approach, the vulnerable birds produce alarm calls to warn other small birds in the vicinity. But the alarm call is a double-edged sword: at the same time that it is sending out a general

[64] *Jinaki* can be compared to words that have meanings:「地鳴きは（人間の言語における）意味をもった単語に喩えることができる」。数行下の the sounds of *jinaki* are equivalent to words that have individual meanings と同じ内容。

[66] cannot be broken down into separate meaningful elements:「…はそれぞれ意味を持つ別々の要素に分解することができない」。break A down (into B) は「A を (B に) 分解する」という意味の決まった言い方（名詞 breakdown にも a breakdown on the amount due のように「内訳」「明細」の意味がある）。

[70] the sound elements are combined in certain ways:「音の要素は特定のパターンで組み合わされる」。直前の *Saezuri* does have a grammar の内容を具体的に述べたもの。

[72] the grammar cannot be manipulated to produce variant meanings:「文法を操作してさまざまな意味を創り出すことはできない」。（人間の言語とは異なり）「文」を構成する「単語」を一定に保ったまま，「単語」の組み合わせ方を変化させることによって異なる意味を表すことはできない，ということ。

[73] patterns quite different to those of human language:「人間の言語の場合とは大きく異なるパターン」（9 章 [110]）。

[78] *saezuri* (songs) do not have any explicit meaning in themselves:「さえずり自体には明確な意味がない」。explicit は implicit「暗示的な」の反意語で「明示的な」「はっきりした」。

[79] are intended merely to sound attractive to female birds:「メスの鳥にとって魅力的に聞こえることだけが目的である」。be intended to . . . は「…するためのものである」「することを目的としている」という意味を表す決まった表現。

[83] every now and then:「時として」。

[85] show that it has no feelings of animosity:「自分に敵意がないことを示す」。

[93] Interestingly:「興味深いことに」。いわゆる文副詞で，すぐ後に続く分の内容に対するコメントを表明する機能を果たしている (cf. curiously (enough) / strangely (enough))。

[95] which makes it possible to tell exactly which bird in a group is chirping:「このため一体どの鳥が鳴いているのかがわかる」。このように tell は「（五感を働かせることによって）わかる」という意味でよく用いられる（6 章 [102]）。その場合には通常 can や can't などの(不)可能または難易を表す表現とともに使われる (e.g. I *could tell* she was upset from her expression [her tone of voice]./It's sometimes *hard to tell* how he really feels.)。tell A from B, tell A and B apart, tell the difference between A and B はいずれも「A と B の違いがわかる」という意味を表す頻出表現。

[99] predators:「捕食者」(cf. prey「被食者」[194])。

[100] vulnerable:「攻撃されやすい」「脆い」(e.g. Newborn babies are *vulnerable to* this kind of disease.)。

[101] warn other small birds in the vicinity:「近くに (in the vicinity) いる小鳥に警告を与える」。

[101] a double-edged sword: something that has both advantages and disadvantages「両刃の剣」。

[102] at the same time that . . . :「…と同時に」(cf. He says he is too busy to talk to me *every time* I call him.)。

warning, it can also let the predator know where the bird making the alarm is hiding. In order to counteract this threat, small birds have developed some very useful refinements to their alarm calls. [105] The diagram below shows the alarm calls of various small birds. The sound of these calls is concentrated at around 7 kHz. The call starts gradually and lasts for half a second or so, and then it comes to an end also gradually. Because the beginning and ending are vague, the predator bird would have a hard time telling the precise [110] amount of time the sound had taken to reach its right and left ears. This makes it hard for the predator to determine precisely the source location of the call. The fact that there are few sound components in the call (in other words, the fact that the frequency is limited) also makes it hard for the enemy to tell exactly where the bird sounding [115] the alarm is hiding. Moreover, birds like hawks and eagles have difficulty in detecting sounds of around 7 kHz. Although they have extremely sharp hearing — they are even able to detect the sound of mice scurrying along under leaves on the ground — they tend to be

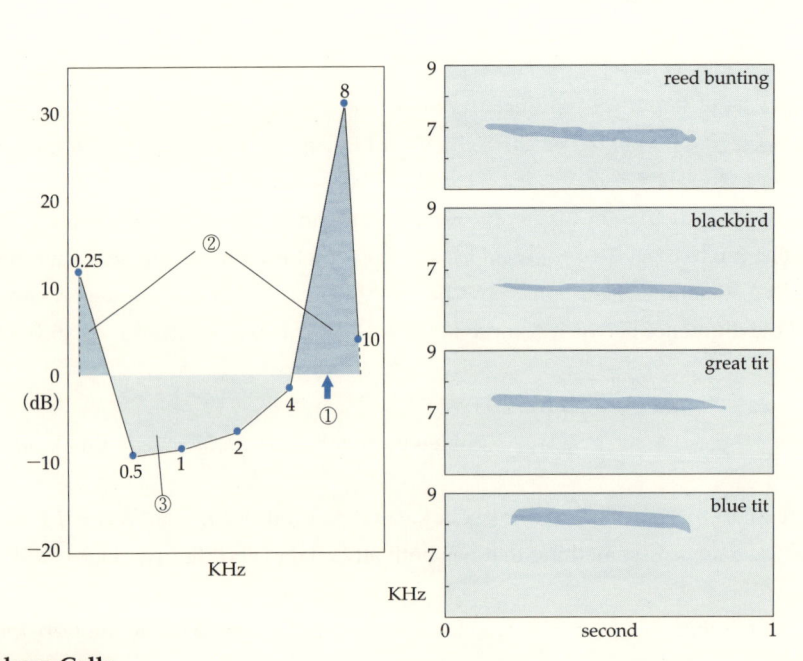

Alarm Calls
The boxes on the right show the different alarm calls of various birds. The box on the left shows the range of sounds audible to finches and hawks. ① Alarm call sound frequencies, ② Range clearly audible to great tits, ③ Range clearly audible to American Kestrels.

[104] **counteract this threat:**「この脅威に対抗する」。counteract は「…の影響を緩和または防止する」。

[107] **7 kHz:** seven kilohertz [kíləhə:rts] と読む。kilohertz は単複同形。

[109] **Because the beginning and ending are vague:**「始まりと終わりがはっきりしていないために」(vague: not clear / cf. a *vague* acquaintance (4章 [52]))。

[110] **have a hard time telling the precise amount of time . . . :**「…の正確な時間の長さがわかりづらい」。have a hard time doing はすぐ後に出てくる have difficulty (in) doing や have trouble doing と並んで「(人が)…するのに苦労する」「(人にとって)…することは難しい」という意味を表す頻出パターン。difficulty と trouble の前に苦労や困難の量を表す表現をつけて「…するのに非常に苦労する，全く苦労しない」などの意味を表せることも習得しておきたい (e.g. He *had a lot of* [*a little*] [*little*] [*no*] *difficulty* [*trouble*] express*ing* himself in Italian.)。

[117] **Although they have extremely sharp hearing:**「タカやワシは聴覚が非常に鋭いけれども」。hearing は「聴覚」「聴力」の意味。「英語のヒアリングテスト」「英語のヒアリングが得意[苦手]」などという場合のヒアリングに相当するのは listening comprehension や listening skills であることに注意。a hearing test は「聴力検査」。

[118] **even able to detect the sound of mice scurrying along . . . :**「落ち葉の下をちょこちょこ走り抜ける (scurry along) ネズミの音さえ探知する (detect) ことができる」。

[119] **tend to be relatively less attuned to . . . :**「比較的(他の波長の音に比べると)…に反応しにくい傾向がある」。be attuned to . . . は「…に慣れている」「…に適切に反応できる」。

relatively less attuned to the sound frequency of the alarm calls. In other words, in the course of the evolution of both the small birds and their larger predators, the more vulnerable birds developed precisely the kind of alarm call sound that would enable them to go undetected, and thereby escape attack.

Let's turn from simple calls to the particular sound sequences of sound signals that make up songs, or *saezuri*. Animals and birds in general use a wide variety of sounds for communication. But the majority of these sounds are just vocalizations. The only creatures that actually pay attention to the meanings of particular sequences of sound signals are birds, human beings, and whales. If you deprive these animals of the chance to learn the sound signals, or if they are raised by different kinds of animals who make different kinds of sounds, then they will lose the ability to produce and interpret speech and song. The finches that I study sing using eight different kinds of sound elements. As the songs are sung by male birds to attract female birds, the female birds actually do not sing themselves. Their role is to listen carefully to the songs of male birds and then decide which one to choose as a mate. The brains of the male birds have a nerve system that enables them to learn and sing songs. The brains of the female birds, on the other hand, while including a nerve system that allows them to learn songs, lack the component that would allow them to produce and sing songs. Instead, it is likely that this part is replaced by a system that enables them to interpret songs.

The sound elements that compose the songs of the finches are not put together in the same sequence every time. Rather, the arrangement changes every time they sing. Because each sound element does not have its own specific meaning, the change in the arrangement does not create any difference in meaning. A basic research question in the study of finch songs therefore has to do with the interpretation of this variety: why do the birds try to come up with different sequences?

Today's Japanese finches are all actually the descendants of one group of *koshijirokinpara* birds which were imported by a Kyushu daimyo about 250 years ago. Interestingly, the *koshijirokinpara* itself has only very simple songs, usually consisting of about eight song components. This itself is no different from the finches, but *koshijirokinpara* always produce these components in the same sequence when singing, while finches produce a variety of sequences in their songs (see graph). So, the second research question in the study of finch songs is why finches and *koshijirokinpara*, which are

- [123] **the kind of alarm call sound that would enable them to go undetected:**「居場所を探知されないですむような(鳴き声による)警告音」。go un- 過去分詞はこのように「…されないままである」「…されずにすむ」という意味を表す表現型 (e.g. I'm afraid quite a few mistakes may have *gone unnoticed*.)。
- [127] **use a wide variety of sounds for communication:**「コミュニケーションのために多種多様な音声を使う」。a wide variety of ... は「多種多様な…」という意味の決まり文句。
- [138] **The brains of the male birds ... :** 口絵［SONG］a 参照。
- [146] **put together:** 頻出の句動詞で，ここでは combine と同じ「…を組み合わせる」という意味。「(複数のものを組み合わせて)…を組み立てる」「(情報を集めて)…(考えなど)をまとめる」「(人を集めて)…を組織する」という意味で用いることも多い (e.g. This bookshelf is very easy to *put together*./We have to *put together* a decent proposal as soon as possible.)。
- [153] **Today's Japanese finches:** 口絵［SONG］b 参照。
- [154] ***koshijirokinpara*:** コシジロキンパラは，台湾，中国南部，インド，マレー半島，スマトラ島に分布している鳥。中国で近縁種との交雑によってこの鳥の変種がつくられ，それが江戸時代に日本に輸入され，さらにジュウシマツに改良されたと言われている。
- [157] **This itself is no different from the finches:**「これ自体はジュウシマツと全く変わらない」。no different from ... は「…と異なるところが全くない」「…と同じ」という意味の決まった言い方。このように no は後に続く表現(この場合は「違う」)と逆の意味(この場合は「同じ」)を強調することが多い (e.g. This is *no* easy task./John is *no* fool.)。

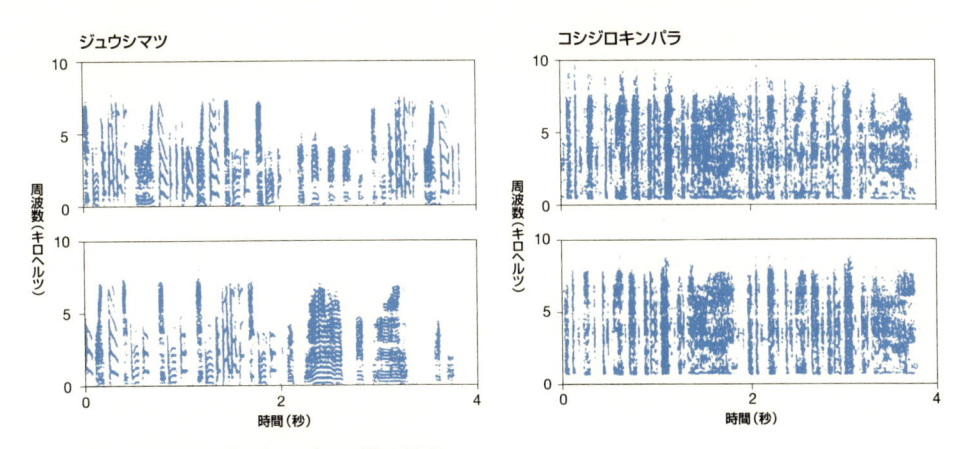

ジュウシマツとコシジロキンパラの歌の比較
ジュウシマツの歌(左)とコシジロキンパラの歌(右)。それぞれ連続した 8 秒分を 4 秒ずつ 2 段に示した。ジュウシマツの歌は多様な音要素が複雑に配列されているが，コシジロキンパラの歌は同じ要素配列で 4 回繰り返してうたわれていることがわかる。

basically the same species, are so different in their singing? The answer to these questions may well lie with sexual selection.

In any species which has sexual differentiation, it's the females that bear the higher cost for reproduction. For this reason, females tend to study the quality of their potential mates carefully, and, as a result, males evolve in such a way as to facilitate the kinds of displays which will appeal to potential mates. The beautiful tail feathers of the male pheasant are a good example of this kind of evolved display. My theory was that the complex grammar of finch songs is a comparable form of display and has evolved through a similar process. In order to test out this theory, I put each female finch into a separate cage and studied its response to various artificial songs. As it turned out, the group who listened to more complex songs laid eggs in half the number of days it took for the group who listened to simple songs. The complex song group also carried almost twice as many twigs to their nests. Then I did a similar experiment with *koshijirokinpara*. I rearranged the simple song of the *koshijirokinpara* to fit the complex grammar of finches and played these altered songs to female *koshijirokinparas*. The female *koshijorokinparas* clearly preferred the artificially rearranged, more complex songs. So it seems clear that the female birds of both groups instinctively prefer complex songs.

But why do complex songs stimulate the birds to be more active sexually? A plausible explanation can be found in the theory put forward by the ornithologist Amotz Zahavi, a theory known as the "handicap principle." Obviously, singing complex songs is a somewhat risky activity for birds in the wild. Singing birds, for example, attract the attention of enemies, and, even more basically, the maintenance of the nerve system needed for singing is an effort that is not really necessary. The possession of this kind of facility for unnecessary ornament is proof that the individual has some extra power and hence a stronger capacity for survival. A *koshijirokinpara* living in the wild would have quickly fallen prey to predators if it had spent too much time and energy trying to lure females by singing complex songs. But the finches which developed the complex songs were human pets and for that reason did not have to be concerned about danger from predators. Their circumstances gave the finches the opportunity to start developing a repertoire of complex songs.

I am convinced that human language (the grammatical arrangement of meaningful elements) evolved similarly: in other words, in relation to sexual activities. The ability to produce varied dances

- [167] **males evolve in such a way as to . . . :**「オスは…する方向に進化する」。in such a way as to . . . は「…するような仕方で」という意味の決まった言い回し。facilitate: make it easier for . . . to happen or proceed.
- [168] **appeal to potential mates:**「自分とつがいになる潜在性のあるメスの気を引く」。ここでの appeal to . . . は「…の気に入る」「…を魅了する」で attract とほぼ同義 (cf. I didn't find his proposal particularly *appealing*. / What do you think is *the appeal of* living in a big city?)。
- [170] **the complex grammar . . . :**「ジュウシマツの歌の複雑な文法もこれに類する誇示行動の一形態で」。comparable [kámpərəbl] はこのように「類似の」という意味で用いることが多い。
- [174] **As it turned out:**「その結果（わかったことは）」。
- [174] **laid eggs:**「卵を産んだ」(cf. The platypus is an *egg-laying* mammal. / How much longer will these *eggs* take to hatch?)。
- [184] **stimulate:** stimulate A to B は「A を刺激して B させる」(e.g. As a good teacher, she knows what she can do *to stimulate* her students *to* study on their own.)。
- [185] **A plausible explanation:**「なるほどと思える説明」。「もっともらしい」という訳語が与えられることの多い plausible だが，ここでは否定的な意味合いはなく，reasonable とほぼ同義。
- [185] **the theory put forward by the ornithologist Amotz Zahavi:**「鳥類学者 (ornithologist) アモツ・ザハヴィが提案した理論」。put forward は「（理論などを）提唱する」「（意見や案を）出す」という意味でよく使われる句動詞。アモツ・ザハヴィはイスラエルの動物行動学者。1970 年代に「ハンディキャップ原理」を提唱。その彼の主張をまとめたのが，Amotz and Avishag Zahavi, *The Handicap Principle: A Missing Piece of Darwin's Puzzle* という 1997 年刊の本（邦訳『生物進化とハンディキャップ原理──性選択と利他行動の謎を解く』)。原著のサブタイトルにある「ダーウィンの謎」とは，あまりに派手なクジャクの羽根，あまりに重すぎるシカの角，猛獣の前で跳ねるガゼルの踊りなど，ダーウィンの進化論によっては完全には説明できない，個体の生存にとってハンディキャップでしかない特徴や行動の進化がどうして起こってきたのか，ということ。
- [188] **birds in the wild:**「野生の鳥」(cf. birds raised *in captivity*)。
- [191] **facility for unnecessary ornament:** facility for . . . は「…を苦もなく行う[身につける]自然に備わった才能」(e.g. His *facility for* languages is truly amazing.)。
- [192] **has . . . a stronger capacity for survival:** have a capacity for . . . で「…する[…を習得する]能力がある」(cf. Some scholars believe that it is *the capacity for* language that sets human beings apart from other species.)。
- [194] **would have quickly fallen prey to predators:**「たちまち捕食者の餌食になっていたであろう」。fall prey to . . . は「…の餌食になる」だが，「…によってネガティブな影響を受ける」という比喩的な意味で用いることも多い (e.g. He often *falls prey to* groundless fears.「理由もないのに恐怖を感じて苦しむことがよくある」)。
- [197] **did not have to be concerned about . . . :**「捕食者によって危険にさらされるという心配をする必要がなかった」。be concerned about . . . は「…のことを心配する」(cf. I'm *concerned that* he might not show up.)。名詞の concern にも「心配」「懸念」の意味がある (e.g. There is grow-ing *concern about* the stagnant economy.)。
- [199] **a repertoire** [répərtwɑːr] **of complex songs:**「複雑な歌のレパートリー」。
- [201] **I am convinced that . . . :**「私は…であることを確信している」。be convinced は「確信している」(e.g. I'm *convinced of* her innocence. / cf. a *convincing* argument「説得力のある主張」)。

and songs — performances used to attract potential mates — would gradually have become more complex, like the song grammar of [205] the finch, and this was what would eventually enable human beings to control the arrangement of a wide variety of signs, like songs and other kinds of performance. Basic to this argument is the idea that in order for something like the layered arrangement of rules which we call *grammar* to evolve, there has to be a form of sexual [210] selection that facilitates the evolution of meaningless complexity. That kind of sexual selection, rather than the evolution of qualities necessary for individual survival, is the mechanism that enables the evolution of "unnecessary" qualities.

[206] **this was what would eventually enable human beings to control . . . :**「これによって人間はついには…をコントロールすることができるようになるのである」。この場合の would は，過去のある時点に基準をおいて，そこからそれより後に（発話時点から見ればやはり過去の）ある事態が生じることになる，という「過去から見た未来」を表している。

[208] **Basic to this argument is the idea that . . . :**「この主張の基本にあるのは…という考え方である」。主語の the idea that . . . の内容を新たに導入するために倒置構文が用いられている。こうした倒置は英語でもごく普通に見られる（3 章 [4, 11, 186]，5 章 [64]）(e.g. *Of particular importance is the fact* that Japan has a much larger number of universities than does Britain.)。

[209] **the layered arrangement of rules:**「多層的に配列された規則」。layered は「層 (layers) をなす」。

14

PHYSICS

Introduction
Takashi Nagata and Kozo Kuchitsu

What are the things that surround us made of? Modern science tells us that all matter is made up of small particles called elementary particles. Neutrinos are one example of such particles. While their exact size and weight is unknown, it is estimated that a neutrino is smaller than 0.0000000000000001 cm and lighter than 0.00000000000000000000000000000001 g.

The neutrino was first postulated in 1930 by the Austrian physicist Wolfgang Pauli. But their existence was not actually proven until the 1950s, when American physicists managed to observe some neutrinos that had been emitted from a nuclear reactor. This difficulty in detecting neutrinos was due to the fact that they hardly ever react with other particles but simply penetrate everything, even the earth. That's why detecting neutrinos has always been regarded as an extremely challenging task. The neutrino has even been characterized as "a ghost particle."

Neutrinos are generated during the process of nuclear fusion. For example, the sun, which radiates light as a result of nuclear reaction, is constantly emitting neutrinos. Many of these neutrinos reach the earth. Neutrinos are also emitted from rocks on the earth's surface, as well as from inside the earth. It is also thought that at the time of the Big Bang, when our universe was born, an enormous number of neutrinos were generated. So in fact our lives are saturated with neutrinos. It is said that there are as many as 300 of them in one cubic centimeter.

On February 23, 1987, at 35 seconds past 4:35 p.m., an incident of historic significance in the field of physics occurred. The neutrino observation apparatus called KamiokaNDE, set up in the Kamioka mine in Gifu Prefecture, successfully detected neutrinos from a su-

[2] **all matter is . . . :** この場合の matter は「物質」。この意味では不可算名詞であることに注意。
[2] **elementary particles:**「素粒子」。
[7] **postulated:** postulate は「措定する(あるものが存在すると考える)」。
[8] **Wolfgang Pauli:** ヴォルフガング・パウリ (1900–1958)。1945 年，ノーベル物理学賞を受賞。
[13] **an extremely challenging task:** challenging は「(技能や能力を試されるという意味で)難しい，手強い」(cf. Teaching here has turned out to be *a rewarding challenge.*)。
[16] **nuclear fusion:**「核融合」。
[21] **the Big Bang:**「ビッグバン」。宇宙のはじめの大爆発。標準的膨張宇宙理論によれば，宇宙は，今から約 140 億年前に起こったその大爆発によって生まれ，現在も膨脹しつづけている。
[22] **are saturated with . . . :**「…で飽和状態にある」「…で満ち満ちている」。
[28] **a supernova explosion:**「超新星の爆発」。

pernova explosion that had taken place at a distance of 170,000 light-years from the earth. It has been calculated that the number of neutrinos generated within the few seconds of that supernova explosion was 10^{58}. Eleven of those neutrinos, having traveled across the universe for 170,000 years, finally reached the earth and became the first neutrinos from a supernova explosion to be observed by human beings. This happened just before the retirement from the University of Tokyo of Professor Masatoshi Koshiba, who had been the driving force behind the construction of KamiokaNDE.

The neutrino is one of the fundamental particles constituting our world. If we can make clear its characteristics, we will be able to understand nature itself. It will also become possible to explain the ultimate origin of the forces that govern the natural world, such as gravity and electromagnetism. The neutrino is also intimately related to the birth and development of the earth, our solar system, and the whole universe. Human beings, who came into existence only a few million years ago in a universe that is now more than ten billion years old, may be able to account for the creation of their magnificent universe by studying these minute particles. Since 1987, research into neutrinos has progressed dramatically in the fields of physics and astronomy. All this progress was made possible by that first observation of the eleven neutrinos. As one physicist has aptly put it: "never has so much science and astronomy been extracted from so few events."

The Thrill of Experiments

Masatoshi Koshiba

*I*n 2001, the Nobel Prize celebrated its centennial with the publication of a book called The Nobel Prize: The First 100 Years. Taking as one of its central themes the meaning of "creativity," the book introduces us to a number of scholars, writers, politicians, and others who have received the Nobel Prize, and encourages us to consider what it means to be creative.

What, after all, is this thing called "creativity"? And what is the engine or source of our creativity? Is it anger? An unquenchable curiosity? Com-

[32] 10^{58}: ten (raised) to the power of fifty-eight, ten (raised) to the fifty-eighth power と読むが，略して ten to the fifty-eighth と言うこともある。

[36] **Professor Masatoshi Koshiba:** 小柴昌俊（1926– ）。1987 年，岐阜県の神岡鉱山に設置したカミオカンデ（KamiokaNDE 神岡陽子崩壊実験装置）において，超新星からのニュートリノを世界で初めて観測。2002 年，「宇宙物理学に対する先駆的功績，特に宇宙ニュートリノの検出」により，ノーベル物理学賞を受賞。

[37] **the driving force behind ...:** 「…の推進力（となる人）」という意味でこのように比喩的に用いられることの多い頻出表現 (4 章 [75], 13 章 [24])。

[50] **As one physicist has aptly put it:** 「一人の物理学者が巧みに表現したように」。as ... put it は誰かの発言を引用する際の決まり文句のひとつ。aptly < apt:「（目的や状況などに）ぴったりかなった」。

[53] **centennial:** 「百周年記念」。

[57] **what it means to be creative:** what it means to be ... は「…であるとはどういうことか」「…であることの意味」という意味を表す決まった言い方（e.g. This movie will make you think about *what it means to be* successful.）。

[59] **What, after all, is this thing called "creativity"?:** What is this thing called ... ? は「…とは一体何なのか」という（しばしば話題になるので知っているようでいて実際にはよくわからないものの正体を問う）場合に用いられる表現。

[60] **An unquenchable curiosity:** 「抑えられない好奇心」（cf. *quench* one's thirst)。3 章にも [137] have *an unquenchable thirst for* knowledge という表現が出てきたが，unquenchable はこのように欲求などが抑え難いことを表すのによく用いられる。

[60] **Compassion for ...:** 「…に対する思いやり」（cf. compassionate）。

passion for other human beings? Competitiveness? Or could it be nothing more than ambition? If nothing else, The Nobel Prize *shows that creativity is multifaceted and difficult to define. It also shows clearly that the process through which creativity is articulated is hugely variable, and depends on the individual in each case.* [65]

What about the case of Dr. Masatoshi Koshiba, professor emeritus of the University of Tokyo, who received the Nobel Prize in physics in 2002? His passionate work led to the successful execution of an enormously ambitious and — to the general public, at least — unlikely project, which attempted to observe particles by installing a huge pool of water in the mines [70] *of Kamioka. What was the source of his enormous creativity? Here is what Professor Koshiba has to say about creativity.*

Science basically has to do with the knowledge shared by all human beings. This knowledge can be shared because scientists (who study) and nature (the object of their studies) can be distin- [75] guished from each other. In other words, there is a clear separation of subjects and objects here. For this reason, the result of an experiment will remain consistent, regardless of who conducts it. Only that kind of replicable result can be accepted universally. This means that, in the field of natural science, something that has been done by [80] one person could always be done by others. If there were no Einstein, someone else would have undoubtedly come up with the same formula. So there is no "originality" for scientists in the sense that unique things, things which can only be performed by certain individuals, do not exist. That is the critical difference between science [85] and art. I believe there would have been no Mozartian music in this world if Mozart had not lived. But science is different. And precisely for this reason what matters for a scientist is to be the first to discover something.

Creativity, in essence, means doing something that has not been [90] done by others. In that sense, good, diligent students who merely remember everything they learn in school and learn from prominent people are lacking something. I once stated in a commencement address at the University of Tokyo that what the students need to aim for is not simply something passive, like getting good [95] grades, but also, more importantly, being active by initiating things themselves. There is absolutely no single, clear formula that shows how creativity can be achieved. One just has to try and test out all sorts of things. That sort of attitude slowly cultivates creativity. There is no magic bullet — you have to work hard on your own. [100]

- [63] **multifaceted:** having many facets (= aspects).
- [64] **creativity is articulated:** articulate [ɑːrtíkjəlèɪt] は「明確に表現する」(12 章 [52])(cf. *articulate* [ɑːrtíkjələt] messages「明晰なメッセージ」)。
- [66] **professor emeritus** [ɪmérətəs] :「名誉教授」。
- [70] **a huge pool of water:** 英語の pool は水泳プール (a swimming pool) を指すとは限らないことに注意。
- [76] **there is a clear separation of subjects and objects:**「主体と客体がはっきりと区別されている」。
- [79] **replicable:** be replicable [réplikəbl]: can be replicated. replicate は repeat や copy と同じような意味であるが，同じ結果を得るために実験を繰り返す，という場合に用いることが多い（e.g. *replicate* the experiment / *replicate* findings）。
- [86] **Mozartian** [moʊtsɑ́ːrʃən]:「モーツァルト (Mozart) の」(cf. Cartesian < Descartes)。
- [93] **a commencement address:**「卒業式の式辞」(cf. an opening *address*/I'm not used to *addressing* a large audience.)。
- [100] **There is no magic bullet:** a magic bullet は「特効薬」「魔法のような解決策」(cf. a silver bullet)。

Professor Koshiba advocates putting promising young people into positions of responsibility, maintaining that those with ability will thrive on that responsibility. This was the advice given him at the start of his career by Italian physicist Giuseppe Occhialini, whom he has always looked up to as a sort of father figure with regard to his involvement in physics experiment. Five years after Dr. Koshiba acquired his doctorate, Occhialini gave him this advice, and Dr. Koshiba has confirmed its truth again and again himself through his experiences in nursing a number of joint international research projects to completion. Here is an excerpt from Dr. Koshiba's memoir which exemplifies how he put this belief into practice at the University of Tokyo soon after assuming a professorship.

In order to educate students as scientists, it is important to make sure that they realize from the earliest stage of their studies that experiments are fun and rewarding. Unless they experience this for themselves, students will not be attracted to the idea of working on experiments.

When I returned to teach at the University of Tokyo from the United States, one of the first things I set out to do was to get students to realize for themselves the thrill of drawing a conclusion from experiments they had performed on their own. I suggested to my colleagues that since experiments are essential to the understanding of physics, we should provide our students with opportunities to experience the joy of experiments. And I told the students, "For any of you who are interested, I will allow you to do whatever experiments you choose, during the summer break. Of course, this is not for credit. But if you still want to do it, I promise that I will let you do whatever experiments you want."

That's how we started our system of summer vacation student experiments. And of all the things I achieved as a professor of the University of Tokyo, this is one of the things that I am most proud of. Every year, quite a few students devoted themselves to their own experiments during the summer vacation, found it to be rewarding, and decided to become scientists. I must say this was quite a successful initiative.

In this kind of way, I was always thinking about how I could enable my students to experience real experimentation during their first two years of graduate school, as Master's students, and then on into their initial years of doctoral education. In fact, this was partly what led me to the proton decay experiment in Kamioka, because it is a particle physics experiment that can be done without an accelerator.

[102] **thrive on that responsibility:** この場合の thrive on ... は「…(困難なことなど)を糧にする[生き甲斐に感じる]」(e.g. It's really amazing the way he *thrives on* hard work.)。

[104] **Giuseppe Occhialini:** ジュゼッペ・オッキャリーニ (1907–93)。1960 年，当時 MIT の客員教授だったオッキャリーニは，弱冠 33 歳の小柴を，原子核乾板を積んだ大きな風船を航空母艦から上げるという，当時としては非常に大規模な計画の責任者に大抜擢する。

[105] **a sort of father figure:** father figure は「父親的存在」だが，理想化された父親のイメージから「助言や援助をしてくれる尊敬できる年長の男性」といった意味 (cf. He wants his girlfriend to *mother* him.)。

[106] **doctorate** [dάktərət]:「博士号」。

[108] **nursing a number of ...:** nurse は「大切に育成する」「面倒を見る」(cf. a nursing home「老人ホーム」)。

[109] **Here is an excerpt ...:** excerpt [éksə̀:rpt] は「抜粋」。memoir [mémwà:r] は「回想録」。exemplify は「例示する」だが，ここでは「…の好例である」という感じ (cf. This anecdote *illustrates* how important it is to develop intercultural communication skills.)。

[114] **experiments are fun and rewarding:** fun はこのように(「楽しい」という意味の)形容詞であるかのように用いられることも多いが，本来は名詞，それも不可算名詞 (e.g. This car is *fun* to drive./cf. We *had* a lot of *fun* last night, didn't we?)。rewarding は，簡潔な日本語にしにくいが，よく使われる重要な形容詞で，「する価値がある」「すると満足感が得られる」といった感じ。

[118] **get students to realize:** get は「…させる」という意味のいわゆる使役動詞のひとつであるが，「説得」や「努力」を伴う使役を表す点で have とは決定的に異なることに注意 (e.g. I somehow managed to *get* them to listen to me./cf. She *had* her secretary make an appointment with the lawyer.)。後で出てくる本文 [196] was finally able to get the president to say "yes" も参照。

[119] **drawing a conclusion from ...:** draw a conclusion from ... は「…から結論を引き[導き]出す」と言う場合の決まった表現。

[125] **Of course, this is not for credit:**「もちろんこれは単位にはならない」(cf. This class is worth four *credits*.)。

[134] **a successful initiative:** initiative は「特定の目標を達成するために始めた新規の事業」。

[139] **proton decay:**「陽子崩壊」。陽子は，中性子とともに原子核を構成する最も基本的な素粒子だが，それがある種の相互作用により電子や他の素粒子に転化する過程を，陽子崩壊と呼ぶ。カミオカンデは，陽子崩壊を観測することを第一の目標として 1983 年に建設された。宇宙からのニュートリノを検出したものの，陽子が壊れたとする実験結果はまだ得られていない。

[140] **accelerator:** 日本語の「アクセル」と同じ意味でも使うが，ここでは「(粒子)加速器」。

I started the Kamioka experiment with a first-year graduate student, Katsufumi Arisaka, who later became a professor at UCLA. We worked closely together and made various simulations to try to find a detector design that could enable us to get the accurate data we wanted, and we came to the conclusion that we needed to develop big photomultiplier tubes. In the end, we got the Kamioka experiment up and running. I was pleased to see that the experiment enabled other students — not only graduate students but also undergraduates — to participate directly in experimental research.

In starting up the now-famous Kamioka Experiment, Professor Koshiba played against the odds and succeeded, by virtue not only of his brilliance but also because of his hard work, tenacity, and personal charm. He was also greatly assisted by colleagues and students who believed in him. Here he explains how his creative ideas came to fruition.

In the mid-1970s, several Grand Unified Theories, which went beyond the Standard Model of elementary particle theory uniting weak and electromagnetic interactions, and included strong interaction in the unification scheme, were proposed. All these theories predicted that the proton, which had been considered to have an infinite lifetime, would decay over a finite lifetime into lighter particles. Elementary particle experimentalists the world over became extremely excited. Two experiments to search for proton decay were proposed in Japan, and one of them was the Kamioka underground experiment. The idea of observing particles in a massive volume of clear water by photomultipliers from the side in an underground space was hatched in my Chicago days and had been mulled over by me since then. I always impressed two things upon entering graduate students: one was that "We are supported by taxpayers' precious money, and it is unthinkable to buy things from companies at their quoted prices," and the other was "If you want to be a researcher, always have three or four topics of research you want someday to carry out. If you do that, you'll be able to select which information to take and which to ignore from among the massive amount of information now available."

The plan to store 3,000 tons of water 1,000 meters underground and to observe the water with 1,000 photomultipliers was realized and was named KamiokaNDE (NDE = Nucleon Decay Experiment). However, I discovered that a similar design, but on a scale several times bigger than ours, was being planned in America. This would mean that taxpayers' money would be spent on a second-rate one-

[146] **we came to the conclusion that . . .**: come to the conclusion that . . . は「…という結論に至る」と言う場合の決まった表現。

[147] **photomultiplier tubes**:「光電子増倍管」。光電効果を利用して光を光電子に変換し，さらにその電子数を増倍する多段電流増幅真空管のこと。カミオカンデでは，世界最大 50 cm 径の光電増倍管が開発され，実験用水槽の内側に多数取り付けられた。このことにより，超新星ニュートリノの検出が可能になった。

[147] **In the end, we got . . . up and running**: get . . . up and running は「…を稼働させる」(cf. The new system will be *up and running* by the end of the year.)。

[152] **play(ed) against the odds**:「障害や困難に立ち向かう」(cf. *The odds* are *against* him. / Miraculously, the Tigers *beat the odds* and won the pennant.)。

[153] **tenacity** [tənǽsəti]: < tenacious [tənéɪʃəs]:「不屈の」。

[155] **came to fruition** [fruíʃən]: come to fruition は「(計画などが)実を結ぶ」(cf. I'm afraid your research project will be pretty hard to *bring to fruition*.)。

[156] **Grand Unified Theories**:「大統一理論」。素粒子の基本的相互作用として知られている 3 つの相互作用──強い相互作用，電磁相互作用，弱い相互作用──を，統一的に記述する理論。陽子崩壊を測定する実験は，この大統一理論の実験的検証を目的として行われている。

[162] **the world over**:「世界中の」(cf. all over the world, all across the world)。

[167] **was hatched**: この場合の hatch は「(考えなどを)思いつく」。

[167] **had been mulled over**: mull over . . . または mull . . . over は「…についてじっくり考える」。

[168] **I always impressed . . .**: impress A upon [on] B は「A (の重要性)を B (人)に力説する」。

[170] **it is unthinkable to . . .**: unthinkable は「考えられない」だが，このように「…するなどということは想像もできない，到底受け入れられない」と言う場合に用いることが多い。

[171] **quoted prices**:「言い値」(cf. asking price)。

[181] **taxpayers' money**:「納税者の金」だが，日本語で「税金の無駄遣い」とか「税金の節約」などと言う場合の「税金」の意味で非常によく用いられる表現。

[181] **one-shot**:「1 回限りの」「単発の」。

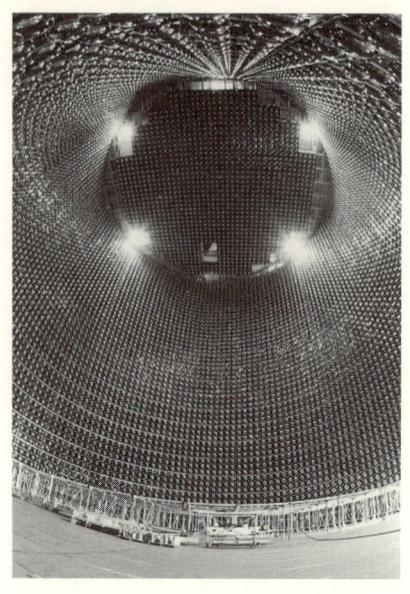

KamiokaNDE in 1983, with the world's largest photomultipliers.

shot experiment. I really thought extremely hard. With the expected budget, we couldn't compete in terms of size, but if we could improve the measurement resolution of the detector enormously, then we should be able to measure the branching ratios of various proton decay modes, and could pick out which Grand Unified Theory was correct, even though we might not be the first to discover proton decay itself. I wondered if this scheme was possible within the limited budget. Then, I thought that instead of increasing the number of photomultipliers, we should improve the light detection sensitivity of each tube as much as possible.

I immediately asked the president and the head of the technical division of Hamamatsu Photonics Company in Shizuoka to come to my office, and spent several hours trying to persuade them to take on the development of such a tube. I offered to assign a research associate and a graduate student to this project, and was finally able to get the president to say "yes." The world's largest photomultiplier with a diameter of 50 cm was developed one year later. This photograph (above) reminds me of that time when I felt a sense of total elation. But, since I haggled over the price of the new tube, the president told me several times that thanks to me the company was in the red to the tune of 300 million yen.

In July 1983, the detector was completed and water started to fill the tank. Eventually, the observation of solar neutrinos was achieved and we were able to make observations inclusive of time, direction and spectrum. These observations and the observation of super-

- [184] **the measurement resolution of . . . :**「…の測定精度」(cf. *high-resolution* images「解像度の高い画像」)。
- [185] **the branching ratios of various proton decay modes:** branching ratio は「分岐比」。陽子が崩壊する過程には，その最終状態(陽電子と中間子になったり，ニュートリノと中間子になったり)によって複数のモード(崩壊のしかた)がある。陽子が崩壊する頻度全体に対する，ある特定のモードで崩壊する頻度の比率を，「そのモードへの分岐比」と言う。
- [194] **take on the development:** この場合の take on は「(任務などを)引き受ける」(cf. I *took it upon myself to* break the news to him.)。
- [199] **I felt a sense of total elation:**「有頂天になった」「嬉しくてたまらなかった」(cf. We were *elated* at the news of her comeback.)。
- [200] **I haggled over the price of . . . :** haggle over the price of . . . は「…をうるさく値切る」。
- [201] **thanks to . . . :**「…のおかげで」だが，日本語と同じく，よくない事態の原因を表す場合にも用いることがある。
- [201] **was in the red to the tune of . . . :** (be) in the red は「赤字で」(cf. go into the red, go bankrupt)。to the tune of . . . は「総額…もの」。
- [206] **spectrum:**「スペクトル」。もともとは，スペクトルというと「光のスペクトル」であったが，拡張されて波長，振動数などの分布という意味で使われることが多い。ここではエネルギー分布の意味。グラフの横軸にエネルギー値を目盛り，縦軸にそのエネルギーをもつニュートリノの個数をプロットしたもの。

nova neutrinos are commonly held to be the foundation of neutrino astrophysics.

Right now [in 2002] Kamioka is the Mecca for global neutrino research, and over 150 researchers from the U.S are engaged in research there. [210]

[207] **are commonly held to be the foundation:** be (commonly) held to... は，be believed [considered/supposed] to... などと同様，「(一般に)…と考えられている」と言う場合によく用いられる表現型のひとつ (cf. a *commonly held* belief)。

> *Dr. Kozo Kuchitsu, a Professor Emeritus of the University of Tokyo and Dr. Masatoshi Koshiba's former classmate, explains why the Nobel Laureate has been such a successful scholar and teacher.*
>
> Dr. Koshiba contracted polio soon after entering junior high school and as a result was forced to abandon his dream of following in his father's footsteps and becoming an army officer. He also had to give up the idea of studying his favorite music. However, a book given to him by his junior high school teacher at the time when he was bed-ridden, entitled *The Evolution of Physics*, lit an unquenchable flame in his mind.*
>
> After recovering from his illness, Dr. Koshiba proceeded to Dai Ichi High School (the ancestor of today's College of Liberal Arts of the University of Tokyo). He and I lived in the dormitory as roommates, and we shared the pleasures of our student life with many good friends around us. This is a fond memory for me. Thanks to his tireless efforts, he managed to be accepted by the Department of Physics at the University of Tokyo.
>
> When Dr. Koshiba was twenty-six years old, he left Japan with a recommendation from Dr. Shinichiro Tomonaga, the future recipient of a Nobel Prize in physics, to continue his graduate work at the University of Rochester. Once there, he immersed himself in the study of cosmic rays. He finished his Ph.D. in a mere 20 months and then, following a period spent working at the University of Chicago, he returned to the University of Tokyo to continue his experiments aimed at understanding the mysteries of the universe.
>
> It goes without saying that the climax of those experiments was the detection of eleven neutrinos at KamiokaNDE. This success was due to the quality of Kamioka's detection equipment, which was at the time the best in the world. Thanks to the accumulation of skills and knowledge nurtured over the years in Dr. Koshiba's laboratory, this equipment was unparalleled in its sensitivity and accuracy. The successful detection of the eleven neutrinos was the culmination of the long and tireless efforts made by Dr. Koshiba, his associates, and his students — efforts made not just in the facilities established on the earth's surface but also way down deep inside the earth, at the bottom of the Kamioka mine.
>
> Dr. Koshiba has always been at the center of a network of people who respect him as a person. This network consists of people of all ages and nationalities, not only from the field of science but also from many other disciplines and many walks of life. If it can be said — and I firmly believe that it can — that this network of people has been the source of his success, then it can also be concluded that what ultimately led to Dr. Koshiba's great achievement was his wonderful humanity, sustained as it always has been by the depth and breadth of his knowledge.
>
> It is certainly the case that the quality of a project's measuring and computing apparatus will be a key factor in successful experiments, but it is also true that such a project is also always a human endeavor. The humanity of the scientist, therefore, plays a crucial role in the study of science. As someone who has known Dr. Koshiba since his high school days, I believe his success is simply a manifestation of his humanity.
>
> * Albert Einstein and Leopold Infeld, *The Evolution of Physics* (Simon & Schuster, 1938)

On Campus

2006年3月27日　初　版

[検印廃止]

編　者　東京大学教養学部英語部会
発行所　財団法人　東京大学出版会
代表者　岡本和夫
113–8654　東京都文京区本郷 7–3–1　東大構内
電話：03–3811–8814・FAX: 03–3812–6958
振替：00160–6–59964

印刷所　研究社印刷株式会社
製本所　株式会社島崎製本

© 2006 Department of English, The University of Tokyo, Komaba
ISBN 4–13–082118–0 Printed in Japan

Ⓡ〈日本複写権センター委託出版物〉
本書の全部または一部を無断で複写複製(コピー)することは，
著作権法上での例外を除き，禁じられています．本書からの複
写を希望される場合は，日本複写権センター (03–3401–2382) に
ご連絡ください．

The Universe of English II

東京大学教養学部英語部会 編

ベストセラーになった東大駒場の1年生用統一テキストが全章新しくなった．最新の英文で語られる知の宇宙と，味わい深い短編小説世界を豊富な注に導かれて散策する「教養英語」の新・定番テキスト．

［テキストのみ］菊判・240頁／定価（本体価格1900円＋税）
［テキスト＋4CD］菊判・函入／定価（本体価格3800円＋税）

広がりゆく知識の宇宙……
The Expanding Universe of English II

東京大学教養学部英語部会 編

「教養英語」の定義を塗りかえたテキスト *The Universe of English* の上級編が全面改訂．

［テキストのみ］菊判・256頁／定価（本体価格1900円＋税）
［テキスト＋4CD］セット・菊判函入／定価（本体価格3800円＋税）

「発信型」英語運用能力をめざして！
The Universe of English

東京大学教養学部英語教室 編
B5判・208頁／定価（本体価格1900円＋税）

The Expanding Universe of English

東京大学教養学部英語教室 編
B5判・288頁／定価（本体価格2000円＋税）

自分の英語を組み立てる〈最初の一手（ファースト・ムーブス）〉！
First Moves: An Introduction to Academic Writing in English

ポール・ロシター＋東京大学教養学部英語部会

「和文英訳」から英語による思考の構成へ．精選されたトピックスとランゲージワークによる画期的ライティング教科書．
B5判・192頁／定価（本体価格2400円＋税）